CONTENTS

*Front cover: Children enjoy exploring
Baconsthorpe Castle, Norfolk*

Copyright © English Heritage 1998
Designed by Collins & Brown Limited
Reproduction by Dot Gradations, Chelmsford, Essex
Printed in Spain
ISBN 1 85074 690 7

GW00372079

FOREWORD

ENGLISH HERITAGE is entrusted with the care of many of the nation's greatest monuments and historic houses and it is my pleasure to introduce them to you in our 1998–99 Handbook.

Last year more than 11 million visitors enjoyed the extraordinary variety of properties contained within these pages. All in all the buildings, monuments and gardens represent the full span of the nation's history. Whether you are visiting a remote standing stone or passing through the portals of a mighty fortress such as Dover Castle, you are encouraged to enjoy not just the building, its setting and its own particular story, but the opportunity to use your imagination.

Our heritage, of course, is all around us – not just in ancient sites. English Heritage works hard to safeguard this rich legacy wherever it is at risk, whether in historic buildings or in your own high street. We do this by offering grants, advice and the unparalleled conservation expertise to others and by working in partnership with many organizations at national and local level.

We attach great importance to new architecture as well. The Government has charged us to look at post-war architecture and to recommend for protection the finest and most innovative examples. It is a challenging job. Modern buildings, built with imagination and flair, need to be protected so that future generations can appreciate our era as well as those that have gone before. So we invite you to open your eyes to our wonderful built heritage, old and new. I would like to thank you for your continuing support. It is you, our members and visitors, who enable us to conserve England's heritage.

SIR JOCELYN STEVENS
Chairman

WHAT'S NEW IN 1998

A NUMBER OF CHANGES have been introduced at English Heritage properties this year in our continuous efforts to enhance your understanding and enjoyment of the heritage.

As part of our plans to bring the Keep at Dover Castle alive, visitors will be able to experience the French siege of 1216, with the aid of a new sound and light display. Pendennis Castle will be displaying for the first time the 20th-century military defences as well as a new Discovery Centre, designed for families and children. Battle Abbey will present 'Prelude to Battle', the first part of a new exhibition explaining the events leading up to the conflict in 1066.

Visitors of all ages can enjoy their heritage

Since the heritage is as much about people as buildings, visitors will be fascinated by the recently acquired Down House, the home of Charles Darwin. Here, the visitor can become immersed in the life of Darwin, the man and the scientist, through the experience of exploring his home and garden and the interactive exhibition on the first floor of his house.

Charles Darwin, whose home, Down House, opens in 1998

At English Heritage we seek to help you, the visitor, to enjoy each property as fully as we can. From guidebooks, audio tours, information panels, exhibitions and historic re-enactments, you will find much that will appeal to you. Historic properties also depend on good visitor facilities. During 1998 a number of new and redesigned shops will offer an exciting range of souvenirs and publications.

The following pages are designed to help you discover the opportunities and facilities that each property has to offer and to plan your visits throughout the year. If you cannot find what you want to know, our Customer Services telephone line is here to help. See inside the back cover for details.

Visit the Dover Castle '1216 Siege Experience'

PLANNING YOUR VISIT

OPENING TIMES

• Full details of opening arrangements are shown under each property.

• A large number of properties are open all year round.

• Where a property can only be visited by prior arrangement, contact details are shown.

And teddy comes too!

• Where a property is described as open 'Any reasonable time', please visit only during daylight hours for safety reasons and to avoid disturbance to nearby properties.

• For reasons of safety, many properties close at 6pm or dusk (whichever is earlier) in October. We define dusk as when light levels prevent a safe and enjoyable visit. You are advised to contact properties beforehand for advice.

• Where a property is opened by a keykeeper, please contact either the keykeeper or ring the number shown under the property, prior to your visit.

State-of-the-art technology at Dover Castle

Free entry to our properties for members

ADMISSION CHARGES

• All admission prices in this Handbook are valid from 1 April 1998 to 31 March 1999.

• Admission to all properties is free to English Heritage members unless otherwise stated. Most special events are also free to members.

• Admission charges for non-members vary from site to site. There are three levels of charge: Adult/concession/children under 16. Throughout the Handbook these are shown as follows: £2.30/£1.70/£1.30.

Concessions are available for senior citizens, unemployed people on production of UB40 and students on production of student union card. Children under five are admitted free.

• The **Family Tickets** available at some of our major properties are a great money saver for a family day out.

GROUP & SCHOOL VISITS

• Discounts of 15% are available at most properties for groups of 11 or more. If you are a group organizer or a tour operator, contact Customer Services (see inside back cover) for a free copy of our Group Visits Guide.

• Student and school groups are admitted free to properties provided they book in advance. For further

Detective work at St Augustine's Abbey

information on this and our other educational facilities, please call 0171 973 3442.

• Our **Windows on the Past** teachers' membership scheme offers many valuable benefits including free admission for up to 4 teachers – contact Customer Services for further details.

TRAVELLING BY CAR, TRAIN, BUS OR FERRY

• Road and public transport details are shown under each entry.

• We are grateful to Barry S. Doe for providing the public transport information. Please contact him with any comments on 01202 528707.

WHEN YOU VISIT

• We welcome families with children of all ages. However, inside some of our grander properties we regret that babies cannot be carried in **back carriers** as this increases the risk of damage to house contents. Alternative means of carrying babies are provided free of charge at these properties.

• **Photography** is welcomed in the grounds of all our properties provided it is not for commercial use. We regret that photography is not permitted inside certain properties for conservation reasons. Please enquire on arrival.

• **Smoking** is not permitted inside any of the historic houses listed in this guide.

• We aim to welcome **dogs** at as many properties as possible. Symbols are shown in individual entries where there are restrictions on dogs. **Guide dogs** and **hearing dogs for the deaf** are welcome at all our properties.

• Some of our properties, due to remoteness or the sensitive historic

Children enjoy a picnic at Castle Acre Castle (above) while another joins in at a special event (left)

fabric of the property, do not have **toilets**. Custodians will be happy to direct visitors to the nearest conveniences.

• **Unforeseen closures** of our properties are extremely rare. However, to avoid possible disappointment we do advise that you check before your visit.

5

SPECIAL FEATURES AND FACILITIES

Visitors enjoying the audio tour at Wenlock Priory

ACCESS FOR ALL

• We aim to make our properties open to everyone who wishes to enjoy them. Over 100 properties in this guide have particular appeal for people with disabilities. Look for the ♿ symbol, indicating that much of the property is easily accessible.

• At many properties there are personal stereo guided tours for wheelchair users or visitors with a visual impairment. At some, there are personal stereo tours in basic language for visitors with learning difficulties.

• Staff will be pleased to assist visitors with special needs, if at all possible. We recommend you contact the property in advance so that preparations can be made to ensure you have a more rewarding visit.

• **Admission is free for the assisting companion** of a visitor with disabilities.

• Our **Guide for Visitors with Disabilities** (also available in braille, large print and on tape) gives full details. For a free copy contact Customer Services (see inside back cover).

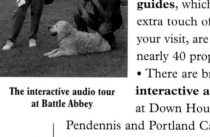

The interactive audio tour at Battle Abbey

BRING YOUR VISITS TO LIFE

• **Souvenir Guides** are on sale at almost all the properties where an entrance fee is charged. If you prefer, you can buy guidebooks through our postal sales service (telephone 01604 781163).

• **Personal stereo guides**, which add an extra touch of realism to your visit, are available at nearly 40 properties.

• There are brand-new **interactive audio tours** at Down House and Pendennis and Portland Castles, which allow you to control the information you hear as you move around – look out for the 🎧★ symbol.

Souvenir guides fascinate all age groups

A WARM WELCOME TO FAMILIES AND CHILDREN

• We welcome families and children to our properties, at many of which special features, exhibitions or educational facilities make visits particularly interesting for children. Look out for properties with free **children's activity sheets**.

• **Baby changing** facilities are available at some of our properties. Look out for the symbol (⭐).

• From April to October, we host a programme of special events, most of which are especially suitable for children.

A SPECIAL WELCOME TO VISITORS FROM OVERSEAS

Visitors to England will find the **Overseas Visitor Pass** the convenient way to visit our properties. For further information, contact Customer Services on 0171 973 3434. Many of our properties display a wide variety of leaflets in different languages, and translations of souvenir guides and audio tours are also available at many properties.

A display panel explains the history of Battle Abbey (right)

SHOPS

• Many properties have shops offering an attractive range of souvenirs, gifts and books. No two shops are exactly the same, as our merchandise is selected to suit each type of building from abbey to castle, historic house to prehistoric monument.

'...I want to be a soldier...'

REFRESHMENTS

• Refreshments are available at many properties. At some you can enjoy a meal in one of our restaurants or tea rooms, which are often located within the historic buildings themselves. Picnics are also welcome in the grounds. Look out for the symbols – (🍴, 🍺, 🥤).

Enjoy a meal in historic surroundings (above)

DISPLAYS AND EXHIBITIONS

• At most properties, display panels explain how the property appeared in the past, often with the help of reconstruction drawings or interactive displays.

• Other properties host temporary exhibitions of paintings and sculpture.

SPECIAL EVENTS AND CONCERTS

BRINGING HISTORY ALIVE

Our special events programme runs from Easter to October and ranges from top-quality living history displays and battle re-enactments to family entertainments, drama and music through the ages. Among this year's highlights are **History in Action III** – our acclaimed historical festival, this year even bigger and more exciting – at Kirby Hall on 1–2 August; **Alice in Wonderland** at various properties; **Roman festivals**

Re-enactments of a siege and battle (above) and Henry VIII (left)

featuring hundreds of enthusiasts from all over Europe in the largest display of its kind ever held in the UK.

Full details of these and over 500 other events taking place this year – nearly all of them free to English Heritage members – can be found in the 1998 Events Diary, available at all properties or from Customer Services (see inside back cover).

Bows, arrows and bonnets for children of all ages (below and below left)

A falconry display involves children at first hand

at Wroxeter Roman City and Richborough Castle; and our **Napoleonic Battle Spectacular** at Battle Abbey on 3–4 May,

Performance at Witley Court

MUSIC ON A SUMMER EVENING

Picnic in the grounds of some of the most beautiful properties in our care before settling down to enjoy world-class performances by acclaimed orchestras and soloists.

The 1998 **Music on a Summer Evening** programme includes concerts and operas at Kenwood Lakeside, Marble Hill House, Audley End and a host of other venues. To coincide with the Tall Ships' Race, there will be also be a jazz concert at Pendennis Castle. Many of the performances are accompanied by spectacular fireworks.

For full details please ask for our free 1998 Concert diary at properties or contact Customer Services (for details see inside back cover).

The finale of a concert at Kenwood Lakeside

🎥 LIGHTS, CAMERA... ACTION 🎥

Many visitors are intrigued to know which properties feature in films and TV programmes. Well-known examples include such productions as **Hamlet, Robin Hood Prince of Thieves, Wuthering Heights** and, most recently, at Osborne House, **Mrs Brown**, which tells the story of Queen Victoria and her ghillie, John Brown. Look out for the new symbol (🎥) under the relevant property.

Dame Judi Dench and Billy Connolly star in *Mrs Brown*, **filmed at Osborne House**

9

JOIN US TODAY

AND GET MORE FROM YOUR HERITAGE...

There are **hundreds** of reasons to join English Heritage – all contained within this Handbook.
* FREE entry to over 400 historic properties.
* FREE entry to over 500 special events and reductions on our open-air concert tickets.
* Half-price admission to historic properties in Scotland and Wales.
* **Welcome Pack** containing Handbook, map, events and concert information.
* *Heritage Today* – the members' quarterly magazine.
* The chance to enjoy cruises, tours and breaks with fellow members.
* You will also be making a personal contribution towards the conservation of your heritage.

Family fun with English Heritage

HOW TO JOIN

Membership is terrific value at £25 for an adult and £43 for the family, with many other categories to choose from. Simply ask a member of staff at one of our properties, ring us on 0171 973 3434 or write to:
English Heritage Membership Dept, PO Box 1BB, London, W1A 1BB

MAKE EVEN MORE OF YOUR MEMBERSHIP

Of course, if you're already a member you'll know that you receive an updated Handbook and events and concerts diaries each Spring, and, after your first year, are entitled to free entry to properties managed by Historic Scotland, Cadw and Manx National Heritage.

MORE FOR YOUR MONEY

The valuable income from members helps create further funding for the heritage. As the country's leading conservation organization, we aim to protect your heritage for all to enjoy, through our expert advice and skills.

Here are three more ways you can help us conserve more of your heritage, without it costing you a penny:

• **PAY YOUR SUBSCRIPTION BY DIRECT DEBIT**
It's convenient for you and means we spend less money and time on administration.

• **COVENANT YOUR MEMBERSHIP**
This allows us to claim back the tax you have already paid in your membership fee. It costs you nothing – and all you need to do is fill in a form.

• **APPLY FOR THE ENGLISH HERITAGE VISA CARD**
As well as offering you benefits, each new account will trigger a £10 donation to English Heritage and a percentage of whatever you spend.
Ring 0171 973 3434 for further information on all of these ways to make your heritage pound go further.

Just two of the many conservation projects your membership supports

---

MAKE A PRESENT OF YOUR PAST

Give a gift of English Heritage membership to family and friends – an original gift they can enjoy all year long.

They'll receive a special gift box with Handbook, map and greetings card (for your own message) and will of course enjoy all the benefits of membership!

To order your gift memberships simply call us on 0171 973 3434.

THE REGIONS

In 1998 we are reorganizing many of our activities across the country into nine regions which will enable us to work more easily and efficiently with others at local level. These regions coincide with the Government regional boundaries. The familiar counties and unitary authorities are listed by region below and shown under each property in the Handbook.

LONDON

SOUTH EAST
Berkshire
Buckinghamshire
Hampshire
Kent
Oxfordshire
Surrey
East Sussex
West Sussex

SOUTH WEST
Cornwall
Devon
Dorset
Gloucestershire
Somerset
Wiltshire
Bath & N. E. Somerset
Bristol
North West Somerset
South Gloucestershire
Isles of Scilly

EASTERN REGION
Bedfordshire
Cambridgeshire
Essex
Hertfordshire
Norfolk
Suffolk

EAST MIDLANDS
Derbyshire
Leicestershire
Lincolnshire
Northamptonshire
Nottinghamshire

WEST MIDLANDS
Hereford & Worcester
Shropshire
Staffordshire
Warwickshire
West Midlands

YORKSHIRE AND THE HUMBER
North Yorkshire
South Yorkshire
West Yorkshire
City of York
East Riding of
    Yorkshire
North East
    Lincolnshire
North Lincolnshire

NORTH WEST
Cheshire
Cumbria
Greater Manchester
Lancashire
Merseyside

NORTH EAST
County Durham
Northumberland
Tyne & Wear
Teesside

Conserving the Past for the Future

Most people know of English Heritage through the 409 historic properties listed in this guide. However, we are also committed to protecting and promoting this country's historic environment in numerous other ways. Here is a brief outline of the key areas of our responsibility.

From the ancient St Swithuns Church, Compton Beauchamp, Oxfordshire...

...to the post-war, Grade 1-listed Willis Corroon Building, Ipswich

- Providing expert advice and grants to England's 365,000 listed buildings, 17,250 ancient monuments and 9,000 conservation areas

- Identifying important buildings and monuments and if necessary recommending that they be protected by the Government, either by listing or scheduling

- Offering conservation grants of £14.3m to churches and cathedrals in 1996–97

- Supporting archaeology, especially on sites threatened by development

- Acting as the main advisor to the Heritage Lottery Fund on the applications for historic buildings and monuments

- Tackling large and complex restoration projects to rescue important historic buildings at risk

- Encouraging schools, visitors and the wider public to understand and enjoy the heritage

Excavation in progress at Stanwick Iron Age Fortifications

To do this we work with Local Authorities, numerous partners and clients throughout the country.

To find out more about our services, please turn to the inside back cover.

Preservation of the medieval Rows in Chester

LONDON

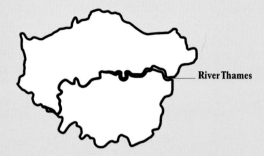

River Thames

Escape the hustle and bustle of the city by visiting one of the magnificent English Heritage properties in London. Chiswick House and Marble Hill House are both original Palladian masterpieces set beside the River Thames. Kenwood, on the edge of Hampstead Heath, is situated in a beautiful landscaped park with a lake which forms the perfect backdrop for summer concerts. It also houses the Iveagh Bequest, one of the most important collections of paintings ever given to the nation.

Kenwood welcomes you to its popular summer concerts

⊙ Albert Memorial

Kensington, LONDON

George Gilbert Scott's elaborate national memorial to the Prince Consort.

Open The Visitor Centre will close in 1998–99 to allow essential conservation work, to be completed in the year 2000.

⊕ Chapter House, Pyx Chamber and Abbey Museum

Westminster Abbey, LONDON (p. 211, 6M)

The Chapter House, built by the royal masons in 1250, contains some of the finest medieval English sculpture to be seen. The octagonal building still has its original floor of newly conserved glazed tiles. The

Mural of the Apocalypse of St John in the Chapter House, Westminster Abbey

11th-century Pyx Chamber houses the Abbey treasures and the Abbey museum medieval royal effigies.

Open all year round.
Open 1 April–1 Nov: daily, 10am–5.30pm. 2 Nov– 31 March: daily, 10am–4pm (closed 24–26 Dec). Liable to be closed at short notice on State occasions. Pyx Chamber 10.30am–4pm all year.
Entry £2.50/£1.90/£1.30.
(0171 222 5897
🦽 ⊗ ♿ 🗋
➔ *Approach either through the Abbey or through Dean's Yard and the cloister.*
🚌 *Tel: 0171 222 1234.*
🚇 *Victoria and Charing Cross both ¾m, Waterloo 1m.*
Tube Westminster ¼m.

⊙ ⊛ Chiswick House

Chiswick, LONDON
(p. 210, 5M)
See p. 16 for full details.

The Chapter House, Westminster Abbey

CHISWICK HOUSE

Chiswick, LONDON (p. 210, 5M)

Inigo Jones

Surrounded by beautiful gardens, close to the centre of London, lies one of England's finest Palladian villas. It was designed by the third Earl of Burlington, a great promoter of the Palladian style first pioneered in England by Inigo Jones, who sought to create the kind of house and garden found in ancient Rome. Today you can enjoy the house's lavish interiors before stepping outside into the classical gardens – a perfect complement to the house itself.

William Kent's sumptuous interiors contrast with Burlington's pure exterior. Enjoy the lavish Blue Velvet Room, with its fabulous gilding, and see the newly redecorated octagonal and domed Saloon. An exhibition and video tell the story of the house, grounds and Lord Burlington.

Open all year round.
Now available for hiring for special occasions, telephone 0171 973 3494.
The Servant, starring James Fox, filmed here.
Open 1 April–30 Sept: daily, 10am–6pm. 1 Oct–21 Oct: daily, 10am–5pm. 22 Oct–31 March:

The extensive grounds include a magnificent Camellia House (above) and the Cascade (below)

Wed–Sun, 10am–4pm (closed 24–26 Dec and 4–17 Jan).
Entry £3.00/£2.30/£1.50.
(0181 995 0508
(in grounds) (off west-bound A4) (also available for the visually impaired, those with learning difficulties, and in French and German)
(exterior & ground floor only) ('Burlington Café'; open daily in summer, weekends only in winter. Not managed by English Heritage.)
Pre-booked tours available.
Burlington Lane, W4.
Local Tourist Information: Tel: 0181 572 8279.
Tel: 0171 222 1234.
Chiswick ½m (trains every 30 minutes from Waterloo).
Tube Turnham Green ¾m.

The Palladian facade (left) and the ornate Blue Velvet Room (right)

⊖ Coombe Conduit

Kingston-Upon-Thames,
LONDON (p. 210, 5M)

Two small buildings (one
now a ruin), connected by
an underground passage,
which supplied water to
Hampton Court Palace.

Open *By appointment only.
Please contact House Manager
at Marble Hill House on 0181
892 5115.*
Entry *Free.*
🚌 *Tel: 0171 222 1234.*
🚆 *Kingston-upon-Thames ¼m.*

⊕ Danson House

Bexley, LONDON (p. 211, 5M)

Built in 1762–67 for a
city merchant, the house
remains in its original form
with many of its principal
interiors restored.

Open *The House is undergoing major building works and
is not currently open to the
public. Access arrangements will
be announced in the members'
magazine,* Heritage Today,
*and the local press. For further
details, contact Customer
Services on 0171 973 3434.*

⊕ ✹ Down House:
Home of
Charles Darwin

Downe, LONDON (p. 211, 5N)
See pp. 18–21 for full details.

⊕ ✹ Eltham Palace

Eltham, LONDON (p. 211, 5M)

A fascinating blend of a
medieval royal palace and

Jewel Tower

a striking 1930s Art Deco
country house.

Open *The Palace is undergoing major building works
and is not currently open to the
public. Access arrangements will
be announced in the members'
magazine,* Heritage Today, *and
the local press. For further
details, contact Customer
Services on 0171 973 3434.*

⊙ Jewel Tower

Westminster, LONDON
(p. 211, 5M)

One of two surviving
buildings of the original
Palace of Westminster, the
Jewel Tower was built
c.1365 to house the
personal treasure of
Edward III. It was later
used as a storehouse and

government office. The
exhibition, 'Parliament
Past and Present', shows
how Parliament works and
a new touch-screen
computer gives a virtual-
reality tour of both Houses
of Parliament.

Open all year round.
Open *1 April–1 Nov: daily,
10am–6pm (6pm/dusk in
Oct). 2 Nov–31 March:
Wed–Sun, 10am–4pm
(closed 24–26 Dec).*
Entry *£1.50/£1.10/80p.*
✆ **0171 222 2219**
✖ 🖰
➔ *Opposite S end of Houses of
Parliament (Victoria Tower).*
🚌 *Tel: 0171 222 1234.*
🚆 *Charing Cross ¾m,
Victoria and Waterloo, both 1m.*
Tube *Westminster ¼m.*

17

Down House:
Home of Charles Darwin

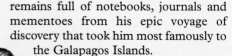

LONDON (p. 211, 5N)

Charles Darwin was perhaps the most influential scientist of the 19th century. It was from his study at Down House that he worked on the scientific theories that first scandalized and then revolutionized the Victorian world, culminating in the publication of the most significant book of the century, *On the Origin of Species by means of Natural Selection*, in 1859. His home for forty years, Down House was the centre of his intellectual world and even now his study remains full of notebooks, journals and mementoes from his epic voyage of discovery that took him most famously to the Galapagos Islands.

The house has recently undergone a major programme of restoration, so that you can visit Darwin's much-loved family home in the tranquil Kent countryside in all its splendour. Visitors can wander in the gardens along the 'Sandwalk', as Darwin did every morning to compose his thoughts before beginning his scientific studies.

Charles Darwin

From the outside, Down House looks like an every-day mid-Victorian family home, lying on the edge of a Kent village. Its significance lies in the influence of its remarkable former owner who made this house his home for forty years.

Charles Darwin returned to Britain from his epic voyage on HMS *Beagle* around South America in 1836 and at first lived in London. He had already achieved a certain fame through the reports he had sent back throughout his five-year journey and his writings continued to be well received. Following marriage to his cousin, Emma Wedgwood, and the first signs of his own poor health, he decided, in 1842, to move away from the capital into the peace and open space of the country.

The house from the gardens

The Cary microscope Darwin used on HMS *Beagle*

A watercolour of Down House painted in 1880 by Goodwin

Although not his ideal choice, he at first thought Down House 'oldish and ugly', it did allow him and his large family the freedom and space that had not been possible in London.

Originally a farmhouse, the main structure of the house was built in the late 18th century. The move to Kent allowed him to live the quiet and happy life of a family man while at the same time correlating the discoveries from which he formed the revolutionary theory of evolution through natural selection. The principal asset of the house is that it remains much as it was when Darwin lived there. Most special of all is the ground-floor study which was the centre of his life, in which are collected some of the 3,500 objects connected with his work that still remain at Down House.

This quiet room contains the chair he used and the desk at which he sat to write his famous works. Further in the house are some of his prized possessions, the most important of which is the huge original bound manuscript of the journal from his five-year voyage on HMS *Beagle*.

Charles Darwin at Down House with his eldest son, William

The study in which Darwin worked as it is today (above) and his notebooks from the *Beagle*

The study also houses the ingenious instruments which he used to collect his data, including the portable microscope, made by Cary of London, his pocket pistols and 'life preserver'. And there are reminders of the vilification Darwin underwent when his theories were published. Going against the conceptions of the age, both scientific and religious, Darwin bore the brunt of the outrage with equanimity. He himself kept *Punch* cartoons that derided his theories and the cruellest caricatures from *Vanity Fair*.

In later life the study became a sanctuary into which Darwin could retreat for hours at a time. He even had his own closet built into the corner of the room, with sink and cold shower, so he could remain in the study for long periods.

Darwin's happiest years were spent at Down House. It was a family home where there were always children present. In fact, his children busied themselves with some of the experiments and investigations that went into the production of his great work, *On the Origin of Species*. Darwin was indeed an encouraging father: early photographs show him affectionately holding his eldest son, William, and his great delight in fatherhood is readily apparent.

He also found time to make several additions to the simple three-storey house. At various times he extended both the drawing room and his wife's bedroom, and he also built the kitchen wing. The restoration of the garden is a long-term conservation project in its own right. Darwin's 'thinking path', the 'sandwalk' which he walked daily, can still be followed, and the rest of the gardens are in the process of detailed restoration.

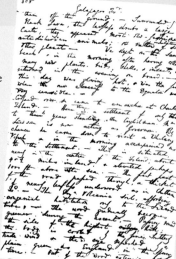

A page from Charles Darwin's *Journal*

Down House has recently undergone extensive development to return the ground-floor rooms to their 1870s' appearance. An interactive exhibition area on the first floor captures the essence of Darwin's life and work and conveys the importance of his ideas.

Down House is a tribute to the memory and influence of this country's best-known scientist: a man who once modestly said, 'I have dabbled in several branches of natural history...'

HMS *Beagle* in the Straits of Magellan

Entry to Down House will be by timed ticket only. Visitors must pre-book, at least 1 day in advance, by telephoning 0870 6030145 (after 1 February 1998).

Darwin's desk in the Old Study (above)

Memorabilia from Darwin's journey on the *Beagle* (right)

Open all year round.
♿ **Down House will be opening to the public in Spring 1998.**
Open 10 April–31 Oct: Wed–Sun, 10am–6pm (6pm/dusk in Oct). 1 Nov–31 Jan: Wed–Sun, 10am–4pm. 1–31 Mar: Wed–Sun, 10am–4pm. (Closed 24–26 Dec and 1–28 Feb.)
Entry £5.00/£3.80/£2.50. Entry will be by timed ticket only. Visitors must pre-book. To pre-book, at least 1 day in advance, telephone the booking line: 0870 6030145 (after 1 February 1998).
✆ **01689 859119** or **Booking line 0870 6030145.**
♿♿ 🅿 (♿ and coaches only during peak season) 🎧 ☕ ♿ (throughout) ⊗ 🛈 📷 ➲ In Luxted Road, Downe, off A21 near Biggin Hill. Parking for coaches and disabled visitors is provided at the House throughout the open season. During peak periods additional car parking is available nearby, signed from Downe village. As Downe is a small village with limited capacity for traffic, English Heritage would like to encourage visitors to travel by public transport. Train services from central London take less than 30 minutes to the nearest mainline stations.
🚆 Tel: 0171 222 1234.
🚌 Orpington (from Charing Cross and Waterloo East) and Bromley South (from Victoria).

21

A portrait by Sir Godfrey Kneller at Marble Hill House

⊕✪ Kenwood

Hampstead, LONDON
(p. 210, 6M)
See pp. 24–25 for full details.

⊘ London Wall

Tower Hill, LONDON
(p. 211, 6M)
The best-preserved piece of the Roman Wall, heightened in the Middle Ages, which formed part of the eastern defences of the City of London.

Open *Any reasonable time.*
Entry *Free.*
🍴 ♿ ⊗
➤ *Near Tower Hill underground station, EC3.*
🚌 *Tel: 0171 222 1234.*
🚆 *Fenchurch Street ¼m.*
Tube *Tower Hill, adjacent.*

⊕✪ Marble Hill House

Twickenham, LONDON
(p. 210, 5M)

A magnificent Thamesside Palladian villa built 1724–29 for Henrietta Howard, Countess of Suffolk, set in 66 acres of parkland. The Great Room has lavish gilded decoration and architectural paintings by Panini. The house also contains an important collection of early Georgian furniture, the Lazenby Bequest Chinoiserie collection and an 18th-century lacquer screen. There is a display on the ground floor with an introductory film about the house, grounds, and the life and times of Henrietta Howard.

Marble Hill House (below): the Great Room (below left) and Lady Suffolk's Bedchamber (right)

Open all year round.
🎥 *Basil, released January 1998, starring Sir Derek Jacobi and Christian Slater, was filmed here.*
• Free Children's Activity Sheet available.
Open *1 April–30 Sept: daily, 10am–6pm. 1 Oct–21 Oct: daily, 10am–5pm. 22 Oct–31 March: Wed–Sun, 10am–4pm (closed 24–26 Dec and 4–17 Jan).*
Entry *£3.00/£2.30/£1.50.*
☎ *0181 892 5115*
🚻 🍴 *('Coach House Cafe', open March–Oct)* 🎧 🅿 *(at Richmond end of Marble Hill Park)* ♿ *(exterior & ground floor only; toilets)* ⊗ 🛍 🚃 *Prebooked group tours available.*

➲ *Richmond Road,*
Twickenham.
🚌 *Tel: 0171 222 1234.*
🚉 *St Margarets ½m,*
Richmond or Twickenham 1m.
Tube *Richmond 1m*

⊕ Ranger's House
Blackheath, LONDON
(p. 211, 5M)

A handsome red brick villa
built *c.*1700, on the edge
of Greenwich Park, with a
splendid bow-windowed
gallery. The house is also
home to the magnificent
Suffolk collection of
paintings, with its stunning
full-length Jacobean
portraits which show
exquisite details of the 'style'
and costume of the day.

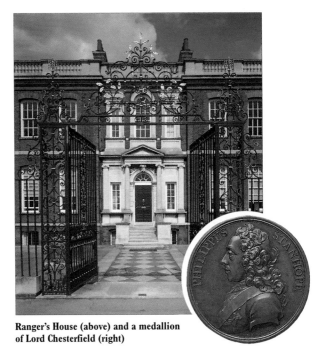

Ranger's House (above) and a medallion
of Lord Chesterfield (right)

Open all year round.
♿ *New exhibition galleries.*

**Jacobian portrait of the Countess
of Oxford at Ranger's House**

♿ *New Children's*
Discovery Centre.
Open *1 April–30 Sept: daily,*
10am–6pm. 1 Oct–21
Oct: daily, 10am–5pm.
22 Oct–31 March:
Wed–Sun, 10am–4pm
(closed 24–26 Dec
and 4–17 Jan).
Entry
£2.50/£1.90/£1.30.
📞 *0181 853 0035*
👪 🅿 *(in Chesterfield*
Walk) ⊗ ♿ 🅔
Pre-booked group
tours available.
➲ *Chesterfield Walk,*
Blackheath, SE10.
🚌 *Tel: 0171 222 1234.*
🚉 *Maze Hill ½m,*
Greenwich or
Blackheath ¼m.

⊕ Winchester Palace
Southwark, LONDON
(p. 211, 6M)

The west gable end, with
its unusual round window,
is the prominent feature of
the remains of the Great
Hall of this 13th-century
town house of the Bishops
of Winchester, damaged
by fire in 1814.

Open *Any reasonable time.*
Entry *Free.*
👪 ♿ ⊗
➲ *Near Southwark*
Cathedral, at corner of Clink
St & Storey St, SE1.
🚌 *Tel: 0171 222 1234.*
🚉 *and* **Tube** *London*
Bridge ¼m.

23

KENWOOD

Hampstead, LONDON (p. 210, 6M)

In splendid grounds beside Hampstead Heath, Kenwood contains the most important collection of paintings ever given to the nation. Among the finest is the 'Self-Portrait' by Rembrandt and 'The Guitar Player' by Vermeer, and works by eminent British artists such as Turner, Gainsborough and Reynolds.

Lord Mansfield's lion

The outstanding neoclassical house was remodelled by Robert Adam, 1764–73, and English Heritage has restored his original colour scheme in the Entrance Hall. Outside, the landscaped park, with sloping lawns and a lake, forms the perfect setting for the concerts held through the summer.

In the 18th century Robert Adam transformed the brick house at Kenwood into a majestic villa for the great judge, Lord Mansfield. Later Earls of Mansfield remodelled the parkland and Kenwood remained in the family until 1922. When developers attempted to buy the estate, the grounds were saved by public purchase; the brewing magnate, the first Earl of Iveagh, bought the house and bequeathed it and his collection of pictures to the nation in 1927.

Open all year round.
101 Dalmations was filmed at Kenwood.
See the exhibition, 'Angels & Urchins: The Fancy Picture in 18th-century British Art.'
• Enjoy a season of summer concerts at the Kenwood Lakeside.
• Free Children's Activity Sheet available.
Open *1 April–31 Oct: daily, 10am–6pm (5pm in Oct). 1 Nov–31 March: daily, 10am–4pm (closed 24–25 Dec).*

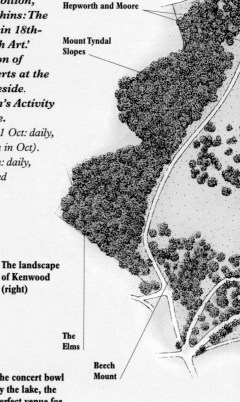

Dairy

Sculptures by Hepworth and Moore

Mount Tyndal Slopes

The landscape of Kenwood (right)

The Elms

Beech Mount

The concert bowl by the lake, the perfect venue for summer concerts

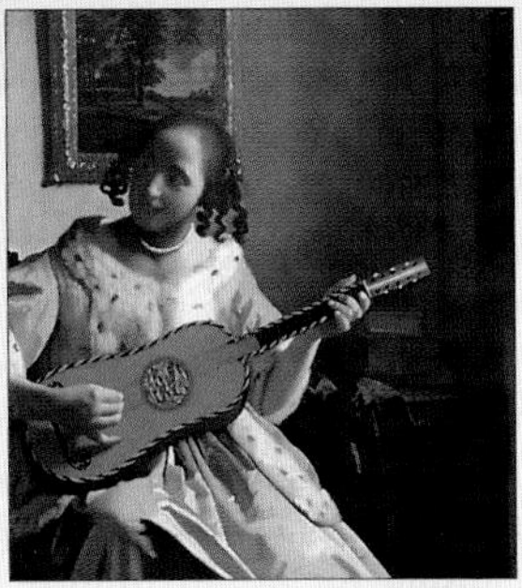

'Guitar Player' by Vermeer, one of Kenwood's fabulous paintings

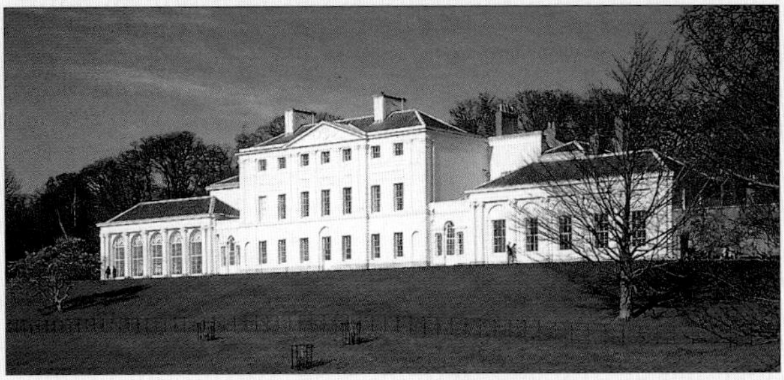

Kenwood House from the south

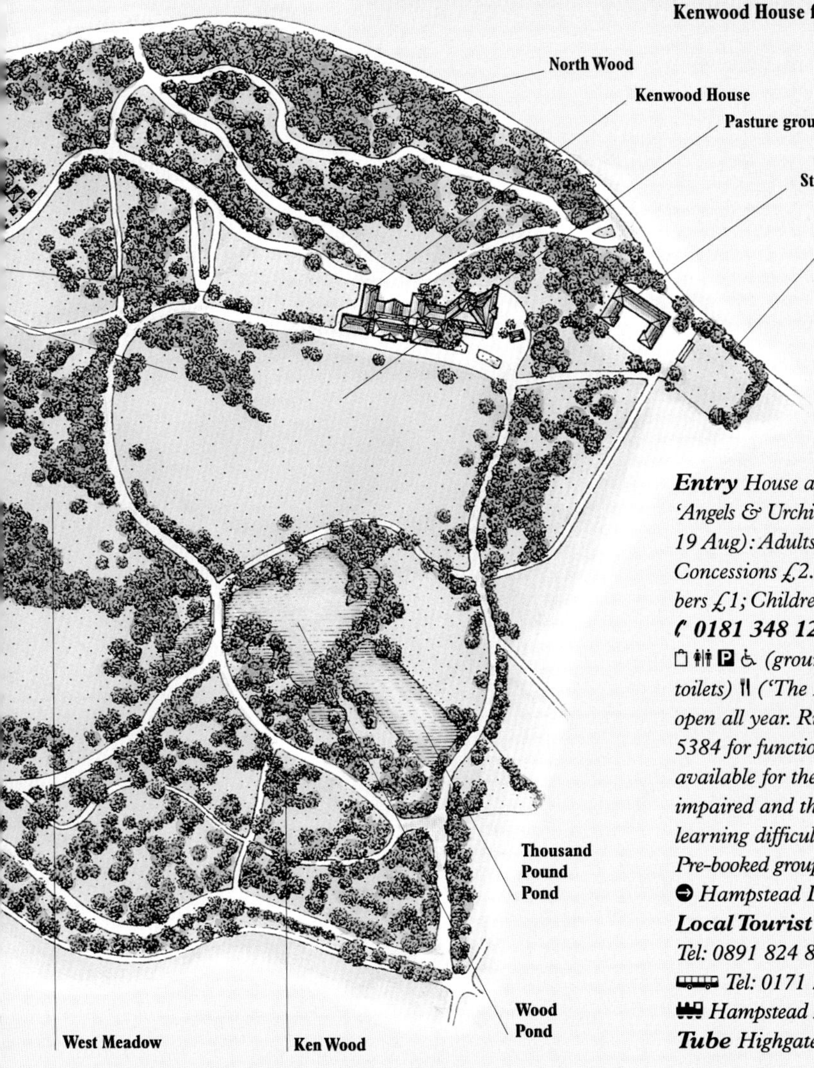
North Wood
Kenwood House
Pasture ground
Stables
Kitchen garden
Thousand Pound Pond
Wood Pond
West Meadow
Ken Wood

Entry *House and grounds free. 'Angels & Urchins' (14 May–19 Aug): Adults £3.50; Concessions £2.50; E.H. members £1; Children under 12 free.*
0181 348 1286
(ground floor only; toilets) *('The Brewhouse', open all year. Ring 0181 341 5384 for functions)* *(also available for the visually impaired and those with learning difficulties)*
Pre-booked group tours available.
Hampstead Lane, NW3.
Local Tourist Information: *Tel: 0891 824 8844.*
Tel: 0171 222 1234.
Hampstead Heath 1½m.
Tube *Highgate 1m.*

SOUTH EAST

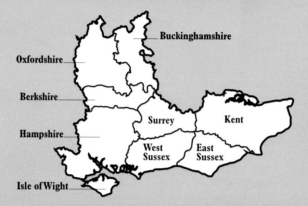

Buckinghamshire
Oxfordshire
Berkshire
Hampshire
Isle of Wight
Surrey
West Sussex
East Sussex
Kent

THE PROPERTIES IN the South East span the centuries. They range from the Roman villa at Lullingstone to Dover Castle where you can explore both the Siege of 1216 Experience and the huge tunnel complex used throughout World War II. Imagine the arrival of St Augustine in Kent with a visit to the Abbey he founded in 598. Explore the battlefield where King Harold fell in 1066 and relive the invasion of William the Conqueror. Royal heritage dominates the Isle of Wight where Carisbrooke Castle, once prison to King Charles I, and Osborne House, Queen Victoria's 'place of one's own', give glimpses of past royal life. The tradition continues at Walmer Castle where you'll see Queen Elizabeth The Queen Mother's beautiful garden.

Travelling in style at Osborne House

Appuldurcombe House

◉ Abingdon County Hall

OXFORDSHIRE (p. 210, 6K)

A grand centrepiece for the market place at Abingdon, this 17th-century public building was built to house the Assize Courts.

Open All year: Tues–Sun, *11am–5pm (4pm outside British Summer Time).* Closed 25–26 Dec. *Entry* Free. ℂ *01235 523703* ⊗ ⑰

◑ In Abingdon, 7m S of Oxford in Market Place. (OS Map 164; ref SU 497971) 🚌 Tel: 01865 785400. 🚄 Radley 2½m.

♡ ◐ Appuldurcombe House

ISLE OF WIGHT (p. 210, 3K)

Although now mainly a shell, Appuldurcombe was once the grandest house on the Isle of Wight. The fine 18th-century baroque-style house stands in its own ornamental grounds, designed by 'Capability' Brown. The rolling green landscape beyond makes this an idyllic setting. An exhibition of prints and photographs depicts the house and its history.

Open 1 April–1 Nov: daily, *10am–6pm (6pm/dusk in Oct).* Last admission 5.30pm (4pm

in Oct). *(Property managed by Mr & Mrs Owen.)* **Entry** £2.00/£1.50/£1.00. ℂ *01983 852484*

👫 🅿 ⅙ 🏠 🏺

◑ ½ m W of Wroxall off B3327. (OS Map 196; ref SZ 543800.) 🚌 Tel: 01983 827005. 🚄 Shanklin 3½ m. 🚢 Ryde 11m (Wightlink. Tel: 0990 827744); West Cowes 12m; East Cowes 12m (Red Funnel. Tel: 01703 334010).

⊕ ♡ Battle Abbey and Battlefield

SUSSEX (p. 211, 4N)

See pp. 28–31 for full details.

⊕ ◐ Bayham Old Abbey

SUSSEX (p. 211, 4N)

Ruins of a house of 'white' canons, founded in c.1208, in an 18th-century land-scaped setting. The Georgian House (Dower House) is also open to the public.

Open all year round. • *Licensed for civil marriage ceremonies.* *Open* 1 April–1 Nov: daily, *10am–6pm (6pm/dusk in Oct). 2 Nov–31 March: Sat–Sun, 10am–4pm.* **Entry** £2.00/£1.50/£1.00. ℂ *01892 890381*

👫 🅿 ⅙ 🏺 🏠 ♨

◑ 1¾m W of Lamberhurst off B2169. (OS Map 188; ref TQ 651366.) 🚌 Tel: 0800 696 996. 🚄 Frant 4m.

Bayham Old Abbey

27

1066 BATTLE OF HASTINGS ABBEY & BATTLEFIELD

✠ ♡ SUSSEX (p. 211, 4N)

The one date in English history that everyone can remember is 1066: the Battle of Hastings, when the conquering Normans vanquished the Anglo-Saxons on 14 October. There is just as much myth surrounding the conflict as known fact. The two armies did not even fight at Hastings, but at the place which became the town of Battle, 6 miles inland. There, on the

William the Conqueror

valley slopes, it is possible to retrace the lines of conflict. In the ruins of the abbey that King William built to atone for the blood spilt, you may stand on the very spot where the defeated King Harold fell. The battlefield itself provides an unparalleled chance to absorb the reality of the conquest. Battle Abbey stands at one of the turning points of English history.

It was never a foregone conclusion that William would win at Battle. Only days before, Harold had won a famous victory in the north at Stamford Bridge against the King of Norway. William *did* win, but only after a great struggle. Today an interactive audio tour re-creates the sounds of the battle, as you stand exactly where the English were, watching the Normans advance towards them. With the English occupying the high ground,

A scene of the Battle of Hastings (above). The great abbey gatehouse (below) and the Battle Abbey seal showing the west front of the church (right)

the Normans were forced to fight uphill. They overcame this disadvantage by fighting both on foot and horseback, while the English dismounted, using swords or their huge two-handed axes. The course of the battle was reversed when the Normans pretended to flee, but then turned back to cut down the English who had broken ranks in pursuit.

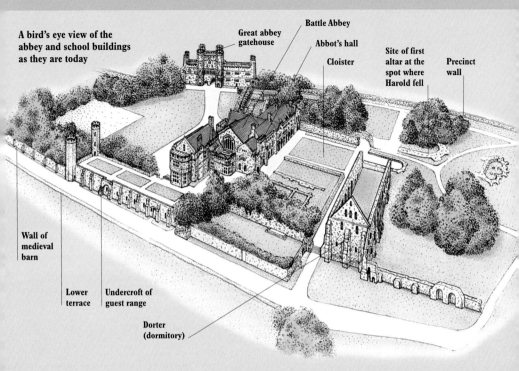

A bird's eye view of the abbey and school buildings as they are today

Great abbey gatehouse

Battle Abbey

Abbot's hall

Cloister

Site of first altar at the spot where Harold fell

Precinct wall

Wall of medieval barn

Lower terrace

Undercroft of guest range

Dorter (dormitory)

The final assault by William was preceded by a devastating volley of arrows. The Bayeux Tapestry depicts an arrow hitting Harold in the eye. He did not die directly from that wound, but was later cut down by a Norman sword. On Harold's death his army fled, the Normans in pursuit. Once William had quelled the nation in 1070, ruthlessly crushing any opposition to his rule, he founded Battle Abbey to atone for the terrible loss of life at the Battle of Hastings.

The site of the battle, with the abbey remains in the background

29

Site where
Harold fell

English lines

Map of the site of the Battle of Hastings.
Harold's army controlled the higher ground
to the left, facing William's forces in the
marshy bottoms to the right.

Norman lines

Powdermill Lane

Battle High
Street

Battle Abbey
School grounds

Children discover
Battle's history
(right)

A few portions of the abbey
remain today, but little of
the church or features dating
back to the early Normans.
The best-preserved and
most impressive part is the
Great Gatehouse, finest of

all surviving medieval abbey
entrances, which was built
around 1338. The great hall
and other monastic buildings
were incorporated into the
Tudor and Georgian houses
that occupied the site

Section of Bayeux Tapestry

Battle Abbey museum (left)

after Henry VIII's dissolution of the monasteries. The battlefield, though, remains little touched: a generous gift from the USA enabling it to be purchased for the nation in 1976.

Open all year round.
♿ New interpretation and exhibition on the run-up to the Battle of Hastings.
♿ New shop in conserved courthouse.
• Exciting range of interactive displays and exhibitions: an audio-visual interpretation of the battle, and an inter-active audio tour of the

history of the battlefield and abbey that guides you around the grounds.
• Special Event highlights include the Napoleonic Battle Spectacular, 3–4 May, and the 1066 Living History and Skirmish, 10–11 October.
• Children's activity area with outdoor playground.
• Family Discovery Pack and free Children's Activity Sheet available.
Open 1 April–1 Nov: daily, 10am–6pm (6pm/dusk in Oct). 2 Nov–31 March: daily, 10am–4pm (closed 24–26 Dec). Film/audio-visual – '1066, The Battle of Hastings'; Abbot's Hall open

to the public during school summer holidays only.
Entry £4.00/£3.00/£2.00. Family ticket (2 adults & 3 children) £10.00.
☎ 01424 773792
🅿 (charge payable) 🎧* (also available for the visually impaired, those in wheelchairs or with learning difficulties, and in French, German and Japanese; braille guides in English only) ♿ (some steps) 🚻 (nearby) ▯ ⊙ 🗂 🐾 ▣
➲ In Battle, at S end of High St. Battle is reached by road by turning off A21 onto the A2100.
(OS Map 199; ref TQ 749157.)
Local Tourist Information: Battle (tel: 01424 773721) and Hastings (tel: 01424 781111).
🚌 Tel: 01273 474747.
🚃 Battle ½m.

Norman archer from the audio-visual re-enactment of the battle

✚♡ Bishop's Waltham Palace

HAMPSHIRE (p. 210, 4K)

This medieval seat of the Bishops of Winchester once stood in an enormous park. Wooded grounds still surround the mainly 12th- and 14th-century remains, including the Great Hall and three-storey tower, as well as the moat which once enclosed the palace. Much was destroyed in a fire by Parliamentarians in the Civil War after the Battle of Cheriton in 1644, but the ground floor of the Dower House is intact and furnished as a 19th-century farmhouse, with an exhibition on the powerful Winchester Bishops on the first floor.

Bishop's Waltham Palace

Bishop's Waltham Palace shield

Open *1 April–1 Nov: daily, 10am–6pm (6pm/dusk in Oct). Keykeeper in winter, please telephone 01732 778030.*
Entry *£2.00/£1.50/£1.00.*
☎ *01489 892460*
🅿 ♿ *(grounds only)* 🚻 *(nearby in Bishop's Waltham)* ⊙ ⚑
➲ *In Bishop's Waltham 5m from junction 8 of M27. (OS Map 185; ref SU 552173.)*
🚌 *Tel: 01256 464501 or 01703 226235.*
🚂 *Botley 3½m.*

✚♡ Boxgrove Priory

SUSSEX (p. 210, 4L)

Remains of the Guest House, Chapter House and church of a 12th-century priory.

Open *Any reasonable time.*
Entry *Free.*
⊗ 🅿
➲ *N of Boxgrove, 4m E of Chichester on minor road off A27. (OS Map 197; ref SU 909076.)*
🚌 *Tel: 01243 783251.*
🚂 *Chichester 4m.*

⊖♡ Bramber Castle

SUSSEX (p. 210, 4M)

The remains of a Norman castle gatehouse, walls and earthworks.

Open *Any reasonable time.*
Entry *Free.*
🅿 *(limited)* 🐕
➲ *On W side of Bramber village off A283.*

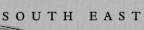

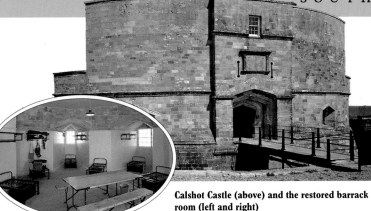
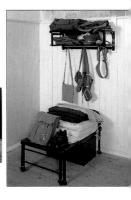

Calshot Castle (above) and the restored barrack room (left and right)

(OS Map 198; ref TQ 187107.)
🚌 *Tel: 01273 886200.*
🚌 *Shoreham-by-Sea 4½m.*

Calshot Castle
HAMPSHIRE (p. 210, 3K)

This century, the fort has been part of both an RN and an RAF base. Spectacular views of the Solent can be seen from the roof. Henry VIII built this coastal fort to command the sea passage to Southampton. The barrack room has been restored to its pre-World War I artillery garrison appearance, complete with bunks and uniform.

Open 1 April–1 Nov: daily, 10am–4pm.
Entry £1.80/£1.40/90p.
(*01703 892023*
🅿 🕴 ⚓ ♿ *(Keep: ground floor only; toilets)* ⊗ 🗂
➲ *On spit 2m SE of Fawley off B3053.*
(OS Map 196; ref SU 488025.)
🚌 *Tel: 01703 226235.*

Camber Castle
SUSSEX (p. 211, 4O)

A rare example of an Henrician fort surviving in its original plan.

Open 1 July–30 Sept: Sat, 2–5pm. Monthly guided walks of Rye Harbour Nature Reserve including Camber Castle. Please telephone the Reserve Manager (01797 223862) for further information. (Property managed by Rye Harbour Nature Reserve.)
Entry £2.00/£1.50/£1.00. Friends of Rye Harbour Nature Reserve free.
(*01797 223862*
⊗
➲ *Access by a delightful 1m walk across fields, off the A259, 1m S of Rye off harbour road. (OS Map 189; ref TQ 922185.)*
🚌 *Tel: 01273 474747.*
🚌 *Rye 1¼m.*

Carisbrooke Castle
ISLE OF WIGHT (p. 210, 3K)
See pp. 34–35 for full details.

Conduit House
Canterbury, KENT (p. 211, 5P)

The Conduit House is the monastic waterworks which supplied nearby St Augustine's Abbey.

Open Any reasonable time. Exterior viewing only.
Entry Free.
➲ *From ring road turn right into Havelock St, right into North Holmes Rd, right into St Martin's Rd, right into Kings Park. Approximately 5–10 minutes' walk from St Augustine's Abbey. (OS Map 179; ref TR 159585.)*
🚌 *Tel: 01227 472082.*
🚌 *Canterbury East or West, both 1½m.*

Camber Castle

CARISBROOKE CASTLE

◉ ISLE OF WIGHT (p. 210, 3K)

From time immemorial, whosoever controlled Carisbrooke controlled the Isle of Wight. The castle sits at the heart of the island, and has been a fixture since its foundation as a Saxon camp during the 8th century. Carisbrooke's royal connections date from the 13th century when

The Redvers Shield of Arms

Edward I bought it from the Redvers family. For a brief period the castle occupied centre stage when Charles I was imprisoned there from 1647 to 1648, before being taken for trial and execution in London. His story is commemorated in the museum.

The compact castle buildings demonstrate every phase of construction from the Saxon era to the present. Remnants of the Saxon wall run below the Norman keep, high on its artificial mound. Built up by the Redvers family, who ruled the island until 1293, Carisbrooke was bought by Edward I on the death of Countess Isabella, whose individual taste is seen in the beautiful chapel she built.

The castle was refortified in the late 16th century by its Governor, Sir George Carey, against continued threats of invasion by Catholic Spain. Although it saw no action in the English Civil War, Carisbrooke was prison to King Charles I in 1647–48. He twice tried escaping before he was taken to London to be tried. Lesser prisoners were made to tread the waterwheel, drawing water up the well's 49-metre (161-feet) depth until donkeys – still there today – were introduced in the 17th century. Today, an interactive museum in the Old Coach House displays the history of the castle.

The 12th-century keep, on its artificial mound, towers above the later great hall and private apartments (above)

Open all year round.
♿ New hands-on interpretation for children at the Donkey Centre.
• Free Children's Activity Sheet available.
• An exciting CD-Rom unit provides information on the castles of England, their functions and purpose.
• See military displays, music and dance set during the Spanish Armada, 25–27 August.
***Open** 1 April–1 Nov: daily, 10am–6pm (6pm/dusk in Oct). 2 Nov–31 March: daily, 10am–4pm (closed 24–26 Dec).*

A re-enaction of King Charles I when imprisoned at Carisbrooke (left), and a replica of the seal of Sir George Carey, Governor of the castle from 1583 to 1603 (below)

The St Nicholas Chapel

Entry £4.00/£3.00/£2.00. Family ticket (2 adults & 3 children) £10.

(**01983 522107**

♦♦ 🅿 ♦♦ *(The Coach House Tea Room; open April–October)*
(also available for the visually impaired and those with learning difficulties)
(grounds & lower levels

Children in the shop at Carisbrooke (right) and at the donkey centre (below)

only) 🖶 🖂 ⓜ Ⓔ 🖂
➤ *1¼m SW of Newport. (OS Map 196; ref SZ 486877.)*
Local Tourist Information:
Newport (tel: 01983 525450) and Cowes (tel: 01983 291914).
🚌 *Tel: 01983 827005.*
🚃 *Ryde Esplanade 9m; Wootton (IoW Steam Rly) 5m.*
⛴ *West Cowes 5m; East Cowes 6m (Red Funnel, tel: 01703 334010); Fishbourne 6m; Ryde 8m; Yarmouth 9m (Wightlink, tel: 0990 827744).*

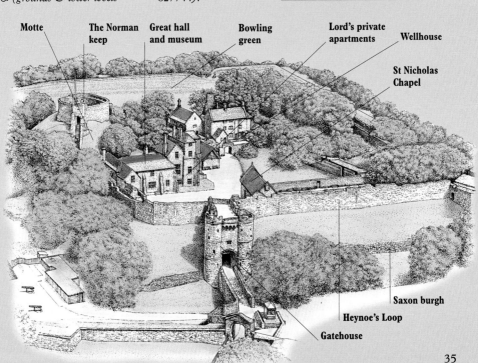

Motte — The Norman keep — Great hall and museum — Bowling green — Lord's private apartments — Wellhouse — St Nicholas Chapel — Saxon burgh — Heynoe's Loop — Gatehouse

◎ Deal Castle

KENT (p. 211, 5P)
See p. 38 for full details.

◎ Deddington Castle

OXFORDSHIRE
(pp. 210/214/217, 7K)

Extensive earthworks
conceal the remains of a
12th-century castle.

*Open Any reasonable time.
(Property managed by
Deddington Parish Council.)*
Entry Free.

🏹

➲ *S of B4031 on E side of
Deddington, 17m N of
Oxford on A423.
(OS Map 151; ref SP 471316.)*
🚌 *Tel: 01788 535555.*
🚉 *King's Sutton 5m.*

◎ Donnington Castle

BERKSHIRE (p. 210, 5K)

Built in the late 14th
century, the twin-towered
gatehouse of this castle
survives amidst some
impressive earthworks.

*Open Any reasonable time
(exterior viewing only).*
Entry Free.
🅿 ♿ *(steep slopes within
grounds)* 🏹
➲ *1m N of Newbury
off B4494.
(OS Map 174; ref
SU 461694.)*
🚌 *Tel: 01635 248423.*
🚉 *Newbury 1¼m.*

◎ Dover Castle

KENT (p. 211, 4P)
See pp. 40–47 for full details.

36

◎ Down House

Downe, GREATER LONDON
(p. 211, 5N)
See pp. 18–21 for full details.

◎ Dymchurch
Martello Tower

KENT (p. 211, 4O)

One of many artillery
towers which formed part
of a chain of strongholds
intended to resist invasion
by Napoleon. It is fully
restored, with a 24-
pounder gun on the roof.

*Open 10–13 April and
2–4 May: 2–5.30pm.
9 May–11 July: weekends and
Bank Holiday Mondays:
2–5.30pm. 18 July–31 Aug:
daily, 2–5.30pm. 1–30 Sept:
Sat–Sun, 2–5.30pm. For
further details please telephone
Area Manager, Dover Castle,
01304 211067.*
Entry £1.00/80p/50p.
❌
➲ *Access from High Street,
not from seafront.
(OS Map 189; ref TR 102294.)*

Eynsford Castle

🚌 *Tel: 0345 696 996.*
🚉 *Sandling 7m; Dymchurch
(R H & D Rly), adjacent.*

◎ Eynsford Castle

KENT (p. 211, 5N)

One of the first stone
castles built by the
Normans. The moat and
remains of the curtain wall
and hall can still be seen.

*Open 1 March–30 Sept:
daily, 10am–6pm. 1 Oct–
28 Feb: 10am–4pm.*
Entry Free.
🅿 ♿ 🏹
➲ *In Eynsford off A225.
(OS Map 177; ref TQ 542658.)*
🚌 *Tel: 0345 696 996.*
🚉 *Eynsford 1m.*

◎ Farnham
Castle Keep

SURREY (p. 210, 5L)

A motte and bailey castle,
once one of the seats of the
Bishop of Winchester,
which has been in
continuous occupation
since the 12th century.

Farnham Castle Keep

Open *1 April–1 Nov:*
daily, 10am–6pm
(6pm/dusk in Oct).
Entry *£2.00/£1.50/£1.00.*
(01252 713393
P ⌂ ☂
➲ *½m N of Farnham town*
centre on A287.
(OS Map 186; ref
SU 839474.)
🚌 *Tel: 01737 223000.*
🚏 *Farnham ¾m.*

✛ Faversham:
Stone Chapel
KENT (p. 211, 5O)

The remains of a small
medieval church incor-
porating part of a 4th-
century Romano-British
pagan mausoleum.

Open *Any reasonable time.*
(Property managed by the
Faversham Society.)
Entry *Free.*
☂
➲ *1¼m W of Faversham on A2.*
(OS Map 178; ref TQ 992614.)
🚌 *Tel: 0345 696 996.*
🚏 *Faversham 1½m.*

⊕ Flowerdown
Barrows
HAMPSHIRE (p. 210, 4K)

Round barrows of a Bronze
Age burial site which were
once part of a larger group.

Open *Any reasonable time.*
Entry *Free.*
☂
➲ *In Littleton, 2½m NW of*
Winchester off A272.
(OS Map 185; ref SU 459320.)
🚌 *Tel: 01256 464501.*
🚏 *Winchester 2m.*

⊕ Fort Brockhurst
HAMPSHIRE (p. 210, 3K)

This was a new type of fort,
built in the 19th century to
protect Portsmouth with
formidable fire-power.
Largely unaltered, the
parade ground, gun ramps
and moated keep can all
be viewed. An exhibition
illustrates the history of
Portsmouth's defences.

⟳ The fort is available
for private hire for

functions and events.
• *See nesting birds,*
and look out for ghostly
activity in Prisoner
Cell No. 3!
• *View the RAF Gosport*
Aviation Heritage
Exhibition.
Open *1 April–1 Nov:*
Sat–Sun, 10am–6pm
(6pm/dusk in Oct).
Entry *£2.00/£1.50/£1.00.*
(01705 581059
E ⍩ P ◑ ⅋ *(grounds &*
ground floor only; toilets)
➲ *Off A32, in Gunner's Way,*
Elson, on N side of Gosport.
(OS Map 196; ref SU 596020.)
🚌 *Tel: 01329 232208.*
🚏 *Fareham 3m.*

⊕ Fort Cumberland
HAMPSHIRE (p. 210, 3K)

Constructed in the shape
of a wide pentagon by the
Duke of Cumberland in
1746. The fort was occu-
pied by the Royal Marines
until 1973 and is perhaps
the most impressive piece
of 18th-century defensive
architecture in England.

Open *19 July, 20 Sept: by*
guided tour only. Advance
booking is required for tours,
please telephone 01732 778030.
Entry *£2.00/£1.00.*
➲ *In the Eastney district of*
Portsmouth on the estuary
approach via Henderson Road,
a turning off Eastney Road, or
from the Esplanade.
(OS Map 196; ref SZ 682992.)
🚌 *Tel: 01705 650967.*
🚏 *Fratton 2m.*

DEAL CASTLE
ⓜ KENT (p. 211, 5P)

Crouching low and menacing, the huge, rounded bastions of this austere fort, built by Henry VIII, once carried 119 guns. Designed to resemble a Tudor Rose, Deal Castle is one of three artillery forts on the Kent coast built to counter the threat of invasion during the mid-16th century. Today the castle still appears exactly as it was originally intended to look: powerful and virtually impregnable. Its remarkable coastal position affords breathtaking views out to sea. It is a fascinating castle to explore, with long, dark passages, battlements and a massive basement with an exciting exhibition.

Of the three castles built by Henry VIII to counter the threat of invasion from the Catholic alliance of France and Spain, Deal was the largest. Built purely as a defensive fortress, it was probably completed by 1540 and had at least 145 embrasures for firearms. The rounded bastions were designed to deflect shot, making the fort almost impregnable.

Deal's bastions protected the castle and held many gunports

Looking out to sea (below) from Deal Castle (bottom)

Open all year round.
♿ New interpretation exhibition.
• Free Children's Activity Sheet available.
Open 1 April–1 Nov: daily, 10am–6pm (6pm/dusk in Oct). 2 Nov–31 Mar: Wed–Sun, 10am–4pm (closed 24–26 Dec).
Entry £3.00/£2.30/£1.50.
ℂ 01304 372762
👪🚻🏛🎧 (also available for the visually impaired, those with learning difficulties, and in French and German)
♿ (courtyards & ground floor only, parking available) ⊗
➜ SW of Deal town centre. (OS Map 179; ref TR 378521.)
Local Tourist Information: Deal (tel: 01304 369576).
🚌 Tel: 0345 696 996.
🚉 Deal ½m.

✚ Horne's Place Chapel

Appledore, KENT (p. 211, 4O)

This 14th-century domestic chapel was once attached to the manor house. The house and chapel are privately owned.

Open *By arrangement. Please telephone 01304 211067.*
Entry *Free.*
🅿 *(nearby)* ✖
➡ *1½ m N of Appledore. (OS Map 189; ref TQ 957307.)*
🚃 *Appledore 2½ m.*

Horne's Place Chapel

✪ Hurst Castle

HAMPSHIRE (pp. 210/213, 3J)

This was one of the most sophisticated fortresses built by Henry VIII, and later strengthened in the 19th and 20th centuries, to command the narrow entrance to the Solent. There are two exhibitions in the castle, and two huge 38-ton guns from the fort's armaments.

Open *1 April–31 Oct: daily, 10am–5.30pm (6pm in July and Aug). (Property managed by Hurst Castle Services.)*
Entry *£2.50/£2.00/£1.50.*
☎ *01590 642344*
🍴 🍽 *('Castle Cafe'; weekends only April and May, daily June–Sept)* ✪
➡ *On Pebble Spit S of Keyhaven. Best approached by ferry from Keyhaven, telephone 01590 642500 (June–Sept,*

9am–2pm) or answerphone 01425 610784, for ferry details. (OS Map 196; ref SZ 319898.)
🚌 *Tel: 01202 673555.*
🚃 *Lymington Town 4½ m to Keyhaven, 6½ m to Fort.*

✪ King James's and Landport Gates

Portsmouth, HAMPSHIRE (p. 210, 3K)

These gates were once part of the 17th-century defences of Portsmouth.

Open *Exterior any reasonable time.*
Entry *Free.*
✈
➡ *King James's Gate: forms entrance to United Services Recreation Ground (officers) on Park Rd; Landport Gate: as above, men's entrance on St George's Rd. (OS Map 196; King James's Gate ref SU 638000, Landport Gate ref SU 634998.)*
🚃 *Portsmouth Harbour ⅓ m.*

Hurst Castle

THE SECRET WARTIME TUNNELS AT DOVER CASTLE

ⓗ KENT (p. 211, 4P)

The White Cliffs of Dover are among England's most celebrated sights, yet hidden inside them is a fascinating and secret world. Above stands the mighty fortress of Dover Castle but below, deep underground, are miles of tunnels. First used in the Napoleonic Wars, their great moment came nearly 150 years later when they became a nerve centre in World War II as the headquarters from which the Dunkirk evacuation was masterminded.

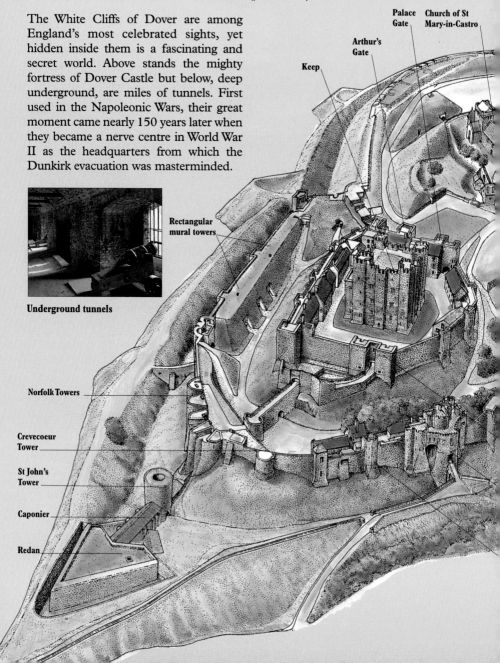

Underground tunnels

Palace Gate

Church of St Mary-in-Castro

Arthur's Gate

Keep

Rectangular mural towers

Norfolk Towers

Crevecoeur Tower

St John's Tower

Caponier

Redan

The labyrinth of tunnels under Dover Castle reached the height of their importance during World War II when they were a vital headquarters during the darkest hours of Britain's struggle.

Today you can experience life as it was for the 700 personnel in the worst days of the war. Relive the drama as a wounded Battle of Britain pilot is taken into the underground hospital

to fight for his life in the operating theatre, then move on to see the Command Centre in which Churchill hatched the most desperate plans – the ones that eventually led to victory.

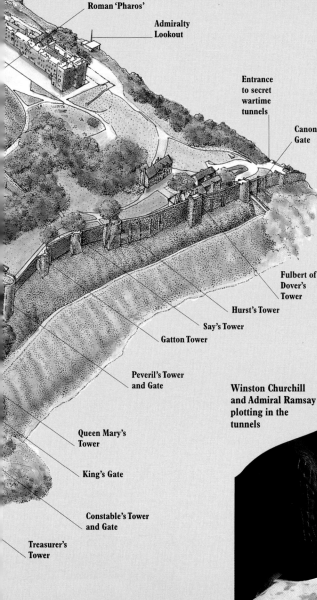

Roman 'Pharos'

Admiralty Lookout

Entrance to secret wartime tunnels

Canon's Gate

Fulbert of Dover's Tower

Hurst's Tower

Say's Tower

Gatton Tower

Peveril's Tower and Gate

Queen Mary's Tower

King's Gate

Constable's Tower and Gate

Treasurer's Tower

The Admiralty Lookout station

Reconstructed repeater station

Winston Churchill and Admiral Ramsay plotting in the tunnels

SECRET WARTIME TUNNELS
Whoever first had the idea of tunnelling under Dover Castle can hardly have anticipated the dramas that would unfold underground. The rabbit warren of tunnels has been the centre of military operations from the Napoleonic Wars almost to the present. The Dunkirk evacuation in 1940 was its finest hour. Visitors may experience for themselves what military life was like underground.

Tunnelling operations began in earnest in the late 1790s when the castle was fortified in readiness for a French invasion. Seven tunnels (running with damp and prone to collapse) were dug for the soldiers and officers who were filling both castle and town to overflowing.

When French threats ended, the tunnels fell into disuse until they came back into their own in World War II. Admiral Ramsay, who was commanding the Straits of Dover, occupied the underground tunnels from the outbreak of war.

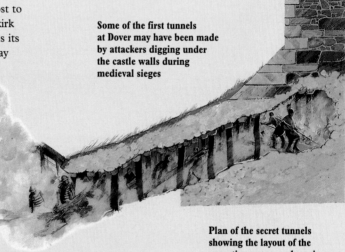

Some of the first tunnels at Dover may have been made by attackers digging under the castle walls during medieval sieges

Plan of the secret tunnels showing the layout of the operation rooms and services as they were in mid-1943. These, together with the Hospital Annexe level above, are open to the public

Entrance to secret wartime tunnels

Visitors' entrance

Ventilation shaft

Coastal artillery operations room during World War II

Children learn about life in the tunnels

The reconstructed
telephone exchange

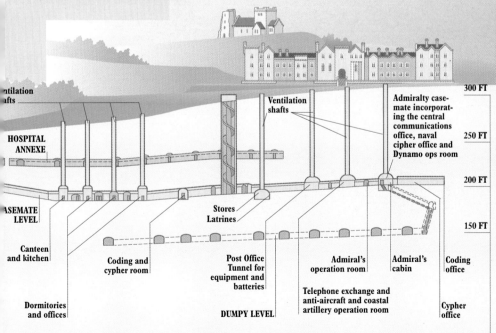

Ventilation
shafts

HOSPITAL
ANNEXE

Ventilation
shafts

Admiralty case-
mate incorporat-
ing the central
communications
office, naval
cipher office and
Dynamo ops room

300 FT

250 FT

200 FT

CASEMATE
LEVEL

Stores
Latrines

150 FT

Canteen
and kitchen

Coding and
cypher room

Post Office
Tunnel for
equipment and
batteries

Admiral's
operation room

Admiral's
cabin

Coding
office

Dormitories
and offices

DUMPY LEVEL

Telephone exchange and
anti-aircraft and coastal
artillery operation room

Cypher
office

SEA LEVEL

In May 1940, as France fell before the German advance, these tunnels became the nerve centre for Operation Dynamo – the evacuation of the British Expeditionary Force (BEF) and French troops from Dunkirk's beaches.

Ramsay and his staff worked round the clock for nine days. On 26 May some 400,000 troops were awaiting rescue. The best estimate was that 45,000 could be brought back. Dunkirk was ablaze. Pleasure craft, fishing boats, sailing barges streamed across the Channel as tenders from the beaches. The Allied forces and rescue ships were sitting targets. Yet, by 4 June, all were evacuated. In total, 338,000 men came back: the BEF and 139,000 French soldiers.

Anti-aircraft operations room

Under sustained German air attack through the war, Dover's tunnels acquired a new importance as shelter for the Combined Headquarters. Additional tunnels were dug, telecommunications systems were installed, and even a hospital was established. Hundreds of men and women worked and lived underground in the most unpleasant conditions of damp and piercing cold.

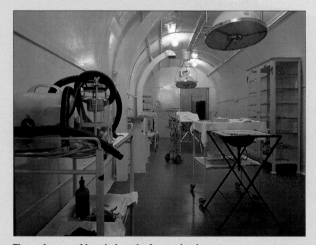

The underground hospital on the Annexe level

A WWII re-enactment at Dover

A TOUR OF DOVER CASTLE

Dover Castle is a sturdy reminder of some of the toughest fighting days in England's past. William the

Henry II

Conqueror strengthened the defences that Harold built, while the monumental keep was built for Henry II, as were the walls of the Inner Bailey and the eastern part of the outer curtain wall. Their designs were innovative, with regularly spaced towers for the Inner Bailey, and the curtain wall's gatehouses and flanking towers. The works were completed under Henry III.

Medieval siege

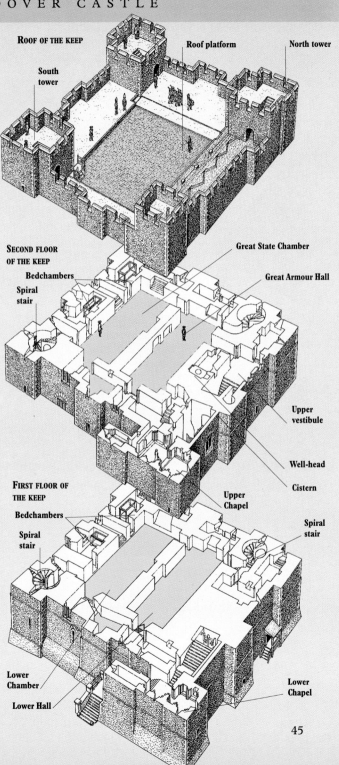

ROOF OF THE KEEP

Roof platform

North tower

South tower

SECOND FLOOR OF THE KEEP

Bedchambers

Spiral stair

Great State Chamber

Great Armour Hall

Upper vestibule

Well-head

Cistern

FIRST FLOOR OF THE KEEP

Bedchambers

Spiral stair

Upper Chapel

Spiral stair

Lower Chamber

Lower Hall

Lower Chapel

45

The keep, the central strong tower built in the 1180s, is the obvious starting point for visitors. Its three-towered forebuilding, carrying the entry staircase and two chapels, is one of the most elaborate of all. The upper chapel, reserved for the royal family's use, is especially fine, with its rich decoration and its style of Norman building, crossing over into Gothic. The former royal apartments, with their central halls and intimate chambers, are still most impressive in their monumental scale, despite having lost most of their original decoration. Although most of

The Pocket Pistol

The Prince of Wales, later George V, a notable Constable

the medieval buildings have gone, Henry III's great hall survives. It is incorporated into the Georgian barracks which are one of the features of Dover's continued military importance, long after many other castles have fallen into picturesque decay. Queen Elizabeth's 'Pocket Pistol' is a survival of the Tudor age of defence. A great gun, 7.3 metres (24 feet) long, it was actually made in 1544 for Henry VIII. The castle's outer defences, which were innovative in military design, provide a fascinating, and lengthy, walk through history.

The Avranches Tower, purpose-built in the 1180s for archers, is approached via the magazines and the artillery works of the

Napoleonic Wars. The Bell Battery, originally for six guns, was built as part of the programme of refortification that began in the 1750s. On the cliff edge, with panoramic views over the town and out to sea, there are the remains of the Admiralty Lookout and Signal Station used in both World Wars. Soldiers and sailors have guarded the English approaches from this spot for well over 800 years.

Dover Castle has something for everyone interested in the nation's past. With the end of World War II, the tunnels were adapted to become a Regional Seat of Government in the event of nuclear catastrophe, before being finally abandoned by

The castle seen from the east

the Home Office in 1984. In the 1990s, the tunnels' wartime secrets are open for all to see.

Open all year round.
♿ For easy access around the castle take a free ride on the land train.
♿ New for 1998 – come and see a dramatic interpretation of life at Dover in 1216 under siege from the French.

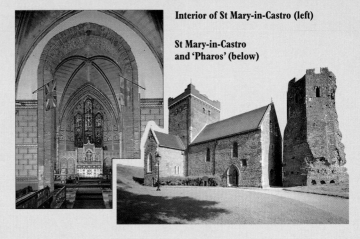

Interior of St Mary-in-Castro (left)

St Mary-in-Castro and 'Pharos' (below)

The land train whisks visitors around Dover Castle (above)

♟ *Zeffirelli's* Hamlet *starring Mel Gibson was shot on location at Dover Castle.*
• Can the French take Dover Castle from the English garrison? See the famous siege of 1216 re-enacted, 27–28 June.
• Exciting CD-Rom unit with information on English castles' functions and purpose.

Open *1 April–1 Nov: daily, 10am–6pm (6pm/dusk in Oct). 2 Nov–31 March: daily, 10am–4pm (closed 24–26 Dec).* **Entry** *£6.50/£5.00/£3.30. (includes admission to secret wartime tunnels, by guided tour only – last tour begins at 5pm (summer) and 3pm (winter). Family ticket (2 adults & 3 children) £16.50.*
📞 01304 201628
🅴 🏠 🚻 ♿ 🅿 🍽 *(The Keep Restaurant, open all year; The Tunnel Café, open April–Oct; for private functions tel: 01304 205830.)* 🌐 *(Two separate tours – for grounds only and for medieval underground works only – available in French, German and Japanese.)* 🎧★ *(underground hospital.)* ♿ *(courtyard & grounds – some very steep slopes)* ♿ 📱
● On E side of Dover. (OS Map 179; ref TR 326416.) **Local Tourist Information:** *Dover (tel: 01304 205108).* 🚌 *Tel: 0345 696 996.* 🚉 *Dover Priory 1½m.*

Constable's Gate

Kit's Coty House

⬡ Kit's Coty House and Little Kit's Coty House

KENT (p. 211, 5N)

Ruins of two prehistoric burial chambers, taking their name from the Celtic phrase for 'tomb in the woods'.

Open *Any reasonable time.*
Entry *Free.*
🏋

➲ *W of A229 2m N of Maidstone. (OS Map 188; ref TQ 745608 & TQ 745604.)*
🚌 *Tel: 0345 696 996.*
🚉 *Aylesford 2½m.*

⊕ Knights Templar Church

Dover, KENT (p. 211, 4P)

Standing across the valley from Dover Castle are the foundations of a small circular 12th-century church.

Open *Any reasonable time.*
Entry *Free.*
🅿

➲ *On the Western Heights above Dover.*
(OS Map 179; ref TR 313408.)
🚉 *Dover Priory ¾m.*

⊘ Lullingstone Roman Villa

KENT (p. 211, 5N)
See p. 50 for full details.

⊘ Maison Dieu

Ospringe, KENT (p. 211, 5O)

Part of a medieval complex of royal lodge, almshouses and hospital, this is much as it was 400 years ago, with a crown-post roof and a decorative 16th-century ceiling. It contains an exhibition about Ospringe in Roman times.

Open *11 April–31 Oct: weekends and Bank Holidays, 2–5pm. For further details contact The Faversham Society on 01795 534542. Keykeeper in winter. (Property managed by The Faversham Society.)*
Entry *£1/80p/50p.*
⚦ ⊗

Maison Dieu

Medieval Merchant's House

➲ *In Ospringe on A2, ½m W of Faversham.*
(OS Map 178; ref TR 002608.)
🚌 *Tel: 0345 696 996.*
🚉 *Faversham ¾m.*

⊕ Medieval Merchant's House

Southampton, HAMPSHIRE (p. 210, 4K)

Life in the Middle Ages is vividly evoked by the brightly painted cabinets and colourful wall hangings authentically re-created for this 13th-century town house, originally built as shop and home for a prosperous wine merchant.

Free Children's Activity Sheet available.
Open *1 April–1 Nov: daily, 10am–6pm (6pm/dusk in Oct).*
Entry *£2.00/£1.50/£1.00.*
☎ 01703 221503
⚦ ⌒ *(also available for the visually impaired and those with learning difficulties)*
♿ *(one step)* ⌂ ⊗
➲ *58 French Street, ¼m S of city centre just off Castle Way*

Minster Lovell Hall

(between High St and Bugle St).
(OS Map 196; ref SU 419112.)
🚌 *Tel: 01703 224854.*
🚉 *Southampton ¼ m.*

✛ Milton Chantry

Gravesend, KENT (p. 211, 5N)

A small 14th-century building which housed the chapel of a leper hospital and a family chantry. It later became a tavern and, in 1780, part of a fort.

Open *1 March–23 Dec: Wed–Sun and Bank Holiday Mondays, 10am–4pm. Closed Jan–Feb. (Property managed by Gravesend Borough Council.)*
Entry *£1.50/75p.*
📞 *01474 321520*
🚫
➲ *In New Tavern Fort Gardens E of central Gravesend off A226.*
(OS Map 177; ref TQ 652743.)
🚌 *Tel: 0345 696 996.*
🚉 *Gravesend ¼ m.*

○ Minster Lovell Hall and Dovecote

OXFORDSHIRE (p. 210, 6J)

The handsome ruins of Lord Lovell's 15th-century manor house stand in a lovely setting on the banks of the River Windrush.

Open *Any reasonable time. Dovecote – exterior only.*
Entry *Free.*
🅿 🐕
➲ *Adjacent to Minster Lovell church, 3m W of Witney off A40.*
(OS Map 164; ref SP 324114.)
🚌 *Tel: 01865 772250.*
🚉 *Charlbury 7m.*

✛ ○ Netley Abbey

HAMPSHIRE (p. 210, 4K)

A 13th-century Cistercian abbey converted in Tudor times for use as a house. Watch out for ghostly figures drifting amongst the ruins.

Open *Any reasonable time.*
Entry *Free.*
📞 *01703 453076*
🅿 ♿ 🐕 🚻 *(nearby, across road near estuary)*
➲ *In Netley, 4m SE of Southampton, facing Southampton Water.*
(OS Map 196; ref SU 453089.)
🚌 *Tel: 01703 224854.*
🚉 *Netley 1m.*

Netley Abbey

LULLINGSTONE ROMAN VILLA

❻ KENT (p. 211, 5N)

The villa, discovered in 1939, was one of the finds of the century. Built *c.* AD 100, but extended during 300 years of Roman occupation, much is visible today. The original villa was fronted by a verandah, with projecting wings. Later, the bath houses were extended and a dining room, with two mosaic panels depicting scenes from classical legend, was added. An early shrine in the cellar has frescoes of water nymphs. Grave goods are evidence of the paganism practised here before Christianity arrived, when some rooms were converted into a chapel. The villa had been abandoned by AD 420, to lie hidden for 1,500 years.

A bronze flagon from Lullingstone

Open all year round.
• Free Children's Activity Sheet available.
Open 1 April–1 Nov:
daily, 10am–6pm
(6pm/dusk in Oct).
2 Nov–31 March: daily,
10am–4pm (closed 24–26 Dec).
Entry £2.50/£1.90/£1.30
℄ 01322 863467
♿ P 🎧 (also available for the
visually impaired and those
with learning difficulties and
in French and German) 🐕 📱
➲ ½m SW of Eynsford
off A225, off junction 3 of
M25. Follow A20 towards
Brands Hatch.
(OS Map 177; ref
TQ 529651.)
Local Tourist Information:
Clacketts Lane (tel: 01959
565063); Sevenoaks (tel:
01732 450305).
🚃 Eynsford ¾m.

**The mosaic floor (left)
lies at the heart of
Lullingstone Roman Villa**

Plan labels: Recreation room; Stairs to bath complex; West verandah; Dining room; Cellar (later site of the Christian chapel); Kitchen; Hot dry room; Large cold plunge bath; South wing room; Heated rooms

◉ North Hinksey Conduit House

OXFORDSHIRE (p. 217, 6K)

Roofed reservoir for Oxford's first water mains, built in the early 17th century.

Open *Any reasonable time (exterior only).*
Entry *Free.*
🐾
◗ *In North Hinksey off A34, 2½m W of Oxford. Located off track leading from Harcourt Hill; use footpath from Ferry Hinksey Lane (near station). (OS Map 164; ref SP 494049.)*
🚉 *Oxford 1½m.*

◉ North Leigh Roman Villa

OXFORDSHIRE (pp. 210/214/217, 7J)

The remains of a large and well-built Roman courtyard villa. The most important feature is an almost complete mosaic tile floor,

Northington Grange

intricately patterned in reds and browns.

Open *Grounds – any reasonable time. Viewing window for mosaic. Pedestrian access only from main road (550 metres).*
Entry *Free.*
🐾 🅿 *(in layby, not in access lane)*
◗ *2m N of North Leigh, 10m W of Oxford off A4095. (OS Map 164; ref SP 397154.)*
🚉 *Tel: 01865 772250.*
🚉 *Handborough 3½m.*

♡◓ Northington Grange

HAMPSHIRE (p. 210, 4K)

Magnificent neoclassical country house, built at the beginning of the 18th century.

Open *Any reasonable time (exterior viewing only).*
Entry *Free.*
🅿 ♿ *(with assistance)* 🐾
◗ *4m N of New Alresford off B3046 along farm track (450 metres).*

(OS Map 185; ref SU 562362.)
🚉 *Tel: 0345 023 067.*
🚉 *Winchester 8m.*

◉ Old Soar Manor

Plaxtol, KENT (p. 211, 5N)

Remains of a late 13th-century knight's manor house, comprising the two-storey solar and chapel. There is also an exhibition to see.

Open *1 April–30 Sept: daily, 10am–6pm. Keykeeper. (Property maintained, managed and owned by the National Trust.)*
Entry *Free.*
✆ *01732 810378*
❌ 🅿 *(limited) (National Trust Kent & East Sussex office)*
◗ *1m E of Plaxtol. (OS Map 188; ref TQ 619541.)*
🚉 *Tel: 0345 696 996.*
🚉 *Borough Green & Wrotham 2½m.*

⊕❀ Osborne House

ISLE OF WIGHT (p. 210, 3K)
See pp. 54–57 for full details.

Tiled floor at North Leigh Roman Villa

are Roman walls, the most complete in Europe, substantial remains of the castle and an exhibition telling the story of Portchester.

**Pevensey Castle
(above and left)**

⊙ Pevensey Castle

EAST SUSSEX (p. 211, 3N)

William the Conqueror landed at Pevensey on 28 September 1066. He may have used the Roman Shore Fort as a shelter for his troops. Today you can see the ruins of the medieval castle including remains of an unusual keep enclosed within its walls, originally dating back to the 4th-century Roman fort Anderida.

Open all year round.
Open *1 April–1 Nov: daily, 10am–6pm (6pm/dusk in Oct). 2 Nov–31 March: Wed–Sun, 10am–4pm (closed 24–26 Dec).*

Entry *£2.50/£1.90/£1.30.*
(01323 762604
🅿 *(charge payable)* ♿ ♟ *(nearby)* ⊙ ∩ *(also available for the visually impaired and those with learning difficulties)* ⑪ *('Castle Cottage Tearoom and Restaurant', closed early Jan.)*
➡ *In Pevensey off A259. (OS Map 199; ref TQ 645048.)*
🚌 *Tel: 01273 474747.*
🚉 *Pevensey & Westham ½m.*

⊙ Portchester Castle

HAMPSHIRE (p. 210, 3K)

A residence for kings and a rallying point for troops, this grand castle has a history stretching back nearly 2,000 years. There

Open all year round.
*• **Watch military displays, music and dance from the Spanish Armada of 1588,** 22–23 August.*
*• **Free Children's Activity Sheet and CD-Rom showing details of English castles.***
Open *1 April–1 Nov: daily, 10am–6pm (6pm/dusk in Oct). 2 Nov–31 March: daily, 10am–4pm (closed 24–26 Dec).*
Entry *£2.50/£1.90/£1.30.*
(01705 378291
🅿 ♿ *(grounds & lower levels only)* ♟ *(in car park)* ⊙ 🗋 🗋 🅴
➡ *On S side of Portchester off A27, Junction 11 on M27. (OS Map 196; ref SU 625046.)*
🚌 *Tel: 01705 650967.*
🚉 *Portchester 1m.*

**Portchester Castle
(below and left)**

⊖ Reculver Towers and Roman Fort

KENT (p. 211, 5P)

Standing in a country park, a 12th-century landmark of twin towers and the walls of a Roman fort.

Open *Any reasonable time (external viewing only).*
Entry *Free.*
☎ **01227 366444**
⚕ 🅿 ✕ ⌷ *(ground floor only – long slope up from car park)*
➲ *At Reculver 3m E of Herne Bay.*
(OS Map 179; ref TR 228694.)
🚌 *Tel: 0345 696 996.*
🚌 *Herne Bay 4m.*

⊘ ⊖ Richborough Roman Fort

KENT (p. 211, 5P)

This fort and township date back to the Roman landing in AD43. The fortified walls and the massive foundations of a triumphal arch which stood 25 metres (80 feet) high still survive. A new updated museum shows aspects of Roman life and artefacts from this busy Roman township.

Open all year round.
♨ *Roman Handling Collection, children's club – phone property for details.*
• *Beautiful picnic spot.*
Open *1 April–1 Nov: daily, 10am–6pm (6pm/dusk in Oct). 2–30 Nov: Wed–Sun, 10am–4pm. 1 Dec–28 Feb: Sat–Sun, 10am–4pm. 1–31 March: Wed–Sun, 10am–4pm.*
Entry *£2.50/£1.90/£1.30.*
☎ **01304 612013**
🅿 ⌷ ⌒ ⊕ ⑦
➲ *1½m N of Sandwich off A257. (OS Map 179; ref TR 324602.)*
🚌 *Sandwich 2m.*

⊘ ⊖ Richborough Roman Amphitheatre

KENT (p. 211, 5P)

Ditch associated with the nearby 3rd-century castle.

Open *Difficult access through farmed field. Please telephone Richborough Roman Fort (01304 612013) for details.*
Entry *Free.*
➲ *1¼m N of Sandwich off A257, Junction 7 of M2, onto A2. (OS Map 179; ref TR 321598.)*
🚌 *Sandwich 1¼m.*

Rochester Castle with the tide out

⊘ Rochester Castle

KENT (p. 211, 5N)

Built on the Roman city wall, this Norman bishop's castle was a vital royal stronghold.

Open all year round.
Open *1 April–31 Oct: daily, 10am–6pm (4pm/dusk in Oct). 1 Nov–31 March: daily, 10am–4pm (closed 24–27 Dec). (Property managed by Rochester upon Medway City Council.)*
Entry *£2.60/£2.00/£1.30.*
☎ **01634 402276**
⚕ *(in castle grounds)*
⌒ ⊗ ⌷ ⌷
➲ *By Rochester Bridge (A2), Junction 1 of M2 and Junction 2 of M25. (OS Map 178; ref TQ 742686.)*
🚌 *Tel: 0345 696 996.*
🚌 *Rochester ½m.*

Richborough Roman Fort

OSBORNE HOUSE

🏛 ✺ ISLE OF WIGHT (p. 210, 3K)

Osborne House was 'a place of one's own, quiet and retired', for Queen Victoria and Prince Albert. They found tranquillity on the Isle of Wight, far from the formality of court life at Buckingham Palace and Windsor Castle. The house they built for themselves and their family was set among terraced gardens and filled

Prince Albert and Queen Victoria

with treasured mementoes. Victoria died at Osborne in 1901, still mourning her beloved Albert, who had died in middle age. Edward VII gave the house to the nation shortly afterwards. With recent restoration, it has become one of the most evocative memorials to Britain's longest-reigning monarch.

With royalty, most things are relative. When visitors see Osborne for the first time, knowing that the young Victoria and Albert had wanted a modest country home, they are surprised by its scale and magnificence. The house is set on rising ground overlooking the Solent, where the ships that helped Britannia rule the waves sailed to and fro. Two tall towers in an Italian style dominate, above fountains set on terraces and rolling wooded parkland. Inside, magnificence abounds – the

Osborne House from the east with the Italian garden and terraces prior to their restoration to their appearance at the end of Queen Victoria's reign

Household wing

Main wing

Durbar wing

Royal appartments

Upper terrace

Lower terrace

Andromeda fountain

Pergola

Queen Victoria's bedroom

Indian room, marbled pillars, gilding, statuary, grand paintings. The full, even overfull, interiors seem typically Victorian, but the contents remind us that this family had links with all the crowned heads of Europe. Despite the idea of cosy domesticity at Osborne, the formality of monarchy and its role as head of the British empire are never far away.

Victoria married Albert in 1840, three years after she had come to the throne. They were dismayed by the places in which they were expected to live. Windsor

The Billiard Room

was a rambling old castle, with smelly drains – their typhoid germs killed Prince Albert in 1861.

Victoria and Albert bought Osborne in 1845, and began dismantling the existing relatively small house. Its ambitious replacement was the work of

Thomas Cubitt, best known for his buildings in London.

The new house was Italianate, rather than in the Gothic idiom one often associates with the Victorians. The first part was ready for occupation by 1846 and the main structure was completed by 1851.

Queen Victoria photographed with many of her family in 1898

This speed was the result of both Cubitt's skill and Albert's unflagging Teutonic zeal. Osborne's completion was also the year of the Great Exhibition – Albert's greatest achievement – held in the Crystal Palace in Hyde Park. Victoria and Albert with their many children embodied the family ideal and helped restore respect for the monarchy following its low esteem under George IV and William IV. Queen Victoria enthused to her uncle Leopold, King of the Belgians, that Albert had 'raised monarchy to the highest pinnacle of respect,

and rendered it popular beyond what it ever was in this country'. Although of necessity State affairs took place at Osborne, it was essentially a family holiday home. The Queen had her first experience of sea bathing there – she liked it until she put her head under the water.

Victoria and Albert's nine children were given more freedom at Osborne. They could play in their own little home, Swiss Cottage, which was given to them on Victoria's birthday in 1854. As a memento of their youth, Victoria commissioned

The Grand corridor

marble sculptures of their infant arms, which still lie in ghostly display.

A new routine helped ease painful memories after Albert died and Victoria went into the mourning from which she never fully emerged. Growing numbers of grand- and great-grand-children filled the house at Christmas, while Princess Beatrice, Victoria's youngest

Cubitt's striking Italianate towers dominate the architectural composition of Osborne

daughter, became her mother's companion. The princess lived in the Durbar wing, Osborne's last addition, built by craftsmen from India in 1890–91 to provide more formal State rooms.

Queen Victoria died on 22 January 1901 on a couch bed in the Queen's Bedroom. The private royal suite was closed to all except members of the royal family until the Queen gave permission in 1954 for full public access.

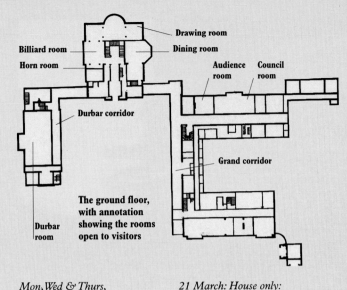

The ground floor, with annotation showing the rooms open to visitors

Open all year round.
♿ *Brand new children's play area.*
🎬 Mrs Brown, *starring Dame Judi Dench and Billy Connolly, filmed here.*
• *Free Children's Activity Sheet available.*
Open *1 April–1 Nov: daily, House & Gardens, 10am–6pm (6pm/dusk in Oct), last admission to house 4pm. 2 Nov–13 Dec & 7 Feb–21 March: Sun,*

Mon, Wed & Thurs, 10am–2pm (1-hour guided tour only. To book tel: 01983 200022 or 01983 281784.)
Entry *1 April–1 Nov: House & Gardens: £6.50/£4.90/£3.30. Family ticket (2 adults & 3 children) £16.30. Grounds only: £3.50/£2.60/£1.80. 2 Nov–13 Dec & 7 Feb–*

21 March: House only: £4.50/£3.50/£2.00.
☎ 01983 200022
🏠 🅴 🚻 🅿 🍴 ('*Keepers Kitchen*') ♿ *(exterior and ground floor only; vehicles with disabled passengers may set them down at the house entrance before returning to car park)* 🛍 ❌ 🐕 ♿
➲ *1m SE of East Cowes. (OS Map 196; ref SZ 516948.)*
Local Tourist Information: *Cowes (tel: 01983 291914) and Newport (tel: 01983 525450).*
🚌 *Tel: 01983 827005.*
🚂 *Ryde Esplanade 7m; Wootton (IoW Steam Rly) 3m.*
⛴ *East Cowes (Red Funnel) 1½m (Tel: 01703 334010); Fishbourne (Wightlink) 4m; Ryde (Wightlink) 7m (Tel: 0990 827744).*

The Durbar room, the last addition to Osborne

◓ Rollright Stones

OXFORDSHIRE
(pp. 210/214/217, 7J)

Three groups of stones, known as 'The King's Men', 'The Whispering Knights' and 'The King Stone', spanning nearly 2,000 years of the Neolithic and Bronze Ages.

Open *The King's Men any reasonable time by courtesy of the owner, who may levy a charge. The King Stone & The Whispering Knights any reasonable time, by footpath.*
Entry *Free.*
🅿 *(in layby)* 🛱
➥ *Off unclassified road between A44 and A3400, 2m NW of Chipping Norton near villages of Little Rollright and Long Compton.*
(OS Map 185; ref SP 297308.)

✛ Royal Garrison Church

Portsmouth, HAMPSHIRE
(p. 211, 3K)

Originally a hospice for pilgrims, this 16th-century chapel became the Garrison Church after the dissolution. Expertly restored in the 1860s but fire-bombed in 1941, the chancel survived and there is still plenty to see.

Open *1 April–30 Sept: Mon–Fri, 11am–4pm. Keykeeper in winter (tel: 01705 378291).*
Entry *Free.*
✆ **01705 378291**
🅿 *(nearby)* ♿ ⊗

Rycote Chapel

➥ *On Grand Parade S of Portsmouth High St.*
(OS Map 196; ref SU 633992.)
🚌 *Tel: 01705 650967.*
🚉 *Portsmouth Harbour ¼m.*

✛ Rycote Chapel

OXFORDSHIRE
(pp. 210/217, 6K)

This lovely 15th-century chapel, with exquisitely carved and painted wood-work, has many intriguing features, including two roofed pews and a musicians' gallery.

🎬 ***The wedding scene from LWT's* Jane Eyre *was filmed at Rycote Chapel.***
Open *1 April–30 Sept: Fri–Sun & Bank Holidays, 2–6pm.*
Entry *£1.60/£1.20/80p.*
🅿 ⊗ ♿ *(assistance required)*
➥ *3m SW of Thame off A329.*
(OS Map 165; ref SP 667046.)
🚌 *Tel: 0345 382 000.*
🚉 *Haddenham & Thame Parkway 5m.*

✛ St Augustine's Abbey

Canterbury, KENT
(p. 211, 5O)
See p. 59 for full details.

✛ St Augustine's Cross

Cliffsend, KENT (p. 211, 5P)

19th-century cross, in Celtic design, marking the traditional site of St Augustine's landing in 597.

Open *Any reasonable time.*
Entry *Free.*
♿ 🛱
➥ *2m E of Minster off B29048.*
(OS Map 179; ref TR 340641.)
🚌 *Tel: 0345 696 996.*
🚉 *Minster 2m.*

St Augustine's Cross

ST AUGUSTINE'S ABBEY

✛ Canterbury, KENT (p. 211, 5O)

This great shrine, built the year after St Augustine arrived in England, became the centre of the country's Christian movement and the burial place of St Augustine. Along with the Cathedral, the Abbey is part of the Canterbury World Heritage

Copper cloisonné mount from 10th or 11th century

property – representing the most important change in English life since Roman times. Today you can see the remains of the earliest parts of the Abbey with the help of the interactive audio tour and follow its history through displays in the interpretation centre.

In 596 St Augustine was sent by the Pope to convert the pagan King of Kent. Landing the next year, he travelled to Canterbury where the King took up the faith. St Augustine was granted an old church within the city walls – 'built long ago by Roman Christians' – to found his

The St Pancras Chapel, which forms part of the Abbey complex

church and the abbey which now bears his name, so succeeding in making Christianity the official faith of both Kent and England.

Although much was destroyed by Henry VIII, remarkable remains of the original 6th-century church survive. An interactive audio tour guides you around the property and computer-generated displays give insight into the whole of the Abbey.

Open all year round.
• Enjoy the museum and interactive audio tour.

Open *1 April–1 Nov: daily, 10am–6pm (6pm/dusk in Oct). 2 Nov–31 March: daily, 10am–4pm (closed 24–26 Dec).* ***Entry*** *£2.50/£1.90/£1.30.*
℡ *01227 767345*
🦽 *(some steps)* 🚶 🅿 *(nearby)*
🎧★ Ⓔ ⓦ
➲ *In Longport ¼m E of Cathedral Close. (OS Map 179; ref TR 154578.)*
Local Tourist Information: *Canterbury (tel: 01227 766567)*
🚌 *Tel: 0800 696 996.*
🚉 *Canterbury East & West, both ¾m.*

The Abbey crypt

Reconstruction of the Abbey from the air

➲☉ St Catherine's Oratory

ISLE OF WIGHT (p. 210, 3K)

Affectionately known as the Pepperpot, this 14th-century lighthouse, erected following the wreck of the wine ship *St Marie*, stands on the highest point of the island.

Open *Any reasonable time (external viewing only). (Property maintained and managed by the National Trust.)*
Entry *Free.*
🅿 🛖
➲ *¾m NW of Niton.*
(OS Map 196; ref SZ 494773.)
🚌 *Tel: 01983 827005.*
🚌 *Shanklin 9m.*
🚢 *West Cowes 14m; East Cowes 14m (Red Funnel. Tel: 01703 334010); Yarmouth 15m (Wightlink. Tel: 0990 827744).*

✠ St John's Commandery

Swingfield, KENT (p. 211, 4P)

A medieval chapel, converted into a farmhouse in the 16th century. It has a fine moulded plaster ceiling and a remarkable timber roof.

Open *Any reasonable time for exterior viewing. Internal viewing by appointment only, tel. 01304 211067 for details.*
Entry *Free.*
🚫
➲ *2m NE of Densole off A260.*
(OS Map 179; ref TR 232440.)
🚌 *Tel: 0345 696 996.*
🚌 *Kearsney 4m.*

✠ St Leonard's Tower

West Malling, KENT (p. 211, 5N)

An early and particularly fine example of a Norman

Temple Manor

tower keep, built *c.*1080 by Gundulf, Bishop of Rochester.

Open *Any reasonable time for exterior viewing. To view interior, contact West Malling Parish Council Mon–Fri, 9am–12pm, tel: 01732 870872.*
Entry *Free.*
♿ *(grounds only)* 🛖
➲ *On unclassified road W of A228.*
(OS Map 188; ref TQ 675570.)
🚌 *Tel: 0345 696 996.*
🚌 *West Malling 1m.*

☉➲ Silchester Roman City Walls and Amphitheatre

HAMPSHIRE (p. 210, 5K)

The best-preserved Roman town walls in Britain, almost one-and-a-half miles around, with an impressive, recently restored amphitheatre.

Open *Any reasonable time.*
Entry *Free.*
🅿 🛖
➲ *On minor road 1m E of Silchester.*
(OS Map 175; ref SU 643624.)

St Leonard's Tower

Titchfield Abbey

🚌 *Tel: 01256 464501.*
🚌 *Bramley or Mortimer,*
both 2¾m.

✛ Stone Chapel

See Faversham: Stone
Chapel, p. 37.

○ ⊕ Sutton Valence Castle

KENT (p. 211, 5O)

The ruins of a 12th-century stone keep built to monitor the important medieval route across the Weald from Rye to Maidstone.

Open *Any reasonable time.*
Entry *Free.*
🐕
➲ *5m SE of Maidstone in Sutton Valence village on A274. (OS Map 188; ref TR 815491.)*
🚌 *Tel: 0345 696 996.*
🚌 *Headcorn 4m, Hollingbourne 5m.*

⊕ Temple Manor

Rochester, KENT (p. 211, 5N)

The 13th-century manor house of the Knights Templar.

Open *1 April–30 Sept: Sat–Sun and Bank Holidays,*

10am–6pm. Please telephone 01634 827980 for details. (Property managed by Rochester upon Medway City Council.)
Entry *Free.*
🅿 ♿ *(grounds only)* ⊗
➲ *In Strood (Rochester) off A228. (OS Map 178; ref TQ 733686.)*
🚌 *Tel: 0345 696 996.*
🚌 *Strood ¾m.*

⊕ Titchfield Abbey

HAMPSHIRE (p. 210, 4K)

Remains of a 13th-century abbey overshadowed by a grand Tudor gatehouse.

Open *1 April–31 Oct: daily, 10am–6pm (6pm/dusk in Oct). 1 Nov–31 March:*

Uffington White Horse

daily, 10am–4pm. (Property managed by The Titchfield Abbey Association.)
Entry *Free.*
🅿 ♿ 🐕
➲ *½m N of Titchfield off A27. (OS Map 196; ref SU 541067.)*
🚌 *Tel: 01703 226235.*
🚌 *Fareham 2m.*

◬ Uffington Castle, White Horse and Dragon Hill

OXFORDSHIRE
(pp. 210/213/217, 6J)

A group of sites lying along the Ridgeway, an old prehistoric route. There is a large Iron Age camp enclosed within ramparts, a natural mound known as Dragon Hill and the spectacular White Horse, cut from turf to reveal the chalk.

Open *Any reasonable time. (Property managed by the National Trust.)*
Entry *Free.*
🅿 🐕
➲ *S of B4507, 7m W of Wantage. (OS Map 174; ref SU 301866.)*

Upnor Castle

◐◒ Upnor Castle

KENT (p. 211, 5N)

Well-preserved 16th-century gun fort, built to protect Queen Elizabeth I's warships. However in 1667 it failed to resist the Dutch navy, which stormed up the Medway destroying half the English fleet.

Open *1 April–30 Sept: daily, 10am–6pm. Telephone 01634 827980 for further details. (Site managed by Rochester upon Medway City Council.)* **Entry** *£2.60/£1.90/£1.30.* *℡ 01634 718742* ⚥ 🅿 *(at a slight distance from castle – park before village)* ♿ *(grounds only)* ◑ 🎧 ● *At Upnor, on unclassified road off A228. (OS Map 178; ref TQ 758706.)* 🚌 *Tel: 0345 696 996.* 🚃 *Strood 2m.*

◐✦ Walmer Castle and Gardens

KENT (p. 211, 5P)

See pp. 64–65 for full details.

✚♡ Waverley Abbey

SURREY (p. 210, 4L)

First Cistercian house in England, founded in 1128.

The remaining ruins date from the 13th century.

Open *Any reasonable time.* **Entry** *Free.* 🅿 *(limited)* 🐕 ● *2m SE of Farnham off B3001 and off Junction 10 of M25. (OS Map 186; ref SU 868453.)* 🚃 *Farnham 2m.*

◭ Wayland's Smithy

OXFORDSHIRE
(pp. 210/213/217, 6J)

Near to the Uffington White Horse lies this evocative Neolithic burial site, surrounded by a small circle of trees. It is an unusual property in that two grave types lie one upon the other.

Open *Any reasonable time. (Property managed by the National Trust.)*

Wolvesey Castle

Entry Free.
🦌
➲ *On the Ridgeway ¾ m
NE of B4000 Ashbury–
Lambourn road.
(OS Map 174; ref
SU 281854.)*

⊖ Western Heights
Dover, KENT (p. 211, 4P)

Parts of moat of 19th-century fort built to fend off a French attack. Now part of the White Cliffs Countryside Project.

Open *Any reasonable time.*
Entry *Free.*
☎ *01304 241806*
🦌 **P**
➲ *Above Dover town on
W side of harbour.
(OS Map 179; ref
TR 312408.)*
🚉 *Dover Priory ¾ m.*

⊕ Wolvesey Castle (Old Bishop's Palace)
Wolvesey, HAMPSHIRE (p. 210, 4K)

One of the greatest medieval buildings in England, the Palace was the chief residence of the Bishops of Winchester. Its extensive ruins still reflect their importance and wealth. The last great occasion was on 25 July 1554 when Queen Mary and Philip of Spain held their wedding breakfast in the East Hall.

Open *1 April–1 Nov: daily,
10am–6pm (6pm/dusk in Oct).*

Yarmouth Castle from the air (above) and visitors among the gunpowder barrels (right)

*Keykeeper in winter
(Tel: 01732 778030).*
Entry *£1.80/£1.40/90p.*
☎ *01962 854766*
♿ 🦌
➲ *¾ m SE of Winchester
Cathedral, next to the Bishop's
Palace; access from College St.
(OS Map 185; ref SU 484291.)*
🚌 *Tel: 0345 023 067.*
🚉 *Winchester ¼ m.*

⊘ Yarmouth Castle
ISLE OF WIGHT (p. 210, 3J)

This last addition to Henry VIII's coastal defences was completed in 1547. It houses exhibitions of paintings of the Isle of Wight and photographs of old Yarmouth.

*Picnic spot with views
over the Solent.*
Open *1 April–1 Nov:
daily, 10am–6pm
(6pm/dusk in Oct).*
Entry *£2.00/£1.50/£1.00.*
☎ *01983 760678*
♿ *(ground floor only)* 🗋 🦌
P *(coach & car park 200yards,
limited roadside of 1hr)*
➲ *In Yarmouth adjacent to
car ferry terminal.
(OS Map 196; ref SZ 354898.)*
⛴ *Yarmouth (Wightlink)
adjacent (Tel: 0990 827744).*

WALMER CASTLE AND GARDENS

ⓜ ❀ KENT (p. 211, 5P)

Walmer Castle was one of the forts Henry VIII built along the south coast that were designed to defend against the new threat of attack by gunpowder. Unlike a medieval castle, it is low and squat, with hugely thick walls able to withstand the mightiest bombardment. Its spherical bastions held heavy armaments which could be deployed against an attacking fleet. The castle was later

Wellington's famous boots

transformed into an elegant stately home that serves as the residence of the Lords Warden of the Cinque Ports. Past Wardens include Pitt the Younger, the Duke of Wellington and Sir Winston Churchill. Today's Lord Warden, Queen Elizabeth The Queen Mother, still visits Walmer and some rooms used by her are open to visitors. Another treat is the recently completed magnificent Queen Mother's Garden.

Built to withstand the wrath of the French and Spanish following Henry VIII's break with the Roman Catholic Church, the defences of Walmer Castle have in fact never been put to the test. Early 1539 saw England under the threat of invasion and Henry built a series of castles from Cornwall to Kent, which

ended with the linked fortresses of Deal, Walmer and Sandown. The expected attack never materialized and, although the castles of the Downs were brought to readiness again in 1588 to repel the Spanish Armada, no fighting took place.

Walmer was transformed when it became the official residence of the Lords

Warden of the Cinque Ports, an ancient title that originally involved control of the five most important medieval ports on the south coast. By the 18th century the position was largely ceremonial, although it retained immense prestige and a substantial salary. The Duke of Dorset was the first Lord Warden to use Walmer, turning the fort into a stately home, increasing the number of first-floor rooms by extending the living

The new Queen Mother's Garden

William Pitt's gaming chair

The castle's extensive gardens (above)

quarters out over the bastions. Further additions were made by Earl Granville, Lord Warden from 1865, who commissioned the extension of the gate-house bastion.

The magnificent gardens surrounding the castle owe much to the enthusiasm of another Lord Warden, William Pitt the Younger, and much of his early landscaping remains.

The castle is full of memories of former Lords Warden, including two rooms that are now a museum dedicated to the Duke of Wellington.

Open all year round. New free audio tour available.

♨ *Visit the Lord Wardens' Tea Rooms for home-made lunches and afternoon tea.*
Open *1 April–1 Nov: daily, 10am–6pm (6pm/dusk in Oct). 2 Nov–31 March:*

Wed–Sun, 10am–4pm. (Closed 24–26 Dec, also closed Mon–Fri in Jan & Feb and when Lord Warden is in residence.)
Entry *£4.00/£3.00/£2.00.*
☎ 01304 364288
⚥ 🅿 *(nearby approach to castle)* 🎧 *(also available for the visually impaired, those with learning difficulties, and in French and German)*
♿ *(courtyard & garden only, parking available)* 🍴 *(Lord Wardens' Tea Rooms: open daily, April–Oct, Sun only, Nov–March)* ⊗ 🖙
➲ *On coast S of Walmer on A258. Junction 13 off M20 or from M2 to Deal. (OS Map 179; ref TR 378501.)*
Local Tourist Information: *Deal (tel: 01304 369576) and Dover (tel: 01304 205108).*
🚌 *Tel: 0800 696 996.*
🚆 *Walmer 1m.*

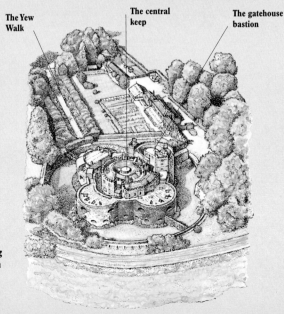

The Yew Walk

The central keep

The gatehouse bastion

Walmer Castle, looking inshore from the beach

SOUTH WEST

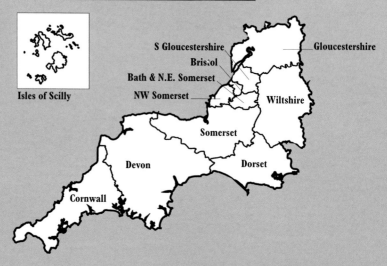

S Gloucestershire
Gloucestershire
Bristol
Bath & N.E. Somerset
NW Somerset
Wiltshire
Isles of Scilly
Somerset
Devon
Dorset
Cornwall

IN THE SOUTH WEST you'll find the greatest wonder of them all – the mysterious stone circle of Stonehenge in Wiltshire. Tintagel Castle, with its spectacular cliff-top location and Arthurian connections, also evokes the spirit of legends. Among other ancient marvels is the huge earthwork of Old Sarum, the original site of Salisbury. Pendennis Castle reveals its wartime secrets for the first time at its new Discovery Centre and the restored 19th- and 20th-century defences. Visit in July and enjoy the Tall Ships' Race or join in the 800th anniversary celebrations at Cleeve Abbey.

The cut and thrust of a 17th-century battle being re-enacted at Pendennis

⊚ Abbotsbury Abbey Remains

DORSET (p. 213, 3G)

The remains of a cloister building of this Benedictine abbey, founded in 1044.

Open *Any reasonable time. (Property managed by the Ilchester Estates.)*
Entry *Free.*
🅿 🐕
➲ *In Abbotsbury, off B3157, near churchyard. (OS Map 194; ref SY 578852.)*
🚌 *Tel: 01305 767023.*
🚌 *Upwey 7½m.*

Alexander Keiller Museum, Avebury

Avebury, WILTSHIRE (pp. 210/213, 5J)

The investigation of Avebury Stone Circles was largely the work of Alexander Keiller in the 1930s. He put together one of the most important prehistoric archaeological collections in Britain, and this can be seen in the museum at Avebury.

Open all year round.
Open *1 April–31 Oct: daily, 10am–6pm. 1 Nov–31 March: daily, 10am–4pm (closed 24–26 Dec, 1 Jan).*
Entry *£1.60 (adult)/80p (child). (Collection on loan to the National Trust.)*
☎ *01672 539250*
👫 🅿 *(in village)* ⊗ ♿ 🅴 📷
➲ *In Avebury 7m W of Marlborough.*

(OS Map 173; ref SU 100700.)
🚌 *Tel: 0345 090 899.*
🚌 *Pewsey 10m, Swindon 11m.*

Avebury

WILTSHIRE
See also Silbury Hill, The Sanctuary, West Kennet Avenue, West Kennet Long Barrow and Windmill Hill.

① Avebury Stone Circles

WILTSHIRE (pp. 210/213, 5J)

Complex, gigantic and mysterious, the Circles were constructed 4,500 years ago, originally comprising more than 180 stones. The remains of the Circles still surround the later village of Avebury.

Open *Any reasonable time. (Property owned and managed by the National Trust.)*
Entry *Free.*
👫 *(in village)* 🅿 ♿ 🐕

Avebury Stone Circles

Alexander Keiller Museum

➲ *In Avebury 7m W of Marlborough. (OS Map 173; ref SU 103700.)*
🚌 *Tel: 0345 090 899.*
🚌 *Pewsey 10m, Swindon 11m.*

⚅ Ballowall Barrow

St Just, CORNWALL
(p. 212, 1A)

In a spectacular position, this is an unusual Bronze Age chambered tomb with a complex layout.

Open *Any reasonable time. (Property managed by the National Trust.)*
Entry *Free.*
🐕
➲ *1m W of St Just, near Carn Gloose.*
(OS Map 203; ref SW 354313.)
🚌 *Tel: 01209 719988.*
🚉 *Penzance 8m.*

➊ Bant's Carn Burial Chamber and Halangy Down Ancient Village

St Mary's, ISLES OF SCILLY
(p. 212, 4A)

In a wonderful scenic location, on a hill above the site of the ancient Iron Age village, lies this

Berry Pomeroy Castle gatehouse (right) and the tower staircase (below)

Bronze Age burial mound with entrance passage and chamber.

Open *Any reasonable time.*
Entry *Free.*
🐕
➲ *1m N of Hugh Town.*
(OS Map 203; ref SV 911124.)

Bant's Carn Burial Chamber

⊘ Bayard's Cove Fort

Dartmouth, DEVON
(p. 213, 2E)

A small artillery fort built before 1534 to defend the harbour entrance.

Open *Any reasonable time. (Property managed by South*

Hams District Council.)
Entry *Free.*
♻
➲ *In Dartmouth, on riverfront.*
(OS Map 202; ref SX 879510.)
🚌 *Tel: 01803 613226 or 01392 382800.*
🚉 *Paignton 7m via vehicle ferry.*

⬟ Belas Knap Long Barrow

GLOUCESTERSHIRE
(pp. 210/217, 7H)

A good example of a Neolithic long barrow, with the mound still intact and surrounded by a stone wall. The chamber tombs, where the remains of 31 people were found, have been opened up so that visitors can see inside.

Open *Any reasonable time. (Property managed by Gloucestershire County Council.)*
Entry *Free.*
🚶
➲ *2m S of Winchcombe, near Charlton Abbots, ½ mile on Cotswold Way. (OS Map 163; ref SP 021254.)*
🚌 *Tel: 01242 602949.*
🚉 *Cheltenham 9m.*

⊕ ♡ Berry Pomeroy Castle

DEVON (p. 213, 2E)

A romantic late-medieval castle, unusual in combining the remains of a large castle with a flamboyant courtier's mansion.

Picnic spot of exceptional beauty.
Open *1 April–1 Nov: daily, 10am–6pm (6pm/dusk in Oct).*
Entry *£2.10/£1.60/£1.10.*
☎ *01803 866618*
🅿 *(no coach access)* ❌ 👫
♿ *(grounds & ground floor only)* 🍽 *(not managed by English Heritage)*

➲ *2½m E of Totnes off A385. (OS Map 202; ref SX 839623.)*
🚉 *Totnes 3½m.*

⬟ Blackbury Camp

DEVON (p. 213, 3F)

An Iron Age hill fort, defended by a bank and ditch.

Open *Any reasonable time.*
Entry *Free.*
🚶 🅿
➲ *1½m SW of Southleigh off B3174/A3052. (OS Map 192; ref SY 188924.)*
🚉 *Honiton 6½m.*

✠ Blackfriars

Gloucester, GLOUCESTER-SHIRE (pp. 210/217, 7H)

A small Dominican priory church. Most of the original 13th-century church remains, including a rare scissor-braced roof.

Belas Knap Long Barrow

Open *Access restricted. Please telephone 0117 975 0700 for further information.*
Entry *Free.*
❌
➲ *In Ladybellegate Street off Southgate Street and Blackfriars Walk. (OS Map 162; ref SO 830186.)*
🚌 *Tel: 01452 425543.*
🚉 *Gloucester ½m.*

Blackfriars

⊕ Bowhill

Exeter, DEVON (p. 213, 3E)

A mansion of considerable status built c.1500 by a member of the Holland family. The impressive Great Hall has been carefully restored by English Heritage craftsmen using traditional materials and techniques.

Open *Limited access after Easter 1998. For details of opening times please telephone 01392 252461. (Property managed by the Devonshire Association.)*
Entry £1.50.
⊗ 🅿
➲ *1½m SW of Exeter on B3212. (OS Map 192; ref SX 906916.)*
▦ *Tel: 01392 427711.*
🚌 *Exeter, St Thomas ¾m.*

⊙ Bradford-on-Avon Tithe Barn

WILTSHIRE (pp. 210/213, 5H)

A medieval stone-built barn with slate roof and wooden beamed interior.

Open *Daily, 10.30am–4pm (closed 25 Dec). Keykeeper.*
Entry *Free.*
🅿 ♿ ⊗
➲ *¼m S of town centre, off B3109. (OS Map 173; ref ST 824604.)*
▦ *Tel: 0345 090 899.*
🚌 *Bradford-on-Avon ¼m.*

⊘ Bratton Camp and White Horse

WILTSHIRE (pp. 210/213, 5H)

A large Iron Age hill fort.

Open *Any reasonable time.*
Entry *Free.*
🅿 🐕
➲ *2m E of Westbury off B3098, 1m SW of Bratton. (OS Map 184; ref ST 900516.)*
🚌 *Westbury 3m.*

⊙ Butter Cross

Dunster, SOMERSET (p. 213, 4E)

A medieval stone cross.

Open *Any reasonable time. (Property managed by the National Trust.)*
Entry *Free.*
🐕

Bradford-on-Avon Tithe Barn

➲ *Beside minor road to Alcombe, 350 metres (400 yards) NW of Dunster parish church. (OS Map 181; ref SS 988439.)*
▦ *Tel: 01823 272033.*
🚌 *Dunster (W Somerset Rly) 1m.*

⊘① Carn Euny Ancient Village

CORNWALL (p. 212, 1A)

The remains of an Iron Age settlement, with foundations of stone huts and an intriguing curved underground passage, or *fogou*.

Open *Any reasonable time. (Property managed by the Cornwall Heritage Trust.)*
Entry *Free.*
🅿 *(600 metre walk to property from car park in Brane)* 🐕
➲ *1¼m SW of Sancreed off A30. (OS Map 203; ref SW 402289.)*
▦ *Tel: 01209 719988.*
🚌 *Penzance 6m.*

Carn Euny Ancient Village

✪ Chisbury Chapel

WILTSHIRE (pp. 210/213, 5J)

A thatched 13th-century chapel rescued from use as a farm building.

Open *Any reasonable time.*
Entry *Free.*
✖

➔ *On unclassified road
¼m E of Chisbury off A4
6m E of Marlborough.
(OS Map 174; ref SU 280658.)*
🚌 *Bedwyn 1m.*

⊙ Christchurch Castle and Norman House

DORSET (pp. 210/213, 3J)

Early 12th-century Norman keep, and Constable's house, built *c.*1160.

Open *Any reasonable time.*
Entry *Free.*
🐾

➔ *In Christchurch, near Priory.
(OS Map 195; ref SZ 160927.)*
🚌 *Tel: 01202 673555.*
🚌 *Christchurch ¼m.*

Chysauster Ancient Village: aerial view (left) and a house entrance (below)

⊘⊙ Chysauster Ancient Village

CORNWALL (p. 212, 1A)

Deserted Romano-Cornish village with a 'street' of eight well-preserved houses, each comprising a number of rooms around an open court.

♿ **New shop for 1998.**
Open *1 April–1 Nov: daily,
10am–6pm (6pm/dusk in Oct).
Tel: 0831 757934 for details.*
Entry *£1.60/£1.20/80p.*
🅿 🐾 ♿ 🔧 ⌂
➔ *2½m NW of Gulval off
B3311.
(OS Map 203; ref SW 473350.)*
🚌 *Tel: 01209 719988.*
🚌 *Penzance 3½m.*

⊘ Cirencester Amphitheatre

GLOUCESTERSHIRE
(pp. 210/213/217, 6H)

A large well-preserved Roman amphitheatre.

Open *Any reasonable time.
(Property managed by
Cotswold District Council.)*
Entry *Free.*
🐾
➔ *Next to bypass W of town –
access from town or along
Chesterton Lane from W end
of bypass onto Cotswold Ave.
Park next to obelisk.
(OS Map 163; ref SP 020014.)*
🚌 *Tel: 01452 425543.*
🚌 *Kemble 4m.*

✪ Cleeve Abbey

SOMERSET (p. 213, 4F)
See p. 73 for full details.

⓿ Cromwell's Castle

Tresco, ISLES OF SCILLY
(p. 212, 5A)

Standing on a promontory guarding the lovely anchorage between Bryher and Tresco, this 17th-century round tower was built to command the haven of New Grimsby.

Open *Any reasonable time.*
Entry *Free.*
🏃
➲ *On shoreline, ¾m NW of New Grimsby.*
(OS Map 203; ref SV 882159.)

⓿ Dartmouth Castle

DEVON (p. 213, 2E)
See p. 75 for full details.

⓿ Daws Castle

SOMERSET (p. 213, 4F)

The site where the people of the Saxon town of Watchet sought refuge against the threat of Viking attack.

Open *Any reasonable time.*
Entry *Free.*
🅿 *(layby 200 metres)* 🏃
➲ *⅓m W of Watchet off B3191 on cliff edge.*
(OS Map 181; ref ST 062434.)
🚊 *Tel: 01823 272033.*
🚌 *Watchet (West Somerset Rly) ¾m.*

❻➲ Dupath Well

Callington, CORNWALL
(p. 212, 2D)

A charming granite-built well house set over a holy well of *c.*1500 and almost complete.

Open *Any reasonable time.*
(Property managed by the Cornwall Heritage Trust.)
Entry *Free.*
⊗
➲ *1m E of Callington off A388.*
(OS Map 201; ref SX 374693.)

Cromwell's Castle

🚊 *Tel: 01752 222666.*
🚌 *Gunnislake 4½m.*

⓿ Farleigh Hungerford Castle

SOMERSET (pp. 210/213, 5H)

14th-century castle ruins with a chapel containing wall paintings, stained glass and the fine tomb of Sir Thomas Hungerford, the builder of the castle.

Open all year round.
🎬 **Robin of Sherwood** *filmed on location here.*
• **See the Redcoats of 1777, with the chance for children to join the army, 12–13 April.**
Open *1 April–1 Nov: daily, 10am–6pm (6pm/dusk in Oct). 2 Nov–31 March: Wed–Sun, 10am–4pm (closed 24–26 Dec). Closed 1–2pm in winter.*
Entry *£2.10/£1.60/£1.10.*
☎ *01225 754026*
👫🅿⊗🗋🎧♿ *(exterior only)*
➲ *In Farleigh Hungerford 3½m W of Trowbridge on A366.*
(OS Map 173; ref ST 801577.)
🚊 *Tel: 0117 955 3231.*
🚌 *Avoncliff 2m; Trowbridge 3½m.*

Farleigh Hungerford Castle

CLEEVE ABBEY
✪ SOMERSET (p. 213, 4F)

Celebrating its 800th anniversary this year, Cleeve is one of the few 13th-century monastic sites where you can still see such a complete set of cloister buildings. Originally named Vallis Florida, or Vale of Flowers, Cleeve Abbey enjoys an idyllic riverside location. Although parts of the abbey were remodelled in the 15th century and in later years other parts were used as a farmhouse, the cloister buildings remain among England's finest.

On 25 June 1198 the first abbot, Ralph, and twelve monks of the Cistercian order arrived at Cleeve. In accordance with the Cistercian custom, the new abbey was dedicated to the Blessed Virgin and probably took up to a century to complete. Shortly after Cleeve was dissolved in 1536 the abbey church was destroyed, yet some of the finest cloister buildings in England still survive. The impressive 15th-century refectory, the painted chamber and the tiled pavement of the original 13th-century refectory can all be seen to this day.

Open all year round.
☝ Come and celebrate the 800th anniversary of the founding of Cleeve Abbey at an Interdenominational Celebratory Service, 25 June, and a Monastic Living History event, 27–28 June.

Cleeve Abbey floor tiles

Cleeve Abbey Gatehouse (left)

📹 The BBC TV children's drama, Maid Marion and her Merry Men, *was filmed here.*

Open *1 April–1 Nov: daily, 10am–6pm (6pm/dusk in Oct). 2 Nov–31 March: daily, 10am–4pm (closed 24–26 Dec). Closed 1–2pm in winter.*
Entry *£2.50/£1.90/£1.30.*
☎ 01984 640377
🚻 🅿 ✪ ♿ *(grounds & ground floor only)* 🅴 📖 🏺
➡ *In Washford, ¼m S of A39. (OS Map 181; ref ST 047407.)*
Local Tourist Information: *Minehead (tel: 01643 702624).* 🚌 *Tel: 01823 272033.*
🚍 *Washford (W Somerset Rly) ½m.*

The cloister (above)

73

⊙ Fiddleford Manor

DORSET (pp. 210/213, 4H)

Part of a medieval manor house, with a remarkable interior. The splendid roof structures in the hall and upper living room are the best in Dorset.

Open *1 April–30 Sept: daily, 10am–6pm. 1 Oct–31 March: daily, 10am–4pm (closed 24–26 Dec, 1 Jan).*
Entry *Free.*
🅿 ♿ *(ground floor only – 1 step)* ⊗
➲ *1m E of Sturminster Newton off A357.*
(OS Map 194; ref ST 801136.)
🚌 *Tel: 01258 453731.*

⊙ Gallox Bridge

Dunster, SOMERSET
(p. 213, 4E)

A stone packhorse bridge with two ribbed arches which spans the old mill stream.

Fiddleford Manor

Open *Any reasonable time. (Property managed by the National Trust.)*
Entry *Free.*
♿ 🐕
➲ *Off A396 at S end of Dunster.*
(OS Map 181; ref SS 990432.)
🚌 *Tel: 01823 272033.*
🚉 *Dunster (W Somerset Rly) ¼m.*

⊙ Garrison Walls

St Mary's, ISLES OF SCILLY
(p. 212, 4A)

You can take a pleasant walk along the ramparts of these well-preserved walls and earthworks, built as part of the island's defences.

Open *Any reasonable time.*
Entry *Free.*
🐕
➲ *Around the headland W of Hugh Town.*
(OS Map 203; ref SV 898104.)

⊙⊙ Glastonbury Tribunal

SOMERSET (p. 213, 4G)

A well-preserved medieval town house, probably used by a merchant for commercial purposes.

Open all year round.
Open *10 April–30 Sept: Sun–Thurs, 10am–5pm (Fri & Sat 5.30pm). 1 Oct–2 April: Sun–Thurs, 10am–4pm (Fri & Sat 4.30pm). (Property managed by Glastonbury Tribunal Ltd.)*

Glastonbury Tribunal

Entry *Tourist Information Centre free. Display areas £1.50/£1.00/75p.*
☎ *01458 832954*
⊗ ♿ *(ground floor only – 2 steps)* ⊙
➲ *In Glastonbury High St.*
(OS Map 182; ref ST 499390.)
🚌 *Tel: 0117 955 3231.*

⊙ Great Witcombe Roman Villa

GLOUCESTERSHIRE
(pp. 210/213/217, 6H)

The remains of a large villa. Built around three sides of a courtyard, it had a luxurious bath-house complex.

Open *Exterior any reasonable time. Guided tours arranged by The Cotswold Countryside Service: 25 May, 21 June, 16 Aug, 13 Sept, 11am–4pm.*
Entry *Free.*
🅿 *(no access for coaches)* 🐕
➲ *5m SE of Gloucester, off A417, ½m S of reservoir in Witcombe Park.*
(OS Map 163; ref SO 899144.)
🚌 *Tel: 01452 527516.*
🚉 *Gloucester 6m.*

DARTMOUTH CASTLE

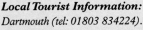 DEVON (p. 213, 2E)

This brilliantly positioned defensive castle juts out into the narrow entrance to the Dart estuary, with the sea lapping at its foot. Begun late in the 14th century, when the merchants of Dartmouth felt the need to protect their homes and warehouses from invasion, it was one of the first castles constructed with artillery in mind. Since then Dartmouth Castle has seen 450 years of fortification and preparation for war. The views from the castle of the town of Dartmouth, the River Dart and out to the Channel are exceptionally beautiful.

Open all year round.
• Special events through the year include 'Thunder of the Guns', 24–25 May.
• Ride from Paignton by steam! Contact Dart Valley Light Railway (tel: 01803 553760).
• Picnic spot of exceptional beauty.
Open *1 April–1 Nov: daily, 10am–6pm (6pm/dusk in Oct). 2 Nov–31 March: Wed–Sun, 10am–4pm (closed 24–26 Dec). Closed 1–2pm in winter.*
Entry *£2.50/£1.90/£1.30.*
(01803 833588
♦♦ P *(limited)* 🛇 ⊗ ♨
➌ *1m SE of Dartmouth off B3205, narrow approach road. (OS Map 202; ref SX 887503.)*

Local Tourist Information:
Dartmouth (tel: 01803 834224).
🚋 *Tel: 01932 382800.*
🚌 *Paignton 8m via vehicle ferry.*

The Victorian Gun Battery (right) and the 15th-century castle (below)

Dartmouth Castle from the air

✚ Greyfriars
Gloucester, GLOUCESTER-
SHIRE (p. 217, 7H)

Remains of a late 15th-
and early 16th-century
Franciscan friary church.

Open *Any reasonable time.
(Property managed by
Gloucester City Council.)*
Entry *Free.*
🚶 🐾
➲ *On Greyfriars Walk,
behind Eastgate Market
off Southgate St.
(OS Map 162; ref SO 830186.)*
🚌 *Tel: 01452 425543.*
🚂 *Gloucester ½m.*

⬟ Grimspound
Dartmoor, DEVON
(p. 212, 3E)

This late Bronze Age
settlement displays the
remains of 24 huts in an
area of four acres enclosed
by a stone wall.

Open *Any reasonable time.
(Property managed by
Dartmoor National Park
Authority.)*
Entry *Free.*
🐾
➲ *6m SW of Moretonhamp-
stead off B3212.
(OS Map 191; ref SX 701809.)*
🚌 *Tel: 01392 382800.*

✚ Hailes Abbey
GLOUCESTERSHIRE
(pp. 210/214/217, 7H)

13th-century Cistercian
abbey, set in wooded
pastureland, with examples
of high-quality sculpture
in the site museum.

Open all year round.
Open *1 April–1 Nov: daily,
10am–6pm (6pm/dusk in Oct).
2 Nov–31 March: Sat–Sun,*
*10am–4pm (closed 24–26
Dec). (Property maintained
and managed by English
Heritage, and owned by the
National Trust.)*
Entry *£2.50/£1.90/£1.30.
National Trust members
admitted free.*
📞 *01242 602398*
🚻 🅿 🎧 *(also available for the
visually impaired, those with
learning difficulties and
wheelchair users)* 🚶 *(general
access, 1 step to museum)*
🚌 🐾 📷
➲ *2m NE of Winchcombe
off B4632.
(OS Map 150; ref SP 050300.)*
🚌 *Tel: 01242 602949.*
🚂 *Cheltenham 10m.*

**Hailes Abbey (left) with
Christ/Sampson boss
(above) and a manuscript
and seal (below)**

❍ Halliggye Fogou

CORNWALL (p. 212, 1B)

One of several strange underground tunnels, associated with Iron Age villages, which are unique to Cornwall.

Open *Any reasonable time, but completely blocked between 31 Oct and 31 March. A torch is advisable. (Property managed by the Trelowarren Estate.)*
Entry *Free.*

➲ *5m SE of Helston off B3293 E of Garras on Trelowarren Estate. (OS Map 203; ref SW 714239.)*
Tel: 01872 73453 or 01209 719988.
Penryn 10m.

❍ Harry's Walls

St Mary's, ISLES OF SCILLY (p. 212, 4B)

An uncompleted 16th-century fort intended to command the harbour of St Mary's Pool.

Open *Any reasonable time.*
Entry *Free.*

➲ *¼m NE of Hugh Town. (OS Map 203; ref SV 910110.)*

❍ Hatfield Earthworks

WILTSHIRE (pp. 210/213, 5J)

Part of a Neolithic enclosure complex 3,500 years old, formerly with a Bronze Age barrow in its centre.

Open *Any reasonable time.*
Entry *Free.*

➲ *5½m SE of Devizes off A342 NE of village of Marden. (OS Map 173; ref SU 091583 or SU 092583.)*
Pewsey 5m.

❍ Hound Tor Deserted Medieval Village

Dartmoor, DEVON (p. 212, 3E)

Remains of three or four medieval farmsteads, first occupied in the Bronze Age.

Open *Any reasonable time. (Property managed by Dartmoor National Park*

Authority.)
Entry *Free.*

➲ *1½m S of Manaton off the Ashburton road. Park in Hound Tor car park, ½m walk. (OS Map 191; ref SX 746788.)*
Tel: 01392 382800.

❍ Hurlers Stone Circles

CORNWALL (p. 212, 2C)

These three Bronze Age stone circles in a line are some of the best examples of ceremonial standing stones in the South West.

Open *Any reasonable time. (Property managed by the Cornwall Heritage Trust.)*
Entry *Free.*

➲ *½m NW of Minions off B3254. (OS Map 201; ref SX 258714.)*
Tel: 01209 719988.
Liskeard 7m.

❍ Innisidgen Lower and Upper Burial Chambers

St Mary's, ISLES OF SCILLY (p. 212, 4B)

Two Bronze Age cairns, about 30 metres (200 feet) apart, with stunning views towards St Martins.

Open *Any reasonable time.*
Entry *Free.*

➲ *1¾m NE of Hugh Town. (OS Map 203; ref SV 921127.)*

77

King Doniert's Stone

⚲⊚ Jordan Hill Roman Temple
Weymouth, DORSET
(pp. 210/213, 3H)

Foundations of a Romano-Celtic temple enclosing an area of about 22 square metres (240 square feet).

Open *Any reasonable time.*
Entry *Free.*
⚲
➲ *2m NE of Weymouth off A353.*
(OS Map 194; ref SY 698821.)
🚌 *Tel: 01305 783645.*
🚉 *Upwey or Weymouth, both 2m.*

⚙ King Charles's Castle
Tresco, ISLES OF SCILLY
(p. 212, 5A)

At the end of a bracing coastal walk to the northern end of Tresco you will find the remains of this castle built for coastal defence.

Open *Any reasonable time.*
Entry *Free.*
⚲

➲ *¾ m NW of New Grimsby.*
(OS Map 203; ref SV 882161.)

⊚ King Doniert's Stone
St Cleer, CORNWALL
(p. 212, 2C)

Two decorated pieces of a 9th-century cross with an inscription believed to commemorate Durngarth, King of Cornwall, who drowned *c.* 875.

Open *Any reasonable time.*
(Property managed by the Cornwall Heritage Trust.)
Entry *Free.*
⚲ 🅿 *(layby)*
➲ *1m NW of St Cleer off B3254.*
(OS Map 201; ref SX 236688.)
🚌 *Tel: 01209 719988.*
🚉 *Liskeard 4m.*

⛰ Kingston Russell Stone Circle
DORSET (p. 213, 3G)

A Bronze Age stone circle of 18 stones.

Open *Any reasonable time.*
Entry *Free.*
⚲ 🅿 *(on verge near entrance to Gorwell Farm)*
➲ *2m N of Abbotsbury, 1m along footpath off minor road to Hardy Monument.*
(OS Map 194; ref SY 577878.)
🚉 *Dorchester West or South, both 8m.*

Kingswood Abbey Gatehouse

78

✠ Kingswood Abbey Gatehouse
GLOUCESTERSHIRE
(pp. 210/213/217, 6H)

The 16th-century gatehouse, with a richly carved mullioned window, is all that remains of the Cistercian abbey.

Open Exterior any reasonable time. Key for interior obtainable from shop nearby during opening hours.
Entry Free.
♗ *(adjacent to monument)* ⊗
➲ *In Kingswood off B4060 1m SW of Wotton-under-Edge.*
(OS Map 162; ref ST 748919.)
🚌 *Tel: 0117 955 3231.*
🚉 *Yate 8m.*

◉ ⊕ Kirkham House
Paignton, DEVON (p. 213, 2E)

A well-preserved, medieval stone house, much restored and repaired, which gives a fascinating insight into life in a town residence in the 15th century.

Kirkham House

Launceston Castle

Open 15 April, 20 May, 17 June, 15 July, 19 Aug, 16 Sept only, 10am–5pm.
Entry Free.
⊗
➲ *In Kirkham St, off Cecil Rd, Paignton.*
(OS Map 202; ref SX 885610.)
🚌 *Tel: 01803 613226.*
🚉 *Paignton ½m.*

✠ ⓝ Knowlton Church and Earthworks
DORSET (pp. 210/213, 4J)

The ruins of this Norman church stand in the middle of Neolithic earthworks, symbolizing the transition from pagan to Christian worship.

Open Any reasonable time.
Entry Free.
🏇
➲ *3m SW of Cranborne on B3078.*
(OS Map 195; ref SU 024100.)

ⓞ Launceston Castle
CORNWALL (p. 212, 3D)

Set on the motte of a Norman castle and commanding the town and surrounding countryside, this medieval castle controlled the main route into Cornwall. The shell keep and tower survive.

Open 1 April–1 Nov: daily 10am–6pm (6pm/dusk in Oct).
Entry £1.60/£1.20/80p.
✆ *01566 772365*
♿ *(outer bailey)* 🏇 🛍
➲ *In Launceston.*
(OS Map 201; ref SX 330846.)
🚌 *Tel: 01392 382800.*

Lulworth Castle

⊖✿ Ludgershall Castle and Cross

WILTSHIRE (pp. 210/213, 5J)

Ruins of an early 12th-century royal hunting palace and a late-medieval cross.

Open *Any reasonable time.*
Entry *Free.*
🅿 *(limited)* ♿ *(part of site only & village cross)* 🐕
➲ *On N side of Ludgershall off A342.*
(OS Map 184; ref SU 264513.)
🚌 *Tel: 0345 090 899.*
🚉 *Andover 7m.*

✪ Lulworth Castle

DORSET
(pp. 210/213, 3H)

An early 17th-century romantic hunting lodge, Lulworth Castle became a fashionable country house set in beautiful parkland during the 18th century. Gutted by fire in 1929, the exterior has been restored by English Heritage.

Open all year round.
Open *4 April–1 Nov: daily, 10am–6pm. 2 Nov–26 March: daily, 10am–4pm.*
Entry *£3.00/£2.60/£2.00. Castle free to E.H. members. E.H. members will be charged for entry to the parklands and for certain special events. (Property managed by the Lulworth Estate.)*
☎ *01929 400510*
👫 🅿 🐕 ♿ *(by ramp)* 🚻 🏠 🍴 🎁
➲ *In east Lulworth off B3070, 3 miles NE of Lulworth Cove.*
(OS Map 194; ref SY 853822.)
🚌 *Tel: 01305 852829.*
🚉 *Wool 4m.*

⊖ Lydford Castles and Saxon Town

DEVON (p. 212, 3D)

Standing above the gorge of the River Lyd, this 12th-century tower was notorious as a prison. The earthworks of the original Norman fort are to the south.

Open *Any reasonable time. (Property managed by the National Trust.)*
Entry *Free.*
🐕 🅿
➲ *In Lydford off A386, 8m S of Okehampton. (OS Map 191; Castle ref SX 510848, Fort ref SX 509847.)*
🚌 *Tel: 01392 382800.*

⊘⊖ Maiden Castle

DORSET (p. 213, 3G)

This is the finest Iron Age hill fort in Britain. The earthworks are enormous, with a series of ramparts and complicated entrances, but they could not prevent the fort's capture by the Romans *c.* AD43.

Open *Any reasonable time.*
Entry *Free.*
🅿 🐕
➲ *2m S of Dorchester. Access off A354, N of bypass.*

Lydford Castle

Maiden Castle

🏃

➲ *1m E of Merrivale.*
(OS Map 191; ref SX 553746.)
🚌 *Tel: 01392 382800.*
🚉 *Gunnislake 10m.*

⊕ Muchelney Abbey
SOMERSET (p. 213, 4G)

The well-preserved remains of the cloisters and abbot's lodging of this Benedictine abbey.

Open *1 April–1 Nov: daily, 10am–6pm (6pm/dusk in Oct).*
Entry *£1.60/£1.20/80p.*
☎ *01458 250664*
🚹 🅿 🏠 ✗ 🍴 ♿ *(grounds and part of ground floor only).*
➲ *In Muchelney 2m S of Langport.*
(OS Map 193; ref ST 428248.)
🚌 *Tel: 01823 272033.*

(OS Map 194; ref SY 670885.)
🚉 *Dorchester South or West, both 2m.*

⊖ Meare Fish House
SOMERSET (p. 213, 4G)

A simple, well-preserved stone dwelling.

Open *Any reasonable time. Key from Manor House farm.*
Entry *Free.*
✗
➲ *In Meare village on B3151.*
(OS Map 182; ref ST 458418.)

⊚ Merrivale Prehistoric Settlement
Dartmoor, DEVON
(p. 212, 3D)

Two rows of standing stones stretching up to 263 metres (864 feet) across the moors, together with the remains of an early Bronze Age village.

Open *Any reasonable time. (Property managed by Dartmoor National Park Authority.)*
Entry *Free.*

Muchelney Abbey (right). A Tudor wedding at Muchelney Abbey (below) and a stone corbel (far right)

⊙ Netheravon Dovecote
WILTSHIRE
(pp. 210/213, 5J)

A charming 18th-century brick dovecote, standing in a pleasant orchard, with most of its 700 or more nesting boxes still present.

Open *Exterior viewing only.*
Entry *Free.*

🏕

⊃ *In Netheravon, 4½m N of Amesbury on A345.*
(OS Map 184; ref SU 146485.)
🚌 *Tel: 01722 336855.*
🚆 *Pewsey 9m, Grateley 11m.*

⊙ The Nine Stones
Winterbourne Abbas,
DORSET (p. 213, 3G)

Remains of a prehistoric circle of nine standing stones constructed about 4,000 years ago.

Open *Any reasonable time.*
Entry *Free.*
🏕 🅿 *(small layby opposite, next to barn; cross road with care)*
⊃ *½m W of Winterbourne Abbas, on A35.*
(OS Map 194; ref SY 611904.)
🚌 *Tel: 01305 783645.*
🚆 *Dorchester West or South, both 5m.*

⊙ Notgrove Long Barrow
GLOUCESTERSHIRE
(pp. 210/214/217, 7J)

A Neolithic burial mound with chambers for human remains opening from a stone-built central passage.

Open *Any reasonable time.*
(Property managed by Gloucestershire County Council.)
Entry *Free.*
🅿 🏕
⊃ *1½m NW of Notgrove on A436.*
(OS Map 163; ref SP 096211.)
🚌 *Tel: 01451 20369.*

⊙⊙ Nunney Castle
SOMERSET (p. 210/213, 5H)

A small 14th-century moated castle which is distinctly French in style.

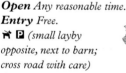

Nunney Castle

Open *Any reasonable time.*
Entry *Free.*
⅙ *(exterior only)* 🏕
⊃ *In Nunney 3½m SW of Frome, off A361 (no coach access).*
(OS Map 183; ref ST 737457.)
🚌 *Tel: 01749 673084.*
🚆 *Frome 3½m.*

⊙ Nympsfield Long Barrow
GLOUCESTERSHIRE
(pp. 210/213/217, 6H)

A chambered Neolithic long barrow 30 metres (90 feet) in length.

Open *Any reasonable time.*
(Property managed by Gloucestershire County Council.)
Entry *Free.*
🅿 🏕 🚻 *(public; 50 metres)*
⊃ *1m NW of Nympsfield on B4066.*
(OS Map 162; ref SO 795014.)

Okehampton Castle motte and keep (above) and viewed from the bluebell wood (left)

Tel: 01452 425543.
Stroud 5m.

⊕ Odda's Chapel

Deerhurst, GLOUCESTER-SHIRE (pp. 210/217, 7H)

A rare Anglo-Saxon chapel attached, unusually, to a half-timbered farmhouse.

Open *1 April–30 Sept: daily, 10am–6pm. 1 Oct–31 March: daily, 10am–4pm (closed 24–26 Dec, 1 Jan). (Property managed by Deerhurst Parish Council.)*

Entry *Free.*

● *In Deerhurst (off B4213) at Abbots Court SW of parish church. (OS Map 150; ref SO 869298.)*
Tel: 01452 425543.
Cheltenham 8m.

⊕● Offa's Dyke

GLOUCESTERSHIRE (pp. 213/217, 6G)

Three-mile section of the great earthwork built by Offa, King of Mercia 757–96, from the Severn estuary to the Welsh coast as a defensive boundary to his kingdom.

Open *Any reasonable time. (Property managed by Forest Enterprise.)*
Entry *Free.*

● *3m NE of Chepstow off B4228. Access via Forestry Commission Tidenham car park. 1m walk (waymarked) down to Devil's Pulpit on Offa's Dyke. (Access suitable only for those wearing proper walking shoes; not suitable for very young, old or infirm.) (OS Map 162; ref SO 545005–549977.)*
Tel: 01633 266366.
Chepstow 7m.

⊕○ Okehampton Castle

DEVON (p. 212, 3D)

The ruins of the largest castle in Devon include the Norman motte and the keep's jagged remains. There is a picnic area and there are also lovely woodland walks.

Picnic spot of exceptional beauty.
Open *1 April–1 Nov: daily, 10am–6pm (6pm/dusk in Oct).*
Entry *£2.30/£1.70/£1.20.*
(*01837 52844*
(picnic tables available) (also available for the visually impaired and those with learning difficulties)
● *1m SW of Okehampton town centre. (OS Map 191; ref SX 584942.)*
Tel: 01392 382800.

✪ Old Blockhouse

Tresco, ISLES OF SCILLY
(p. 212, 5A)

The remains of a small
16th-century gun tower
overlooking the white
sandy bay at Old Grimsby.

Open *Any reasonable time.*
Entry *Free.*
🛪
➲ *On Blockhouse Point, at S
end of Old Grimsby harbour.
(OS Map 203; ref SV 898155.)*

✪✪✪ Old Sarum

WILTSHIRE (pp. 210/213, 4J)
See pp. 86–7 for full details.

✪♡✪ Old Wardour Castle

WILTSHIRE (pp. 210/213, 4H)

The unusual hexagonal
ruins of this 14th-century
castle are on the edge of a
beautiful lake, surrounded
by landscaped grounds,

which include an elaborate
rockwork grotto.

Open all year round.
♿ **New interpretation
depicting the history of
this romantic ruin.**
🎬 **Robin Hood Prince of
Thieves**, *with Kevin
Costner, was filmed here.*
Open *1 April–1 Nov: daily,
10am–6pm (6pm/dusk in Oct).
2 Nov–31 March: Wed–Sun,
10am–4pm (closed 24–26 Dec).
Closed 1–2pm in winter.*
Entry *£1.70/£1.30/90p.*
✆ **01747 870487**
👫 🅿 ♿ *(grounds only)* 🛪 🎨
➲ *Off A30 2m SW of Tisbury.
(OS Map 184; ref ST 939263.)*
🚌 *Tel: 01722 336855.*
🚉 *Tisbury 2½m.*

✪ Over Bridge

GLOUCESTERSHIRE
(pp. 210/217, 7H)

A single-arch masonry
bridge spanning the River

Severn, built by Thomas
Telford 1825–27.

Open *Any reasonable time.
(Property managed by
Gloucester City Council.)*
Entry *Free.*
🛪 🅿 *(in layby)*
➲ *1m NW of Gloucester city
centre at junction of A40
(Ross) & A419 (Ledbury).
(OS Map 162; ref SO 817196.)*
🚌 *Tel: 01452 425543.*
🚉 *Gloucester 2m.*

✪ Pendennis Castle

CORNWALL (p. 212, 1B)
See pp 90–1 for full details.

✪ Penhallam

CORNWALL (p. 212, 3C)

Ruins of a medieval manor
house surrounded by a
protective moat.

Open *Any reasonable time.*
Entry *Free.*
🛪 🅿 *(limited)*
➲ *1m NW of Week St Mary,*

**Old Wardour Castle from the
south (left). Castle stairway to
Grand Hall (below)**

off minor road off A39 from Treskinnick Cross (10-minute walk from car park). (OS Map 190; ref SX 224974.)

❤️ ⛰️ Porth Hellick Down Burial Chamber

St Mary's, ISLES OF SCILLY
(p. 212, 4B)

Probably the best-preserved Bronze Age burial mound on the Islands, with an entrance passage and chamber.

Open *Any reasonable time.*
Entry *Free.*
🐕
➲ *1½ m E of Hugh Town. (OS Map 203; ref SV 929108.)*

⚙️ Portland Castle

DORSET (pp. 210/213, 3H)

One of the best-preserved of Henry VIII's coastal forts, built of white Portland stone. It was originally intended to repel the Spanish and French, and changed hands several times during the Civil War.

Portland Castle from the harbour

♿ *Audio tour of the castle's history up to WWII.*
Open *1 April–1 Nov: daily, 10am–6pm (6pm/dusk in Oct).*
Entry £2.30/£1.70/£1.20.
☎ *01305 820539*
🅿️ ❌ ♿ *(ground floor only – 1 deep step)* 🎧 🛍️ 🍴
➲ *Overlooking Portland harbour adjacent to RN helicopter base. (OS Map 194; ref SY 684743.)*
🚌 *Tel: 01305 783645. (Waterbus from Brewer's Quay.)*
🚆 *Weymouth 4½m.*

⛰️ Ratfyn Barrows

WILTSHIRE (pp. 210/213, 4J)

Part of a Bronze Age cemetery containing burial mounds of different styles.

Open *Access by written consent of owner only.*
Contact 0117 975 0700.
Entry *Free.*
➲ *1½ m E of Amesbury on both sides of A303. Barrows can be seen from A303 (no stopping). (OS Map 184; ref SU 180417.)*
🚌 *Tel: 01722 336855.*
🚆 *Salisbury 10m.*

⚙️ ◯ Restormel Castle

CORNWALL (p. 212, 2C)

Perched on a high mound, surrounded by a deep moat, the huge circular keep of this splendid Norman castle survives in remarkably good condition. It offers splendid views over the surrounding countryside.

♿ *Brand-new shop opening for 1998.*
Open *1 April–1 Nov: daily, 10am–6pm (6pm/dusk in Oct).*
Entry £1.60/£1.20/80p.
☎ *01208 872687*
🚻 🅿️ 🐕 🛍️ 🍴
➲ *1½m N of Lostwithiel off A390. (OS Map 200; ref SX 104614.)*
🚆 *Lostwithiel 1½m.*

Restormel Castle

OLD SARUM

✚ 🅝 🅜 WILTSHIRE (pp. 210/213, 4J)

This great earthwork with its huge banks and ditch lies near Salisbury, on the edge of the Wiltshire chalk plains. It was built by Iron Age peoples around 500BC and was taken over by succeeding settlers and conquerors. Romans, Saxons and, most importantly, the Normans have all occupied what is now known as Old Sarum. The Normans made it into one of their major strongholds, with a royal castle and a great cathedral. But when the new city that we know as Salisbury was founded in the early 13th century, the settlement faded away. Despite its virtual abandonment, a handful of electors still returned a member of Parliament to Westminster until 1832, when a wave of anti-corruption electoral reform swept through the whole of Britain.

Stone carving from Old Sarum cathedral

Today the remains – of the prehistoric fortress, of the Norman palace, castle and cathedral – evoke powerful memories of the people who have ruled England over the millennia. In addition, the chalk downland, with its many wild flowers, makes it a magical spot.

The great earth banks and ditches, a mile round, of the Iron Age hill fort at Old Sarum were used by successive invaders. It was here, in 1070, that William the Conqueror paid off his army and, in 1085, demanded loyalty from his nobles. A castle, a sumptuous palace and a great cathedral were built within the earthwork. However, disputes between soldiers and priests, and inadequate water supplies, were huge hindrances. In 1226 cathedral and town moved. New Sarum, modern Salisbury with its magnificent cathedral, was built in the valley with plentiful water. The cathedral at Old Sarum was then abandoned, although the castle remained in use until Tudor times.

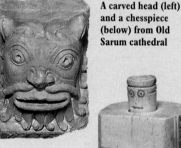

A carved head (left) and a chesspiece (below) from Old Sarum cathedral

A Romano-British brooch found at Old Sarum (below)

The Cathedral foundations marked out in the grass

Open all year round.
• Major special events include 'The Imperial Roman Army', with military displays and the shooting of artillery weapons, 24–25 May.
Open *1 April–1 Nov: daily, 10am–6pm (6pm/dusk in Oct). 2 Nov–31 March: daily, 10am–4pm (closed 24–26 Dec).*
Entry *£2.00/£1.50/£1.00.*
℡ *01722 335398*
🅿 ⛎ 🛥 ♿ *(outer bailey & grounds only)* 🐕 🖨 🎱
➲ *2m N of Salisbury, Wiltshire off A345. (OS Map 184; ref SU 138327.)*
Local Tourist Information: *Salisbury (tel: 01722 334956).*
🚌 *Tel: 01722 336855.*
🚉 *Salisbury 2m.*

Saxon period re-enactors

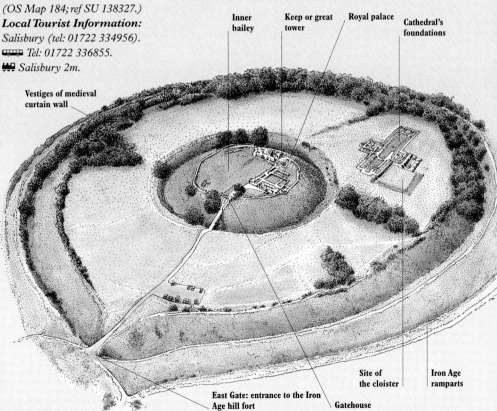

Inner bailey

Keep or great tower

Royal palace

Cathedral's foundations

Vestiges of medieval curtain wall

Site of the cloister

Iron Age ramparts

East Gate: entrance to the Iron Age hill fort

Gatehouse

St Briavel's Castle

⊕⊙ Royal Citadel
Plymouth, DEVON (p. 212, 2D)

A dramatic 17th-century fortress, with walls up to 21 metres (70 feet) high, built to defend the coastline from the Dutch, and still in use today.

Open *By guided tour only (1¼ hours) 1 May–30 Sept: 2pm and 3.30pm. Tickets from Plymouth Dome below Smeaton's Tower on Hoe. For security reasons tours may be suspended at short notice.*
Entry *£3.00/£2.50/£2.00.*
(01752 775841
⊗
➲ *At E end of Plymouth Hoe. (OS Map 201; ref SX 480538.)*
🚌 *Tel: 01752 222666.*
🚃 *Plymouth 1¼ m.*

⊛⊙ St Breock Downs Monolith
CORNWALL (p. 212, 2C)

A prehistoric standing stone, originally about 5 metres (16 feet) high, set in beautiful countryside.

Open *Any reasonable time. (Property managed by the Cornwall Heritage Trust.)*
Entry *Free.*
🛪
➲ *On St Breock Downs, 3¾ m SW of Wadebridge off unclassified road to Rosenannon. (OS Map 200; ref SW 968683.)*
🚃 *Roche 5½ m.*

⊕⊙ St Briavel's Castle
GLOUCESTERSHIRE (pp. 213/217, 6G)

A splendid 12th-century castle now used as a youth hostel, which is appropriate for a building set in such marvellous walking country.

Open *Exterior any reasonable time. Bailey 1 April–30 Sept: daily, 1pm–4pm.*
Entry *Free.*
⊗
➲ *In St Briavel's, 7m NE of Chepstow off B4228. (OS Map 162; ref SO 559046.)*
🚃 *Chepstow 8m.*

⊙ St Catherine's Castle
Fowey, CORNWALL (p. 212, 2C)

A small fort built by Henry VIII to defend Fowey Harbour.

Open *Any reasonable time.*
Entry *Free.*
🛪 🅿 *(in Fowey; ½ m walk)*
➲ *¾ m SW of Fowey along footpath off A3082. (OS Map 200; ref SX 118508.)*
🚌 *Tel: 01209 719988.*
🚃 *Par 4m.*

⊕ St Catherine's Chapel
Abbotsbury, DORSET (p. 213, 3G)

A small stone chapel, set on a hilltop, with an unusual roof and small turret used as a lighthouse.

Open *Any reasonable time. (Property managed by the Ilchester Estates.)*
Entry *Free.*
⊗
➲ *½ m S of Abbotsbury by pedestrian track from village off B3157. (OS Map 194; ref SY 572848.)*
🚌 *Tel: 01305 767023.*
🚃 *Upwey 7½ m.*

⊕ St Mary's Church
Kempley, GLOUCESTERSHIRE (p. 217, 7G)

A Norman church with superb wall paintings from the 12th–14th centuries.

Open *1 April–30 Sept: daily, 10am–6pm. 1 Oct–31 March: daily, 10am–4pm (closed 24–26 Dec, 1 Jan). (Property managed by the Friends of Kempley Church.)*
Entry *Free.*
⊗
➲ *1m N of Kempley off B4024,*

6m NE of Ross-on-Wye.
(OS Map 149; ref SO 670313.)
🚃 Ledbury 8m.

⊙❀ St Mawes Castle

CORNWALL (p. 212, 1B)

Together with Pendennis, St Mawes Castle was built by Henry VIII to guard the entrance to safe anchorage in the Carrick Roads. Its three huge circular bastions with gun ports were formidable defences indeed. Today the castle stands in landscaped grounds which provide some fine views of the surrounding coastline.

Open all year round.
• Free Children's Activity Sheet available.

Open 1 April–1 Nov: daily, 10am–6pm (6pm/dusk in Oct). 1 Nov–31 March: Fri–Tues, 10am–4pm (closed 24–26 Dec). Closed 1–2pm and all day Wed & Thur in winter.
Entry £2.50/£1.90/£1.30.
☎ **01326 270526**
🚻 🅿 ⊗ 🛍 🍴 🏠 🎧 🐕

➲ In St Mawes on A3078. (OS Map 204; ref SW 842328.)
🚌 Tel: 01209 719988.
⛴ Foot ferry: St Mawes Ferry Co. from Falmouth, Prince of Wales Pier (Tel: 01326 313201). Car via King Harry Ferry at Feock on B3289 (Tel: 01872 72463).
🚃 Falmouth Town, ¾m walk to Prince of Wales Pier.

⬣ The Sanctuary

WILTSHIRE (pp. 210/213, 5J)

Possibly 5,000 years old, The Sanctuary consists of two concentric circles of stones and six of timber uprights indicated by concrete posts. The Sanctuary is connected to Avebury by the West Kennet Avenue of standing stones.

Open Any reasonable time. (Property managed by the National Trust.)
Entry Free.
🐕 🅿 (in layby)
➲ Beside A4, ½m E of West Kennet. (OS Map 173; ref SU 118679.)
🚌 Tel: 0345 090 899.
🚃 Pewsey 9m, Bedwyn 12m.

St Mawes Castle

PENDENNIS CASTLE

CORNWALL (p. 212, 1B)

Pendennis and its neighbour St Mawes Castle face each other across the mouth of the River Fal estuary. They are the Cornish end of a chain of castles built by Henry VIII along the south coast as protection against the threat of attack from France. Few have seen active service but Pendennis was adapted to meet new enemies, from the French and Spanish in the 16th century, through to World

Sir Walter Raleigh, who ordered the refortification of Pendennis

War II. Today the excellent site facilities at Pendennis include an exhibition, museum, the new Discovery Centre and the Guardhouse, which has been returned to its World War I appearance. Also opening for the first time this year are the secret World War II defences and the military tunnels. With its fine seaviews, an extra treat will be the Tall Ships' Race, with a series of firework concerts.

The land on which Pendennis stands was originally owned by the Killigrew family, governors of Pendennis for many years. The lodgings fronting the keep were built around 1550 to provide them with more comfortable accommodation. In the later years of Elizabeth I's reign, a new type of defensive wall with bastions was added around the original fort.

The Battery observation post

The Governor's lodging (left), built in the mid-16th century

Strengthened again prior to the Civil War, Pendennis was host to the future Charles II in 1646, who sailed from there to the Isles of Scilly. It withstood five months of siege before becoming the penultimate Royalist garrison to surrender on the mainland.

Pendennis was rearmed in the late 19th and early 20th centuries, seeing action in World War II. For the first time in 1998, these defences, including the World War II Gun Battery, accompanied by interactive displays, will be open to the public.

Pendennis's development

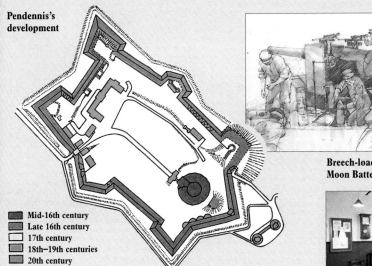

Breech-loading gun at the Half Moon Battery (1911) (above)

- ▪ Mid-16th century
- ▪ Late 16th century
- ☐ 17th century
- ▪ 18th–19th centuries
- ▪ 20th century

Open all year round.
♿ Open from 9am in July and August.
♿ New for 1998 – 'Discovery Centre'.
♿ Re-created WWI Guardhouse complete with cells.
♿ Restored 19th and 20th-century defences.
♿ Underground magazines and tunnels.

• *Re-creation of the gun defences (nearly 40 historic guns on display).*
Open *1 April–1 Nov: daily, 10am–6pm (opens 9am in July & August, closes 6pm/dusk in Oct). 2 Nov–31 March: daily, 10am–4pm (closed 24–26 Dec).*
Entry *£3.00/£2.30/£1.50.*
℡ 01326 316594
🅿 🚹 ♿ *(grounds, parts of keep)* 🚫 📷 E 🍴 *('Pendennis*

Inside the WWI guardroom

Castle Coffee Shop'; open April–Sept) ☐ ☕
➲ *On Pendennis Head, Cornwall, 1m SE of Falmouth. (OS Map 204; ref SW 824318.)*
Local Tourist Information: *Falmouth (tel: 01326 312300).*
🚉 *Falmouth Docks ½m.*

See the Tall Ships' Race from Pendennis Castle, 17–19 July.

Aerial view of Pendennis from the south east

◆ ⓜ Sherborne Old Castle

DORSET (pp. 210/213, 4G)

The ruins of this early 12th-century castle are a testament to the 16 days Cromwell took to capture it during the Civil War. It was then abandoned.

Open all year round.
⌂ Brand-new shop opening for 1998.
Open *1 April–1 Nov: daily, 10am–6pm (6pm/dusk in Oct). 2 Nov–31 March: Wed–Sun, 10am–4pm (closed 24–26 Dec). Closed 1–2pm in winter.*
Entry *£1.60/£1.20/80p.*
℃ *01935 812730*
🅿 ⊗ ⌂ 🛍
◆ *½m E of Sherborne off B3145.*
(OS Map 183; ref ST 647167.)
🚃 *Sherborne ¾m.*

ⓞ Silbury Hill

WILTSHIRE (pp. 210/213, 5J)

An extraordinary artificial prehistoric mound, the largest Neolithic construction of its type in Europe.

Open *Viewing area at any reasonable time (no access to hill itself). (Property managed by the National Trust.)*
Entry *Free.*
⌂ *(viewing area)* 🛉 🅿
◆ *1m W of West Kennet on A4.*
(OS Map 173; ref SU 100685.)
🚌 *Tel: 0345 090 899.*
🚃 *Pewsey 9m, Swindon 13m.*

An aerial view of Sherborne Old Castle

⊙ Sir Bevil Grenville's Monument

Lansdown, BATH & N.E. SOMERSET (pp. 210/213, 5H)

Commemorates the heroism of a Royalist commander and his Cornish pikemen at the Battle of Lansdown.

Open *Any reasonable time.*
Entry *Free.*
🛉 🅿 *(in layby)*
◆ *4m NW of Bath, on N edge of Lansdown Hill, near road to Wick.*
(OS Map 172; ref ST 721703.)
🚌 *Tel: 01225 464446.*
🚃 *Bath Spa 4½m.*

Silbury Hill

◆ⓞ Stanton Drew Circles and Cove

BATH & N.E. SOMERSET (p. 213, 5G)

Recent research at this assembly of stone circles, avenues and a 'Cove' of three standing stones has shown that there was once also a huge timber structure within the Great Circle. The ritual complex dates from about 3000BC.

Open *Cove – any reasonable time. Two main stone circles – access at discretion of owner who may levy a charge. Tel: 0117 975 0700 for details.*
Entry *Free, but see above.*
🛉
◆ *Circles: E of Stanton Drew village; Cove: in garden of Druid's Arms.*
(OS Map 172; Circles ref ST 601634, Cove ref ST 598633.)
🚌 *Tel: 0117 955 3231.*
🚃 *Bristol Temple Meads 7m.*

ⓘ Stonehenge

WILTSHIRE
(pp. 210/213, 5J)
See pp. 94–99 for full details.

⬙ Stoney Littleton Long Barrow

BATH & N.E. SOMERSET
(pp. 210/213, 5H)

This Neolithic burial mound is about 30 metres (100 feet) long and has chambers where human remains once lay.

Open Exterior only – any reasonable time.
Entry Free.
🏠 🅿 *(limited)*
➲ *1m S of Wellow off A367. (OS Map 172; ref ST 735573.)*
🚉 *Bath Spa 6m.*

✚ Temple Church

BRISTOL (p. 213, 5G)

The handsome tower and walls of this 15th-century church defied the bombs of World War II. The graveyard is now a pleasant public garden.

Open Exterior only – any reasonable time.
Entry Free.
♿ 🏠
➲ *In Temple St off Victoria St. (OS Map 172; ref ST 593727.)*
☎ *Tel: 0117 955 3231.*
🚉 *Bristol Temple Meads ¼m.*

◷ ◯ Tintagel Castle

CORNWALL (p. 212, 3C)
See pp. 102–3 for full details.

◷ ◯ Totnes Castle

DEVON (p. 212, 2E)

A superb motte and bailey castle, with splendid views across the roof tops and down to the River Dart – a fine example of Norman fortification.

Open all year round.
• Family Discovery Pack available.
Open 1 April–1 Nov: daily, 10am–6pm (6pm/dusk in Oct).
2 Nov–31 March: Wed–Sun, 10am–4pm (closed 24–26 Dec). Closed 1–2pm in winter.
Entry £1.60/£1.20/80p.
☎ *01803 864406*
🅿 *(64 metres [210 feet], small charge)* 🏠 ⬚
➲ *In Totnes, on hill overlooking the town. (OS Map 202; ref SX 800605.)*
🚉 *Totnes ¼m.*

⬙ Tregiffian Burial Chamber

St Buryan, CORNWALL
(p. 212, 1A)

A Neolithic or early Bronze Age chambered tomb by the side of a country road.

Open Any reasonable time. (Property managed by the Cornwall Heritage Trust.)
Entry Free.
🏠
➲ *2m SE of St Buryan on B3315. (OS Map 203; ref SW 430245.)*
🚉 *Penzance 5½m.*

Totnes Castle

STONEHENGE

① WILTSHIRE (pp. 210/213, 5J)

The great and ancient stone circle of Stonehenge is one of the wonders of the world, as old as many of the great temples and pyramids of Egypt, as old as Troy. Stonehenge is not an isolated monument, however. Although visitors over the centuries have tended to focus on the massive stones, these stand at the centre of an extensive prehistoric landscape that is filled with the remains

Bronze dagger (far left) and gold-plated ornaments (above) from near Stonehenge

of ceremonial and domestic structures. Some are older than the great monument itself. Many of these features – earthworks, burial mounds and other circular 'henge' monuments – are accessible by road or public footpath. Now a World Heritage Site, Stonehenge and all its surroundings remain powerful witnesses to the once great civilization of the Stone and Bronze Ages, between 5,000 and 3,000 years ago.

What visitors see today are the substantial remnants of the last in a sequence of monuments erected between *c.*3000 and 1600BC. Each was a circular structure, aligned along the rising of the sun at the midsummer solstice. The

first 'Stonehenge' consisted of a circular bank and ditch with a ring of 56 wooden posts, now known as Aubrey Holes. Later monuments all used, and re-used, the great stones we see today, which were brought from some

The final phase of Stonehenge's construction

Station stone

The best-surviving section of the outer circle of sarsen stones

Circular ditch and bank

Fallen stones showing the mortice and tenon fixing

distance away. The final phase comprised an outer circle of huge standing stones – super-hard sarsens, from the Marlborough Downs – and topped by lintels making a continuous ring. Inside this stood a horseshoe of still larger stones, five pairs of uprights with a lintel across each pair, known as trilithons. Stones were connected using mortice and tenon and tongue and groove joints, possibly copying previous wood construction techniques. Smaller bluestones, from the Preseli Mountains in south Wales, were arranged in a circle and a horseshoe, within the great sarsen stone circle and horseshoe. In an earlier phase these bluestones had been erected in a different arrangement.

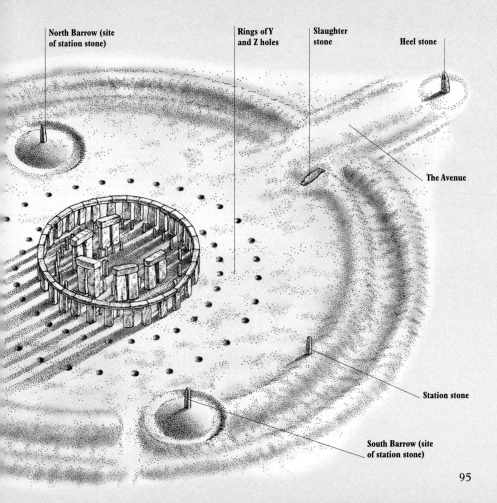

North Barrow (site of station stone)

Rings of Y and Z holes

Slaughter stone

Heel stone

The Avenue

Station stone

South Barrow (site of station stone)

A possible method of raising the sarsen stones into an upright setting

There has always been intense debate over quite what purpose Stonehenge served. Certainly it was the focal point for thousands of years within a ceremonial landscape. It also represented a huge investment of labour and time. The stones were carried tens, sometimes hundreds, of miles by land and water. Huge efforts were needed to transport the stones, and then to shape and raise them. It must have been a sophisticated society to command the amount of labour to design and construct this and the many other surrounding monuments. Stonehenge's orientation on the rising and setting sun has always

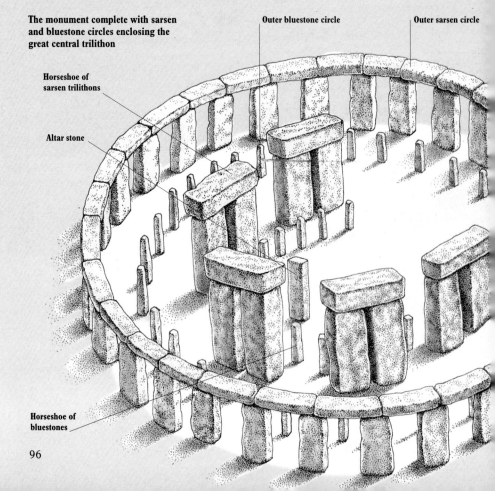

The monument complete with sarsen and bluestone circles enclosing the great central trilithon

Outer bluestone circle

Outer sarsen circle

Horseshoe of sarsen trilithons

Altar stone

Horseshoe of bluestones

A likely method of raising a lintel to the top of two sarsens

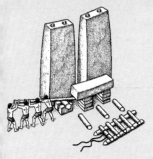

been one of its most remarkable features. Whether this was simply because the builders came from a sun-worshipping culture, or because – as some scholars have believed – the circle and its banks were part of a huge astronomical calendar, remains a mystery.

What cannot be denied is the ingenuity of the builders of Stonehenge. With just very basic tools at their disposal, they shaped the stones and formed the mortices and tenons that linked uprights to lintels. Using antlers and bones, they dug the pits to hold the stones and made the banks and ditches that enclosed them.

Bone and antler digging tools of the type used at Stonehenge

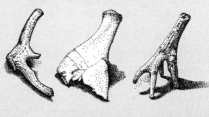

Stonehenge from the air in winter

A dressed sarsen from the outer circle

There are direct links with the people who built Stonehenge in their artefacts: tools, pottery and even the contents of their graves. Some of these are displayed in the museums at Salisbury and Devizes.

Burial mounds, which possibly contained the graves of ruling families, are also integral to the landscape. The long barrows of the

A man buried c.2000 BC, holding a pottery drinking vessel

Pottery funerary vessels of the early Bronze Age

New Stone Age, and the various types of circular barrows that came after, are still visible, as are other earthworks and monuments. Some, such as the long oval earthwork to the north, the Cursus, once thought to be a chariot race course, remain enigmatic.

The Cursus and other parts of the Stonehenge landscape may be visited. Woodhenge, two miles to the north east, was a wooden oval post structure aligned with the summer solstice sun and contemporary with the first phase of Stonehenge.

Map with the barrows and monuments in the Stonehenge area

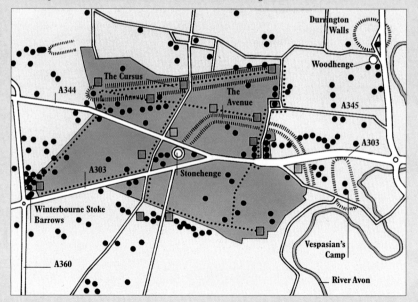

The chalk and grass landscape, with the Cursus, the Stonehenge circle, and clusters of barrow burials

An artist's impression (below) of a possible reconstruction of Woodhenge

✆ *01980 624715*

🅿 ♠ 🚻 📷 🖥 (*'Stonehenge Kitchen', open all year.*)
⊗ ♿ 🎫 (*also available in French, German and Japanese; large print and braille guides in English only*)
🎧* (*available in nine languages & hearing loop*)
➲ *2m W of Amesbury on*

Stonehenge and its surrounding monuments have been an object of fascination and appeal since well before the dawn of recorded history.

Open all year round.
📺 ***LWT's new series,*** **Tess,** ***filmed at Stonehenge.***
• ***Interactive audio tour of the facts and legends of Stonehenge, available in nine languages including Dutch, Russian and Swedish.***

William Cunnington (below), one in a great line of antiquarians, who studied Stonehenge around 1800

• ***Superb gift shop.***
Open *16 March–31 May: daily, 9.30am–6pm. 1 June–31 Aug: daily, 9am–7pm. 1 Sept–15 Oct: daily, 9.30am–6pm. 16 Oct–15 March (1999): daily, 9.30am–4pm (closed 24–26 Dec).*
Entry *£3.90/£2.90/£2.00. Family ticket (2 adults & 3 children) £9.80. National Trust members admitted free. (Under the guardianship and managed by English Heritage. The site is surrounded by 1,500 acres of land owned by the National Trust with excellent walks.)*

junction of A303 and A344/A360. (OS Map 184; ref SU 123422.)
Local Tourist Information: *Amesbury (tel: 01980 622833), Salisbury (tel: 01722 334956).*
🚌 *Tel: 01722 336855.*
🚉 *Salisbury 9½m.*

Hale Bopp comet over Stonehenge

Trethevy Quoit

⏚ Trethevy Quoit

St Cleer, CORNWALL
(p. 212, 2D)

An ancient Neolithic
burial chamber, standing
2.7 metres (9 feet) high
and consisting of five
standing stones
surmounted by a
huge capstone.

Open *Any reasonable time.
(Site managed by the
Cornwall Heritage Trust.)*
Entry *Free.*
⚓
➲ *1m NE of St Cleer near
Darite off B3254.
(OS Map 201; ref
SX 259688.)*
🚌 *Tel: 01209 719988.*
🚌 *Liskeard 3½ m.*

⏚ Uley Long Barrow (Hetty Pegler's Tump)

GLOUCESTERSHIRE
(pp. 210/213/217, 6H)

Dating from around 3000
BC, this 55 metre- (180
foot-) long Neolithic
chambered burial mound is
unusual in that its mound
is still intact.

Open *Any reasonable time.
(Property managed by
Gloucestershire County Council.)*
Entry *Free.*
⚓
➲ *3½ m NE of Dursley
on B4066.
(OS Map 162; ref SO 790000.)*
🚌 *Tel: 01452 425543.*
🚌 *Stroud 6m.*

⏚ Upper Plym Valley

Dartmoor, DEVON (p. 212, 2D)

Scores of prehistoric and
medieval sites covering
six square miles of
ancient landscape.

Open *Any reasonable time.
(Property managed by the
National Trust.)*
Entry *Free.*
⚓
➲ *4m E of Yelverton.
(OS Map 202.)*
🚌 *Tel: 01392 382800.*

⏚ West Kennet Avenue

Avebury, WILTSHIRE
(pp. 210/213, 5J)

An avenue of standing
stones, which ran in a
curve from Avebury Stone
Circles to The Sanctuary,
probably dating from the
late Neolithic Age.

Open *Any reasonable time.
(Property owned and managed
by the National Trust.)*
Entry *Free.*
♿ *(on roadway)* ⚓
➲ *Runs alongside B4003.
(OS Map 173; ref
SU 105695.)*
🚌 *Tel: 0345 090 899.*
🚌 *Pewsey 9m,
Swindon 12m.*

⏚ West Kennet Long Barrow

WILTSHIRE (pp. 210/213, 5J)

A Neolithic chambered
tomb, consisting of a long
earthen mound containing
a passage with side
chambers, and with the
entrance guarded by a
large stone.

Open *Any reasonable time.
(Property managed by the
National Trust.)*
Entry *Free.*
🅿 *(in layby)* ⚓
➲ *¾ m SW of West Kennet
along footpath off A4.
(OS Map 173; ref
SU 104677.)*
🚌 *Tel: 0345 090 899.*
🚌 *Pewsey 9m,
Swindon 13m.*

⏣ Windmill Hill
WILTSHIRE (pp. 210/213, 5J)

Neolithic remains of three concentric rings of ditches, enclosing an area of 21 acres.

Open *Any reasonable time.* *(Property owned and managed by the National Trust.)*
Entry *Free.*
🐕
➲ *1½m NW of Avebury.*
(OS Map 173; ref SU 086714.)
🚌 *Tel: 0345 090 899.*
🚉 *Swindon 11m.*

⏣ Winterbourne Poor Lot Barrows
DORSET (p. 213, 3G)

Part of an extensive 4,000-year-old Bronze Age cemetery.

Open *Any reasonable time.*
Entry *Free.*

⊗
➲ *2m W of Winterbourne Abbas, S of junction of A35 with minor road to Compton Valence. Access via Wellbottom Lodge – 180 metres (200 yards) E along A35 from junction.*
(OS Map 194; ref SY 590906.)
🚌 *Tel: 01305 783645.*
🚉 *Dorchester West or South, both 7m.*

⏣ Woodhenge
WILTSHIRE (pp. 210/213, 5J)

Neolithic ceremonial monument of *c.* 2300 BC, consisting of a bank and ditch and six concentric rings of timber posts, now shown by concrete markers. The entrance and long axis of the oval rings points to the rising sun on Midsummer Day.
See illustration on p. 99.

West Kennet Long Barrow

Open *Any reasonable time.*
Entry *Free.*
🅿️ ♿ 🐕
➲ *1½m N of Amesbury, off A345 just S of Durrington.*
(OS Map 184; ref SU 151434.)
🚌 *Tel: 01722 336855.*
🚉 *Salisbury 9m.*

⏣ Yarn Market
Dunster, SOMERSET
(p. 213, 4E)

A 17th-century octagonal market hall.

Open *Any reasonable time.* *(Property managed by the National Trust.)*
Entry *Free.*
♿ 🐕
➲ *In Dunster High St.*
(OS Map 181; ref SS 992437.)
🚌 *Tel: 01823 272033.*
🚉 *Dunster (W Somerset Rly) ½m.*

Yarn Market

TINTAGEL CASTLE

⬛ ♡ CORNWALL (p. 212, 3C)

With its spectacular location on one of England's most dramatic coastlines, Tintagel is a place of legends. Joined to the mainland by a narrow neck of land, Tintagel Island faces the full force of the Atlantic. On the mainland itself, the gaunt remains of the medieval castle, thought to date from the second quarter of the 13th century, represent only one phase in a long history of occupation. Even before Richard, Earl of Cornwall, built his castle,

Merlin and baby Arthur

Tintagel had come to be associated with King Arthur, as the great warrior leader's birthplace. The legend, depicted in Geoffrey of Monmouth's fabulous History (written *c.* 1139), has lived on. Today, fact and fiction lie inextricably intertwined. We know for sure, however, that with the surf thundering against the cliffs and the waves breaking over the threshold of Merlin's cave, Tintagel remains one of the most awe-inspiring and romantic spots in Britain.

After a period as a Roman settlement and military outpost, Tintagel is thought to have been the stronghold of a Celtic king during the fifth and sixth centuries. Nearby

an early Christian church stands on the site of what may have been a cemetery for important men. Here legend and archaeology come together. Whether one

of those men was King Mark, whose nephew Tristan fell in love with Isolt (or Isolde), history cannot tell. Their doomed romance is part of Tintagel's story, as are Geoffrey of Monmouth's tales, in which Uther Pendragon, aided by Merlin, seduced Queen Igerna at Tintagel. Tintagel's Arthurian connection was later renewed by Alfred, Lord Tennyson in his *Idylls of the King*. The remains of the 13th-century castle are breathtaking. Steep stone steps, stout walls and rugged windswept cliff edges encircle the Great Hall, where Richard, Earl of Cornwall,

Tintagel Castle ruins

The so-called Merlin's cave (left)

King Arthur receives Excalibur from the Lady in the Lake (right)

may once have feasted. The emphasis at Tintagel is always on the word 'may', as it has so many legends and unanswered questions.

Open all year round.
• Family Discovery Pack and free Children's Activity Sheet available.
Open 1 April–1 Nov: daily, 10am–6pm (6pm/dusk in Oct). 2 Nov–31 March: daily, 10am–4pm (closed 24–26 Dec).
Entry £2.80/£2.10/£1.40
(01840 770328
⌂ ♛ ⚓ 🅿 *(in Tintagel village, 600 metres)* 🛏 ⬚ *(Please note steep climb up steps to reach castle.)*
➲ *On Tintagel Head, ½m along uneven track from Tintagel, no vehicles. (OS Map 200; ref SX 048891.)*

Local Tourist Information: *Camelford (tel: 01840 212954, summer only); Padstow (tel: 01841 533449).* 🚌 *Tel: 01209 719988 or 01840 770256).*

The Iron Gate (below), the medieval entrance from the sea

The Island of Tintagel

EASTERN REGION

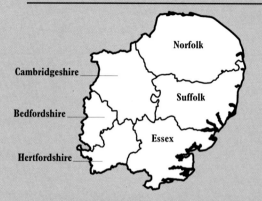

SCATTERED ACROSS the region are Roman sites, castles spanning the centuries, chapels, priories and windmills – you'll even find a prehistoric flint mine. On the grandest scale is Audley End, a Jacobean mansion in Essex with a magnificent landscaped garden.

Medieval castles are epitomized by the impressive solidity of Framlingham in Suffolk and the grandeur of the coastal keep at Orford with its views over the Suffolk marshes, while Tilbury Fort, at the mouth of the Thames, has defended London since Elizabethan times.

Children enjoying the gardens at Audley End

⊕❀ Audley End House and Gardens

ESSEX (pp. 211/214, 7N)
See pp. 106–9 for full details.

⊖⊖ Baconsthorpe Castle

NORFOLK (p. 215, 10O)

Remains of the gatehouses of a large 15th-century fortified manor house, partly surrounded by a moat.

Open *All year: daily, 10am–4pm.*
Entry *Free.*
P 🐾
➲ *¾m N of village of Baconsthorpe off unclassified road 3m E of Holt.*
(OS Map 133; ref TG 122382.)
🚌 *Sheringham 4½m.*

⊕ Berkhamsted Castle

HERTFORDSHIRE
(p. 212, 6L)

The extensive remains of a large 11th-century motte and bailey castle.

Open *All year: daily, 10am–4pm. Please contact keykeeper, Mr Stevens, on 01442 871737.*

Entry *Free.*
🐾
➲ *By Berkhamsted station.*
(OS Map 165; ref SP 996083.)
🚌 *Tel: 0345 244 344.*
🚌 *Berkhamsted, adjacent.*

⊖ Berney Arms Windmill

NORFOLK (p. 215, 9P)

One of the best and largest remaining marsh mills in Norfolk, with seven floors, making it a landmark for miles around. Built to grind a constituent of cement, it was in use until 1951, ending its days pumping water to drain surrounding marshes.

Open *1 April–1 Nov: daily, 9am–5pm. Closed 1–2pm.*
Entry *£1.30/£1.00/70p.*
(*01493 700605*
🐾
➲ *3½m NE of Reedham on N bank of River Yare. Accessible by boat, or by footpath from Halvergate (3½m). (OS Map 134; ref TG 465051.)*
🚌 *Berney Arms ¼m.*

Berney Arms Windmill

⊕ Binham Priory

NORFOLK (p. 215, 10O)

Extensive remains of a Benedictine priory. The original nave of the church is still in use as the parish church.

Open *Any reasonable time.*
Entry *Free.*
🐾
➲ *¼m NW of village of Binham-on-Wells on road off B1388. (OS Map 132; ref TF 982399.)*
🚌 *Tel: 0500 626116.*

⊖ Binham Wayside Cross

NORFOLK (p. 215, 10O)

Medieval cross marking the site of an annual fair held from the reign of Henry I until the 1950s.

Open *Any reasonable time.*
Entry *Free.*
🐾
➲ *On village green adjacent to Priory. (OS Map 132; ref TF 982399.)*
🚌 *Tel: 0500 626116.*

Binham Priory

AUDLEY END HOUSE AND GARDENS

🔵 ✳️ ESSEX (pp. 211/214, 7N)

Audley End was one of the great wonders of the nation when it was built by the first Earl of Suffolk, Lord Treasurer to James I. It was on the scale of a great royal palace, and soon became one after Charles II bought it in 1668 for £50,000, using it as a base when he attended the races at Newmarket. Returned to the Suffolks after his death, substantial parts of the house were demolished. Even so, what remains is one of the most significant Jacobean houses in England. Successive owners have since placed their stylistic imprint both within the graceful exterior and in the surrounding parkland.

As we see it now, Audley End's interior with its historic picture collection and furniture is largely the product of its owner in the mid-19th century, the third Lord Braybrooke. The challenge for the visitor today is to piece together the many changes over time that have created such a harmonious whole.

The first Lord Braybrooke (left) remodelled Audley End in the late 18th century

The rooms at Audley End are a blend of many generations of taste – the differences sometimes subtly combined, sometimes dramatically exploited. The main structure has remained remarkably little-altered since the main front court was demolished in 1708 and the east wing came

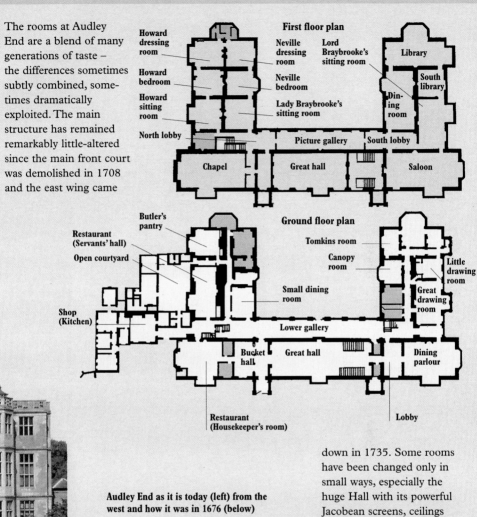

First floor plan

Howard dressing room
Howard bedroom
Howard sitting room
North lobby
Neville dressing room
Neville bedroom
Lady Braybrooke's sitting room
Lord Braybrooke's sitting room
Library
South library
Dining room
Picture gallery
South lobby
Chapel
Great hall
Saloon

Ground floor plan

Butler's pantry
Restaurant (Servants' hall)
Open courtyard
Shop (Kitchen)
Small dining room
Tomkins room
Canopy room
Little drawing room
Great drawing room
Lower gallery
Bucket hall
Great hall
Dining parlour
Restaurant (Housekeeper's room)
Lobby

Audley End as it is today (left) from the west and how it was in 1676 (below)

down in 1735. Some rooms have been changed only in small ways, especially the huge Hall with its powerful Jacobean screens, ceilings and panelling. Other parts of the house, notably the great apartments and bedchambers, have been redecorated, but show a continuity of style. In the 1760s Adam brought his individual brand of graceful neoclassical architecture to the house, while Lancelot 'Capability' Brown transformed the parkland.

William Tomkins' painting of
Audley End and the Ring Hill
Temple, painted *c*. 1785

Sir John Griffin Griffin,
later fourth Baron Howard
de Walden and first Baron
Braybrooke, introduced
sweeping changes before
he died in 1797. The third
Baron Braybrooke, who
inherited house and title
in 1825, stamped his taste
equally firmly and with
longer-lasting results. He
installed his huge picture
collection, filled the rooms
with furnishings, and
reinstated some of the
original Jacobean feel to the
State rooms.

The Georgian 'Gothick'
chapel survives, but many of
the other 18th-century
decorative schemes were
replaced. The fourth Lord
Braybrooke was more
interested in archaeology
and ornithology than
redecorating. His collection
of stuffed birds and animals
are a real
feature of the
house. After
Audley End was
requisitioned in
World War II
the ninth Lord
Braybrooke
resumed
possession and
in 1948 the
house was sold
to English
Heritage's pre-
decessor, the
Ministry of
Works.

Much has
been done recently to
restore the park and the
Victorian gardens, including
the magnificent parterre. A
free exhibition and special
guidebook focus on the
extensive grounds, with

The Little Drawing Room (above)

The fourth Lord Braybrooke's
Natural History Collection (left) –
a great favourite with children

their lake, river and ornamental gardens. On a summer afternoon, Audley End's beauty and historical continuity are readily apparent.

♿ *Free Children's Activity Sheet available.*
• *Winner of a 1996/7 NPI National Heritage Award, voted by the general public as one of Britain's favourite national treasures.*
• *Popular open-air concerts during the summer.*
Open *1 April–30 Sept: Wed–Sun and Bank Holidays, 11am–6pm. Last admissions 5pm. 1 Oct–31 Oct: Wed–Sun, 10am–3pm, house by guided tour only.*
Entry *House and Grounds £5.75/£4.30/£2.90, family ticket (2 adults & 3 children) £14.40. Grounds only £3.50/£2.60/£1.80, family ticket £8.80.*

A tour around the Great Hall at Audley End (above)

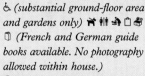

Heraldic crests adorn the plaster ceiling in the Great Hall (right)

☎ **01799 522399** *(information line)*
🅿 ❚❚ *(The Parterre Restaurant)*

♿ *(substantial ground-floor area and gardens only)* 🚗 👪 ♿ 🛍 🍴
🛍 *(French and German guide books available. No photography allowed within house.)*
➲ *1m W of Saffron Walden on B1383 (M11 exits 8, 9, Northbound only, & 10). (OS Map 154; ref TL 525382.)*
Local Tourist Information: *Birchanger (tel: 01279 508656); Cambridge (tel: 01223 322640).*
🚌 *Tel: 0345 000 333.*
🚂 *Audley End 1¼m.*

The Doll's House (left) is a miniature version of early 19th-century highlife at Audley End

⊘ Blakeney Guildhall

NORFOLK (p. 215, 10O)

The surviving basement, most likely used for storage, of a large 14th-century building, probably a merchant's house.

Open *Any reasonable time.*
Entry *Free.*
⊗
➲ *In Blakeney off A149.*
(OS Map 133; ref TG 030441.)
🚌 *Tel: 0500 626116.*
🚃 *Sheringham 9m.*

⊘ Burgh Castle

NORFOLK (p. 215, 9P)

Impressive walls, with projecting bastions, of a Roman fort built in the late 3rd century as one of a chain to defend the coast against Saxon raiders.

Open *Any reasonable time.*
(Property managed by Norfolk Archaeological Trust.)
Entry *Free.*
🏹
➲ *At far W end of Breydon Water, on unclassified road 3m W of Great Yarmouth.*
(OS Map 134; ref TG 475046.)
🚌 *Tel: 0500 626116.*
🚃 *Great Yarmouth 5m.*

✠ Bury St Edmunds Abbey

SUFFOLK (p. 215, 8O)

A Norman tower and 14th-century gatehouse of a ruined Benedictine abbey, church and precinct. The visitor centre has interactive displays.

Open *Abbey all year: Mon–Sat, 7.30am–dusk. Sundays and Bank Holidays, 9am–dusk. Visitor Centre: 1 April–31 Oct, daily, 10am–5pm. (Property managed by St Edmundsbury Borough Council.)*
Entry *Free.*
✆ **01284 764667** *for details.*
🚻 🏹
➲ *E end of town centre.*
(OS Map 155; ref TL 858642.)
🚌 *Tel: 0645 583358.*
🚃 *Bury St Edmunds 1m.*

✠ Bushmead Priory

BEDFORDSHIRE (p. 214, 8M)

A rare survival of the medieval refectory of an Augustinian priory. Its original timber-framed roof is almost intact and contains interesting wall paintings and stained glass.

Open *July–Aug: weekends and Bank Holidays,*

Bushmead Priory

10am–6pm. Closed 1–2pm.
Entry £1.75/£1.30/90p.
✆ **01234 376614**
🅿 ⊗
➲ *On unclassified road near Colmworth, 2m E of B660.*
(OS Map 153; ref TL 115607.)
🚃 *St Neots 6m.*

⊘ Caister Roman Site

NORFOLK (p. 215, 9P)

The remains of a Roman fort, including part of a defensive wall, a gateway and buildings along a main street.

Bury St Edmunds Abbey

Open *Any reasonable time. (Property managed by Great Yarmouth Borough Council.)*
Entry *Free.*

🐾

➲ *Near Caister-on-Sea, 3m N of Great Yarmouth. (OS Map 134; ref TG 518125.)*

🚌 *Tel: 0500 626116.*

🚌 *Great Yarmouth 3m.*

Castle Acre Castle

✪ Castle Acre: Bailey Gate

NORFOLK (p. 215, 9N)

The north gateway to the medieval planned town of Acre, with flint towers.

Open *Any reasonable time.*
Entry *Free.*

🐾

➲ *In Castle Acre, at E end of Stocks Green, 5m N of Swaffham. (OS Map 132; ref TF 817152.)*

✪✪ Castle Acre Castle

NORFOLK (p. 215, 9O)

The remains of a Norman manor house, which became a castle with earthworks, set by the side of the village.

Open *Any reasonable time.*
Entry *Free.*

🐾

➲ *At E end of Castle Acre, 5m N of Swaffham. (OS Map 132; ref TF 819152.)*

✚ Castle Acre Priory

NORFOLK (p. 215, 9N)

The great west front of the 12th-century church of this Cluniac priory still rises to its full height and is elaborately decorated, whilst the prior's lodgings and porch retain their roofs. The herb garden, re-created to show both culinary and medicinal herbs used in medieval times, should not be missed.

Open all year round.
Open *1 April–1 Nov: daily, 10am–6pm (6pm/dusk in Oct). 2 Nov–31 March: Wed–Sun, 10am–4pm (closed 24–26 Dec).*
Entry *£2.95/£2.20/£1.50.*
ℓ 01760 755394

🅿 ♿ *(ground floor & grounds only)* ⅋ 🎧 *(also available for the visually impaired, those with learning difficulties and in French)* 🅗🛍🅦🐾

➲ *¼m W of village of Castle Acre, 5m N of Swaffham. (OS Map 132; ref TF 814148.)*

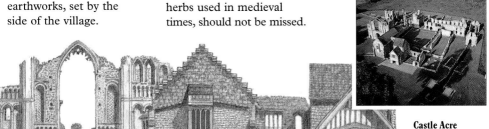

Castle Acre Priory (left and above)

111

◐ Castle Rising Castle

NORFOLK (p. 215, 10N)

A fine mid-12th-century domestic keep, set in the centre of massive defensive earthworks, once palace and prison to Isabella, 'She-Wolf' dowager Queen of England. The keep walls stand to their original height and many of the fortifications are intact.

Open all year round.
Open *1 April–1 Nov: daily, 10am–6pm (6pm/dusk in Oct). 2 Nov–31 March: Wed–Sun, 10am–4pm (closed 24–26 Dec).*
Entry *£2.30/£1.70/£1.20.*
(01553 631330
⌂ ♦♦ ▣ ⅙ *(exterior only; toilets)* ◑ ◉
➔ *4m NE of King's Lynn off A149.*
(OS Map 132; ref TF 666246.)
▩ *Tel: 01553 772343.*
▦ *King's Lynn 4½ m.*

⊕ Church of the Holy Sepulchre

Thetford, NORFOLK
(p. 215, 8O)

The ruined nave of a priory church of the Canons of the Holy Sepulchre, the only surviving remains in England of a house of this order.

Open *Any reasonable time.*
Entry *Free.*
♜

➔ *On W side of Thetford off B1107.*
(OS Map 144; ref TL 865831.)
▩ *Tel: 0500 626116.*
▦ *Thetford ¾ m.*

◐ ⊖ Cow Tower

Norwich, NORFOLK
(p. 215, 9P)

A circular detached brick tower on the riverside which once formed part of the 14th-century city defences.

Open *Any reasonable time. (Property managed by Norwich City Council.)*
Entry *Free.*
(01603 212343
⊗
➔ *In Norwich, near cathedral.*
(OS Map 134; ref TG 240091.)
▩ *Tel: 0500 626116.*
▦ *Norwich ½ m.*

Castle Rising Castle

⊕ Creake Abbey

NORFOLK (p. 215, 10O)

The ruins of the church of an Augustinian abbey.

Open *Any reasonable time.*
Entry *Free.*
♜
➔ *1m N of North Creake off B1355.*
(OS Map 132; ref TF 856395.)
▩ *Tel: 0500 626116.*

⊕ De Grey Mausoleum

Flitton, BEDFORDSHIRE
(pp. 210/214, 7L)

A remarkable treasure-house of sculpted tombs and monuments from the 16th to 19th centuries, dedicated to the de Grey family of Wrest Park.

Open *Weekends only. Access through Flitton Church. Contact keykeeper, Mr Stimson, 3 Highfield Road, Flitton (Tel: 01525 860094).*
Entry *Free.*
⊗
➔ *Flitton, attached to church, on unclassified*

De Grey Mausoleum

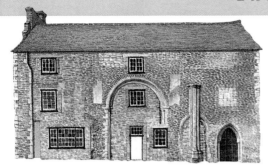

Denny
Abbey

road 1½ m W of A6 at Silsoe.
(OS Map 153; ref TL 059359.)
🚉 *Flitwick 2m.*

✠ Denny Abbey and The Farmland Museum
CAMBRIDGESHIRE
(p. 214, 10N)

What at first appears to be an attractive stone-built farmhouse is actually the remains of a 12th-century Benedictine abbey which, at different times, also housed the Knights Templar, Franciscan nuns and the Countess of Pembroke. The Farmland Museum is ideal for families, with specially designed activities for children, and contains agricultural machinery and displays on village and domestic life.

Open *1 April–1 Nov:*
daily, 12–5pm.
Entry *£3.30/£2.40/£1.20.*
Family ticket £7.80. Joint admission ticket with museum. Abbey free for E.H. members.
(*01223 860489*
🅿 ❂ ⚬ *(grounds & ground floor only)* ❒ ¶ *(weekends only)*
➲ *6m N of Cambridge on A10.*
(OS Map 154; ref TL 495684.)

🚍 *Tel: 01223 423554.*
🚉 *Waterbeach 3m.*

✠ Duxford Chapel
CAMBRIDGESHIRE
(pp. 211/214, 8N)

A medieval chapel once part of the Hospital of St John.

Open *Telephone 01223 443000 for details. (Property managed by South Cambridgeshire District Council.)*
Entry *Free.*
✖
➲ *Adjacent to Whittlesford station off A505.*
(OS Map 154; ref TL 486472.)
🚉 *Whittlesford, adjacent.*

✪ Framlingham Castle
SUFFOLK (p. 215, 8P)
See p 114 for full details.

⚠●✆⓪ Grime's Graves
NORFOLK (p. 215, 9O)

These remarkable Neolithic flint mines, unique in England, comprise over 300 pits and shafts. The visitor can descend some 10m (30ft) by ladder into one excavated shaft, and look along the radiating galleries, where the flint for making axes and knives was extracted.

Open all year round.
• ***Climb down into a prehistoric flint mine.***
• ***Come along to see the special flint-knapping demonstration days.***
• ***Free Children's Activity Sheet available.***
Open *1 April–1 Nov: daily, 10am–6pm (6pm/dusk in Oct). 2 Nov–31 March: Wed–Sun, 10am–4pm (closed 24–26 Dec). Last visit to pit 20 minutes before closing. Closed 1–2pm.*
Entry *£1.75/£1.30/90p.*
(*01842 810656*
🅿 ⚬ *(exhibition area only; access track rough)* ❂ ❒ 🗎
➲ *7m NW of Thetford off A134. (OS Map 144; ref TL 818898.)*
🚍 *Tel: 0645 583358.*
🚉 *Brandon 3½m.*

Grime's Graves (below)

FRAMLINGHAM CASTLE

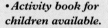 SUFFOLK (p. 215, 8P)

A superb 12th-century castle which, from the outside, looks almost the same as when it was built. From the continuous curtain wall, linking 13 towers, there are excellent views over Framlingham and the charming reed-fringed mere. At different times, the castle has been a fortress, an Elizabethan prison, a poor house and a school. The many alterations over the years have led to a pleasing mixture of historical styles. The Lanman Museum, containing a local history collection, can be seen for a small extra charge.

Open all year round.
• The Tudor Dynasty:
Meet famous Tudor
monarchs, including
Henry VIII and
Elizabeth I, 3–4 May.
• Crisis in the Army, 1648:
Drama and displays as
unrest in Parliament's
New Model Army boils
over into open mutiny,
26–27 Sept.

• Activity book for
children available.
• Walk along the full
length of the towering
castle walls.
Open 1 April–1 Nov:
daily, 10am–6pm (6pm/dusk
in Oct). 2 Nov–31 March:
daily, 10am–4pm
(closed 24–26 Dec).
Entry £2.95/£2.20/£1.50.
℘ 01728 724189
P ⊗ & *(grounds & ground*
floor only) ▢ ▢ E ⑳ ☊*
➔ *In Framlingham*
on B1116.

Framlingham Castle (below)
and a Victorian gunnery
re-enactment (left)

Framlingham Castle

(OS Map 156; ref TM 287637.)
Local Tourist Information:
Stowmarket (tel: 01449 676800).
🚌 *Tel: 0645 583358.*
🚂 *Wickham Market 6½ m;*
Saxmundham 7m.

◐ Hadleigh Castle

ESSEX (p. 211, 6N)

The curtain wall and two towers of this 13th-century castle survive almost to their full height and overlook the Essex marshes and Thames estuary.

Open Any reasonable time.
Entry *Free.*
✆ *01760 755161 for details.*
🐕 ♿ *(hilly)*
➲ *¾m S of A13 at Hadleigh. (OS Map 178; ref TQ 810860.)*
🚌 *Tel: 0345 000 333.*
🚉 *Leigh-on-Sea 1½m by footpath.*

◐◔❀ Hill Hall

ESSEX (p. 211, 6N)

This fine Elizabethan mansion has some of the earliest Renaissance decoration in the country. Rare wall paintings of mythological and biblical subjects date from the same period. The house is surrounded by parkland landscaped by Repton.

Open The Hall is undergoing major building works and is not currently open to the public. Access arrangements will be announced in the members' magazine, Heritage Today, *and the local press. For further details, contact Customer Services on 0171 973 3434.*

◐◔ Houghton House

BEDFORDSHIRE
(pp. 210/214, 7L)

Reputedly the inspiration for 'House Beautiful' in Bunyan's *Pilgrim's Progress*, the remains of this early 17th-century mansion still convey elements that justify the description, including work attributed to Inigo Jones.

Open Any reasonable time.
Entry *Free.*
🅿️ ♿ 🐕
➲ *1m NE of Ampthill off A421, 8m S of Bedford.*
(OS Map 153; ref TL 039394.)
🚌 *Tel: 01604 20077.*
🚉 *Flitwick or Stewartby, both 3m.*

⊕ Isleham Priory Church

CAMBRIDGESHIRE
(p. 215, 8N)

Rare example of an early Norman church. It has survived little altered despite being later converted to a barn.

Open Any reasonable time. Keykeeper (please follow instructions shown at property or telephone 01604 730320 for details).
Entry *Free.*
🚫
➲ *In Isleham, 16m NE of Cambridge on B1104. (OS Map 143; ref TL 642744.)*
🚌 *Tel: 01223 423554.*
🚉 *Newmarket 8½m; Ely 9m.*

Isleham Priory Church

◐ Landguard Fort

Felixstowe, SUFFOLK
(pp. 211/215, 7P)

An 18th-century fort, with later additions. There is a museum featuring displays of local history.

Come to Darells Day, 5 July.
Open *3 May–27 Sept: Sun and Bank Holidays, 10.30am–4.30pm. Small groups at other times (guided tours) by arrangement.*
Entry *Museum £2.00/£1.50/£1.00 (no unaccompanied children).*
(01394 286403 (evenings)
🅿 ⊗ ⏤ 🍴
➲ *1m S of Felixstowe near docks. (OS Map 169; ref TM 284318.)*
🚌 *Tel: 01473 253734.*
🚆 *Felixstowe 2½ m.*

⊕ Leiston Abbey

SUFFOLK (p. 215, 8P)

Remains of an abbey for Premonstratensian canons include a restored chapel.

Open *Any reasonable time.*
Entry *Free.*
🅿 ♿ 🍴
➲ *1m N of Leiston off B1069. (OS Map 156; ref TM 445642.)*
🚌 *Tel: 01645 583358.*
🚆 *Saxmundham 5m.*

⚠ Lexden Earthworks and Bluebottle Grove

Colchester, ESSEX
(pp. 211/215, 7O)

Parts of a series of earthworks, once encompassing 12 square miles, which protected Iron Age Colchester and were subsequently added to by the conquering Romans.

Open *Any reasonable time. (Property managed by Colchester Borough Council.)*
Entry *Free.*
🍴
➲ *2m W of Colchester off A604. (OS Map 168; ref TL 965246 [Lexden Earthworks] and TL 975245 [Bluebottle Grove].)*
🚌 *Tel: 01206 44449.*

🚆 *Colchester or Colchester Town, both 2½ m.*

◉ Longthorpe Tower

CAMBRIDGESHIRE
(p. 214, 9M)

The finest example of 14th-century domestic wall paintings in northern Europe. They show many secular and sacred objects, including the Wheel of Life, the Labours of the Months, the Nativity and King David. The tower, with the Great Chamber that contains the paintings, is part of a fortified manor house.

Open *1 April–1 Nov: weekends and Bank Holidays only, 12–5pm.*
Entry *£1.30/£1.00/70p.*
⊗
(01733 268482
➲ *2m W of Peterborough on A47. (OS Map 142; ref TL 163983.)*
🚌 *Tel: 01733 54571 or 0116 251 1411.*
🚆 *Peterborough 1½ m.*

⊕ Mistley Towers

ESSEX (pp. 211/215, 7O)

The remains of a church designed by Robert Adam and built in 1776. It was unusual in having towers at both the east and west ends.

Leiston Abbey

Open *Key available from Mistley Quay Workshops (Tel: 01206 393884). (Property managed by Mistley Thorn Residents Association.)*
Entry *Free.*
(exterior only)
On B1352, 1½m E of A137 at Lawford, 9m E of Colchester. (OS Map 169; ref TM 116320.)
Tel: 0345 000 333.
Mistley ¼m.

Moulton Packhorse Bridge

SUFFOLK (p. 215, 8N)

Medieval four-arched bridge spanning the River Kennett.

Open *Any reasonable time.*
Entry *Free.*

In Moulton off B1085, 4m E of Newmarket. (OS Map 154; ref TL 698645.)
Kennett 2m.

North Elmham Chapel

NORFOLK (p. 215, 10O)

Remains of a Norman chapel built on the site of the cathedral for the Anglo-Saxon bishops of East Anglia. The chapel was converted into a fortified manor house and enclosed by earthworks in the late 14th century by the notorious Bishop of Norwich, Hugh le Despencer.

Open *Any reasonable time. (Property managed by North Elmham Parish Council.)*
Entry *Free.*

6m N of East Dereham on B1110. (OS Map 132; ref TF 988217.)

Old Gorhambury House

HERTFORDSHIRE (p. 210, 6M)

The remains of this Elizabethan mansion illustrate the impact of the Renaissance on English architecture.

Open *May–Sept: Thurs only, 2–5pm, or at other times by appointment. Call 01604 730320 for more information.*
Entry *Free.*

¼m W of Gorhambury House & accessible only through private drive from A4147 at St Albans (2m). (OS Map 166; ref TL 110077.)
Tel: 0345 244 344.
St Albans Abbey 3m, St Albans 3½m.

Longthorpe Tower (left) and one of the wall paintings (above)

Orford Castle

◗ Orford Castle

SUFFOLK (p. 215, 8P)

A royal castle built for coastal defence in the 12th century. A magnificent keep survives almost intact with three immense towers reaching to 30 metres (90 feet). Inside a spiral stair leads to a maze of rooms and passageways.

Open all year round.
• Free Children's Activity Sheet available.
• CD-Rom unit with information on English castles.
Open 1 April–1 Nov: daily, 10am–6pm (6pm/dusk in Oct). 2 Nov–31 March: Wed–Sun, 10am–4pm (closed 24–26 Dec). Closed 1–2pm in winter.
Entry £2.30/£1.70/£1.20.
℡ 01394 450472

🅿 ⊗ ⬧

➲ *In Orford on B1084 20m NE of Ipswich. (OS Map 169; ref TM 419499.)*

🚌 *Tel: 0645 583358.*
🚆 *Wickham Market 8m.*

◗ Prior's Hall Barn

Widdington, ESSEX
(pp. 211/214, 7N)

One of the finest surviving medieval barns in south-east England and representative of the aisled barns of north-west Essex.

Open 1 April–30 Sept: Sat & Sun, 10am–6pm. Telephone 01799 522842 (Audley End House) for further details.
Entry Free.
⊗ &

➲ *In Widdington, on unclassified road 2m SE of Newport, off B1383. (OS Map 167; ref TL 538319.)*
🚌 *Tel: 0345 000 333.*
🚆 *Newport 2m.*

◗ Roman Wall

St Albans, HERTFORDSHIRE
(p. 210, 6M)

Several hundred yards of the wall, built c. AD200, which enclosed the Roman city of Verulamium. The remains of towers and foundations of a gateway can still be seen.

Open Any reasonable time.
Entry Free.
✈

➲ *On S side of St Albans, ½m from centre off A4147. (OS Map 166; ref TL 135067.)*
🚌 *Tel: 0345 244 344.*
🚆 *St Albans Abbey ½m, St Albans 1¼m.*

⊕ Row 111 House, Old Merchant's House and Greyfriars' Cloisters

Great Yarmouth, NORFOLK
(p. 215, 9P)

Two 17th-century Row Houses, a type of building unique to Great Yarmouth, containing original fixtures and displays of local architectural fittings salvaged from bombing in 1942–43. Nearby are the remains of a Franciscan friary, with rare early wall

Prior's Hall Barn, Widdington

paintings, accidentally discovered during bomb damage repairs.

Open 1 April–1 Nov: daily, 10am–5pm. Guided tours hourly: depart Row 111 House at 10am, 11am, 12pm, 2pm, 3pm & 4pm.
Entry £1.75/£1.30/90p.
(01493 857900
⊗
➡ Great Yarmouth, make for South Quay along riverside and dock, ½m inland from beach. Follow signs to dock and south quay.
(OS Map 134; ref TG 525072 [Houses] and TG 525073 [Cloisters].)
▭ Tel: 0500 626116.
🚌 Great Yarmouth ½m.

◉ St Albans Roman Wall
See Roman Wall, p. 118.

✚ St Botolph's Priory
Colchester, ESSEX
(pp. 211/215, 7O)

The nave, with an impressive arcaded west

end, of the first Augustinian priory in England.

Open Any reasonable time. (Property managed by Colchester Borough Council.)
Entry Free.
🐕
➡ Colchester, near Colchester Town station.
(OS Map 168; ref TL 999249.)
▭ Tel: 0345 000 333.
🚌 Colchester Town, adjacent.

✚ St James's Chapel
Lindsey, SUFFOLK
(pp. 211/215, 7O)

A little 13th-century chapel with thatched roof and lancet windows.

Open All year: daily, 10am–4pm.
Entry Free.
⊗ ♿ (single step)
➡ On unclassified road ½m E of Rose Green, 8m E of Sudbury.
(OS Map 155; ref TL 978443.)
▭ Tel: 0645 583358.
🚌 Sudbury 8m.

Old Merchant's House: glass door panel (left) and interior (below)

St John's Abbey Gate

✚ St John's Abbey Gate
Colchester, ESSEX
(pp. 211/215, 7O)

This fine abbey gatehouse, in East Anglian flintwork, survives from the Benedictine abbey of St John.

Open Any reasonable time. (Property managed by Colchester Borough Council.)
Entry Free.
⊗ ♿
➡ On S side of central Colchester.
(OS Map 168; ref TL 998248.)
▭ Tel: 0345 000 333.
🚌 Colchester Town ¼m.

✠ St Olave's Priory
NORFOLK (p. 215, 9P)

Remains of an Augustinian priory founded nearly 200 years after the death in 1030 of the patron saint of Norway, after whom it is named.

Open Any reasonable time.
Entry Free.
⊛
➲ *5½m SW of Great Yarmouth on A143.*
(OS Map 134; ref TM 459996.)
🚌 *Haddiscoe 1¼m.*

◉ Saxtead Green Post Mill
SUFFOLK (p. 215, 8P)

A fine example of a post mill, where the super-structure turns on a great post to face the wind. The mill, which ceased production in 1947, is still in working order and you can climb the wooden stairs to

Saxtead Green Post Mill

the various floors, which are full of fascinating mill machinery.

Open 1 April–1 Nov: Mon–Sat, 10am–6pm (6pm/dusk in Oct). Closed 1–2pm.
Entry £1.75/£1.30/90p.
✆ *01728 685789*
🍴 🎧
➲ *2½m NW of Framlingham on A1120.*
(OS Map 156; ref TM 253645.)
🚌 *Wickham Market 9m.*

✠ Thetford Priory
NORFOLK (p. 215, 8N)

The 14th-century gatehouse is the best-preserved part of this Cluniac priory built in 1103. The extensive remains include the plan of the cloisters.

Open Any reasonable time.
Entry Free.
🍴
➲ *On W side of Thetford near station.*
(OS Map 144; ref TL 865836.)
🚌 *Tel: 0500 626116.*
🚌 *Thetford ¼m.*

◉ Thetford Warren Lodge
NORFOLK (p. 215, 9O)

The ruins of a small, two-storeyed medieval house, set in pleasant woods, which was probably the home of the priory's gamekeeper.

Open Any reasonable time.
Entry Free.
🍴

➲ *2m W of Thetford off B1107.*
(OS Map 144; ref TL 839841.)
🚌 *Tel: 0500 626116.*
🚌 *Thetford 2½m.*

◐◉ Tilbury Fort
ESSEX (p. 211, 5N)

The largest and best-preserved example of 17th-century military engineering in England, commanding the Thames and showing the development of fortifications over the following 200 years. Exhibitions, the powder magazine and the bunker-like 'casemates' demonstrate how the fort protected London from seaborne attack – there's even a chance to fire an anti-aircraft gun!

Open all year round.
🎬 *Sharpe, the TV drama, was filmed here.*
• *Visit the huge Essex Classic Military Vehicle Rally, 29–31 August.*
• *Free Children's Activity Sheet available.*
Open 1 April–1 Nov: daily, 10am–6pm (6pm/dusk in Oct). 2 Nov–31 March: Wed–Sun, 10am–4pm (closed 24–26 Dec).
Entry £2.30/£1.70/£1.20. £1 to fire anti-aircraft gun.
✆ *01375 858489*
♿ 🅴 ⚧ 🎧 ♿ *(exterior, fort square & magazines)* ⛳
➲ *½m E of Tilbury off A126.*
(OS Map 177; ref TQ 651754.)
🚌 *Tel: 0345 000 333.*
🚌 *Tilbury Town 1½m.*

✛ Waltham Abbey Gatehouse and Bridge

ESSEX (p. 211, 6M)

A late 14th-century abbey gatehouse, part of the cloister and 'Harold's Bridge'.

Open *Any reasonable time. (Properties managed by Lee Valley Park.)*
Entry *Free.*
☎ *01992 702200*
🚩 ♿ *(sensory trail guide)*
➲ *In Waltham Abbey off A112. (OS Map 166; ref TL 381008.)*
🚌 *Tel: 0345 000 333.*
🚉 *Waltham Cross 1¼m.*

➲☉ Weeting Castle

NORFOLK (p. 215, 9N)

The ruins of an early medieval manor house within a shallow rectangular moat.

Open *Any reasonable time.*
Entry *Free.*
🚩
➲ *2m N of Brandon off B1106. (OS Map 144; ref TL 778891.)*
🚉 *Brandon 1½m.*

Wrest Park Gardens

✿☉ Wrest Park Gardens

BEDFORDSHIRE (pp. 210/214, 7M)

Over 90 acres of wonderful gardens originally laid out in the early 18th century, including the Great Garden, with charming buildings and ornaments, and the delightfully intricate French Garden, with statues and fountain. The house, once the home of the de Grey family whose Mausoleum at Flitton is nearby, was inspired by 18th-century French châteaux. It now forms a delightful backdrop to the gardens.

Open *1 April–1 Nov: Sat–Sun & Bank Holidays, 10am–6pm (6pm/dusk in Oct). Last admission 5pm.*
Entry *£2.95/£2.20/£1.50.*
☎ *01525 860152*
🚻 🅿 ☉ 🛍 🎧
➲ *¾m E of Silsoe off A6, 10m S of Bedford. (OS Map 153; ref TL 093356.)*
🚌 *Tel: 01604 20077.*
🚉 *Flitwick 4m.*

Tilbury Fort (left) and the gun emplacement (above)

EAST MIDLANDS

Nottinghamshire

Derbyshire

Lincolnshire

Leicestershire

Northamptonshire

THE CHANGING landscape of the East Midlands contains both Peveril Castle, high on a Peak District crag, and Sibsey Trader Windmill, standing starkly alone among the Lincolnshire fens. The huge shell of Kirby Hall, a grand Elizabethan mansion, now hosts the annual 'History in Action' spectacular, while Bolsover Castle has been voted one of the public's favourite attractions. On a much smaller scale is the delightfully idiosyncratic structure, Rushton Triangular Lodge.

Old traditions never die, morris dancers at Kirby Hall

⬢ Arbor Low Stone Circle and Gib Hill Barrow

DERBYSHIRE (p. 214, 11J)

A fine Neolithic monument, this 'Stonehenge of Derbyshire' comprises many slabs of limestone, surrounded by an unusually large ditch.

Open Daily, 10am–6pm/dusk, whichever is earlier. (Site managed by the Peak Park Joint Planning Board.)
Entry Farmer who owns right of way to property may levy a charge.

🐎
➲ *½m W of A515 2m S of Monyash. (OS Map 119; ref SK 161636.)*
🚌 *Tel: 01332 292200.*
🚌 *Buxton 10m.*

○ Ashby de la Zouch Castle

LEICESTERSHIRE (pp. 214/217, 10J)

The impressive ruins of this late-medieval castle are dominated by a magnificent 24-metre (80-foot) high tower, split in two during the Civil War, from which there are

Arbor Low Stone Circle

panoramic views of the surrounding countryside.

Open all year round.
♿ New for 1998: Inclusive audio tour and shop.
♿ Free Children's Activity Sheet available.
• Attractive picnic spot.
• Bring a torch to explore the tunnels!
Open 1 April–1 Nov: daily, 10am–6pm (6pm/dusk in Oct). 2 Nov–31 March: Wed–Sun, 10am–4pm (closed 24–26 Dec).
Entry £2.30/£1.70/£1.20.
✆ *01530 413343*
🅿 ♿ *(grounds only)* 🐎 🚻 🛍 ☕ 🎧

➲ *In Ashby de la Zouch, 12m S of Derby on A50. (OS Map 128; ref SK 363167.)*
🚌 *Tel: 01332 292200.*
🚌 *Burton-on-Trent 9m.*

⊕ Bishop's Old Palace

Lincoln, LINCOLNSHIRE
See Lincoln Medieval Bishop's Palace, p. 128.

🅑🅐🅜 Bolingbroke Castle

LINCOLNSHIRE (p. 214, 11M)

Remains of a 13th-century hexagonal castle, birthplace of Henry IV in 1367 and besieged by Parliamentary forces in 1643.

Open 1 April–30 Sept: daily, 9am–9pm. 1 Oct–31 March: daily, 9am–7pm. (Site managed by Heritage Lincolnshire.)
Entry Free.
🐎
➲ *In Old Bolingbroke, 16m N of Boston off A16. (OS Map 122; ref TF 349649.)*
🚌 *Thorpe Culvert 10m.*

Ashby de la Zouch Castle with the 80-foot Hasting's Tower

BOLSOVER CASTLE

♡ ⊞ ✾ DERBYSHIRE (pp. 214/217, 11K)

An enchanting and romantic spectacle, Bolsover sits high on a wooded hilltop, dominating the surrounding landscape. The Castle consists of a complex of buildings constructed on the site of a Norman keep. One of the highlights is the Little Castle, a unique celebration of Jacobean romanticism with battlemented walls, elaborate fireplaces, panelling and wall paintings. There is also the Indoor Riding School, one of the oldest in Europe, and the ruins of the great State apartments.

Bolsover Castle

The Little Castle's Pillar Chamber

Bolsover was built in the early 17th century by Charles Cavendish and his heir William, later the first Duke of Newcastle. The Little Castle, which played host to Charles I, contains exceptional examples of high-quality Jacobean decoration. It is currently being restored, as is the Fountain Garden outside it.

Open all year round.
• Winner of a 1996/7 NPI National Heritage Award, voted by the general public as one of Britain's favourite national treasures.
• See the fury of the Norsemen, ferocious Viking military action, 30–31 August.

The Little Castle

• Free Children's Activity Sheet available.
Open 1 April–1 Nov: daily, 10am–6pm (6pm/dusk in Oct). 2 Nov–31 March: Wed–Sun, 10am–4pm (closed 24–26 Dec). Entry £2.95/£2.20/£1.50.
☎ 01246 822844 or 823349
⭍▯ (opposite main gate) ♿ (grounds only) ✗ 🍴 📷 🎧 🐕‍🦺
➔ Off M1 at junction 29, 6m from Mansfield. In Bolsover, 6m E of Chesterfield on A632. (OS Map 120; ref SK 471707.)
Local Tourist Information: Chesterfield (tel: 01246 207777).
🚌 *Tel: 01332 292200.*
🚆 *Chesterfield 6m.*

♡⚫✳ Bolsover Castle
DERBYSHIRE
(pp. 214/217, 11K)
See opposite for full details.

✚ Chichele College
NORTHAMPTONSHIRE
(p. 214, 8L)

Parts of a quadrangle remain of this college for secular canons, founded in 1422.

Open Quadrangle any reasonable time. For chapel please contact keykeeper, Mrs D. Holyoak, 12 Lancaster St, Higham Ferrers; tel. 01933 314157. (Site managed by East Northamptonshire Council.)
Entry *Free.*
⚫
➔ *In Higham Ferrers, on A6. (OS Map 153; ref SP 960687.)*
🚌 *Tel: 01604 20077.*
🚉 *Wellingborough 5m.*

✚ Eleanor Cross
Geddington, NORTHAMP-
TONSHIRE (p. 214, 9L)

One of a series of famous crosses erected by Edward I to mark the resting places of the body of his wife, Eleanor, when brought for burial from Harby in Nottinghamshire to Westminster Abbey.

Open Any reasonable time.
Entry *Free.*
🏹
➔ *In Geddington, off A43 between Kettering and Corby.*

(OS Map 141; ref SP 896830.)
🚌 *Tel: 01604 20077.*
🚉 *Kettering 4m.*

⚫ Gainsborough Old Hall
LINCOLNSHIRE (p. 214, 12L)

A large medieval house with a magnificent Great Hall and suites of rooms. A collection of historic furniture and a re-created medieval kitchen are on display.

Open Easter Sunday–31 Oct: Mon–Sat, 10am–5pm; Sun, 2pm–5.30pm.

Gainsborough Old Hall

1 Nov–Easter Saturday, Mon–Sat, 10am–5pm (closed Good Friday, 24–26 Dec, 1 Jan). (Site managed by Lincolnshire County Council.)
Entry *£2.50/£1.50/£1.00 (no reduction for students/ unemployed). Small charge on Special Event Days for E.H. members.*
☎ **01427 612669**
🚻 🎧 ♿ *(most of ground floor)*
✗ 🛍
➔ *In Gainsborough, opposite the Library. (OS Map 121; ref SK 815895.)*
🚌 *Tel: 01522 553135.*
🚉 *Gainsborough Central ½m, Gainsborough Lea Road 1m.*

Eleanor Cross

✚ Geddington, Eleanor Cross
See Eleanor Cross.

125

♡⊕ Hardwick Old Hall

DERBYSHIRE
(pp. 214/217, 11K)

This large ruined house, finished in 1591, still displays Bess of Hardwick's innovative planning and interesting decorative plasterwork. The views from the top floor over the country park and 'New' Hall are spectacular.

👂 *New for 1998 – audio tour telling the 'Bess of Hardwick' story.*
Open *1 April–1 Nov: Wed–Sun, 10am–6pm (6pm/dusk in Oct).*
Entry *£2.30/£1.70/£1.20. National Trust members admitted free, but small charge at English Heritage events. (Site maintained and managed by English Heritage, and owned by the National Trust. Joint ticket available for the New Hall and Gardens and the Old Hall.)*
☎ *01246 850431*

Hardwick Old Hall

🏹 ❑ ❐ 🎧 *(£1.00 for National Trust members)* 🅿 *(£2.00 vehicle entry charge for access to National Trust Estate, refundable on a visit to Hardwick New Hall)* 🚻 *(in National Trust car park)*
➡ *9½m SE of Chesterfield, off A6175, from J29 of M1. (OS Map 120; ref SK 463638.)*
🚌 *Tel: 01332 292200.*
🚉 *Chesterfield 8m.*

▲➡ Hob Hurst's House

DERBYSHIRE
(pp. 214/217, 11J)

A square prehistoric burial mound with an earthwork ditch and outer bank.

Open *Any reasonable time. (Site managed by the Peak Park Joint Planning Board.)*
Entry *Free.*
🏹
➡ *From unclassified road off B5057, 9m W of Chesterfield. (OS Map 119; ref SK 287692.)*
🚌 *Tel: 01332 292200.*
🚉 *Chesterfield 9m.*

Kirby Muxloe Castle

➡ Jewry Wall

Leicester, LEICESTERSHIRE
(p. 214, 9K)

A length of Roman wall over 9 metres (30 feet) high.

Open *Mon–Sat, 10am–5.30pm; Sun, 2–5.30pm.*
Entry *Free.*
☎ *0116 247 3021 (Jewry Wall Museum)*
🏹
➡ *In St Nicholas St, W of Church of St Nicholas. (OS Map 140; ref SK 583044.)*
🚌 *Tel: 0116 251 1411.*
🚉 *Leicester ¼ m.*

♡✳➡⊕ Kirby Hall

NORTHAMPTONSHIRE
(p. 214, 9L)
See p. 127 for full details.

➡ Kirby Muxloe Castle

LEICESTERSHIRE (p. 214, 9K)

Picturesque, moated, brick-built castle begun in 1480 by William, Lord Hastings.

Open *1 April–1 Nov: Sat–Sun and Bank Holidays only, 12pm–5pm. Closed 1–2pm.*
Entry *£1.75/£1.30/90p.*
☎ *01162 386886*
🅿 ♿ ⊗
➡ *4m W of Leicester off B5380. (OS Map 140; ref SK 524046.)*
🚌 *Tel: 0116 251 1411.*
🚉 *Leicester 5m.*

KIRBY HALL

♡ ❀ ➷ ⓜ NORTHAMPTONSHIRE (p. 214, 9L)

Built of the local Weldon stone, Kirby Hall is an outstanding example of an Elizabethan mansion, including two courtyards, long galleries and a Great Hall. Justly acclaimed for the richness and variety of its architectural detail, by the end of the 17th century the Hall's wonderful gardens had also become renowned as amongst the finest in England. Now home to peacocks, the gardens are being restored, with the introduction of topiary in 1998.

Kirby Hall has a delightful mixture of architectural styles. Begun in 1570 by Sir Humphrey Stafford, it was completed by Sir Christopher Hatton, one of Elizabeth I's most talented courtiers.

Open all year round.
♧ New shop opening in 1998.
• Come to 'History in Action III' – the most spectacular historical event of its kind in Europe. Over 1,500 performers, from the Romans to WWII, bring history to life with displays and living history, 1–2 Aug.

The inner courtyard

Open 1 April–1 Nov: daily, 10am–6pm (6pm/dusk in Oct). 2 Nov–31 March: Sat–Sun, 10am–4pm (closed 24–26 Dec). Closed 1–2pm in winter. Entry £2.30/£1.70/£1.20.

℘ 01536 203230
🅿 ⚥ ♿ *(grounds, gardens & ground floor only)* ⊗ 🗋 🗍 🎧
➷ *On unclassified road off A43, 4m NE of Corby. (OS Map 141; ref SP 926927.)*
Local Tourist Information: *Corby (tel: 01536 407507).*

Kirby Hall: the 'History in Action' spectacular (above) and the Great Garden (below)

⊘ Leicester Jewry Wall

See *Jewry Wall, p.126.*

⊕ Lincoln Medieval Bishop's Palace

Lincoln, LINCOLNSHIRE
(pp. 214/219, 11L)

The remains of this medieval palace of the Bishops of Lincoln are in the shadow of Lincoln Cathedral. You can climb the stairs to the Alnwick Tower, explore the undercroft and see the recently established vineyard, which is one of the most northerly in Europe.

Open all year round.
• Exhibition on the history of the Bishops of Lincoln.
Open *1 April–1 Nov: daily, 10am–6pm (6pm/dusk in Oct). 2 Nov–31 March: weekends only, 10am–4pm. Closed 1–2pm in winter. Special opening for Christmas Market.*
Entry *£1.30/£1.00/70p.*

Lincoln Medieval Bishop's Palace

☎ *01522 527468*
✗ ◻ ◻ ◻
➜ *S side of Lincoln Cathedral. (OS Map 121; ref SK 981717.)*
🚌 *Tel: 01522 553135.*
🚌 *Lincoln 1m.*

⊕ Lyddington Bede House

LEICESTERSHIRE (p. 214, 9L)

Set among picturesque golden stone cottages, the Bede House (house of prayer) was originally a medieval palace of the Bishops of Lincoln. It

was later converted into an almshouse. There are three floors and a number of rooms to explore.

♨ *New audio tour.*
Open *1 April–1 Nov: daily, 10am–6pm (6pm/dusk in Oct). Closed 1–2pm.*
Entry *£2.30/£1.70/£1.20.*
☎ *01572 822438*
✗ ♿ *(ground-floor rooms only)*
🎧 ◻
➜ *In Lyddington, 6m N of Corby, 1m E of A6003. (OS Map 141; ref SP 875970.)*
🚌 *Tel: 0116 251 1411.*

Lyddington Bede House

✪ Mattersey Priory

NOTTINGHAMSHIRE
(pp. 214/217/219, 11K)

Remains of a small Gilbertine monastery founded in 1185.

Open *Any reasonable time.*
Entry *Free.*

🏹

➲ *Rough access down drive ¾m long, 1m E of Mattersey off B6045, 7m N of East Retford. (OS Map 112; ref SK 704896.)*
🚌 *Retford 7m.*

⬟ Nine Ladies Stone Circle

Stanton Moor, DERBYSHIRE
(pp. 214/217, 11J)

Once part of the burial site for 300–400 people, this Early Bronze Age circle is 15 metres (50 feet) across.

Open *Any reasonable time. (Site managed by the Peak Park Joint Planning Board.)*
Entry *Free.*

🏹

➲ *From unclassified road off A6, 5m SE of Bakewell. (OS Map 119; ref SK 249635.)*
🚌 *Tel: 01332 292200.*
🚂 *Matlock 4½m.*

♡ ✪ Peveril Castle

DERBYSHIRE
(pp. 214/217, 11J)

There are breathtaking views of the Peak District from this castle, perched high above the pretty village of Castleton. The great square tower stands almost to its original height.

Picnic spot of exceptional beauty.

Nine Ladies Stone Circle

• *Free Children's Activity Sheet available.*
Open *1 April–1 Nov: daily, 10am–6pm (6pm/dusk in Oct). 2 Nov–31 March: Wed–Sun, 10am–4pm (closed 24–26 Dec).*
Entry *£1.75/£1.30/90p.*
☎ *01433 620613*
🏹 ⬚ ⬚ 🚻 *(in town)*
🅿 *(in town)*
➲ *On S side of Castleton, 15m W of Sheffield on A625. (OS Map 110; ref SK 150827.)*
🚌 *Tel: 01332 292200.*
🚂 *Hope 2½m.*

Peveril Castle (above and left)

✠ Rufford Abbey

NOTTINGHAMSHIRE
(pp. 214/217, 11K)

The remains of a 17th-century country house, built on the foundations of a 12th-century Cistercian abbey, set in the Rufford Country Park.

Open *1 April–31 Oct: daily, 10am–5pm. 1 Nov– 31 March: daily, 10am–4pm (closed 24–26 Dec). (Site managed by Nottinghamshire County Council.)*
Entry *Free.*
☎ *01623 823148*
♀♂ 🅿 🍴 📷 *(craft centre)* ♿ ⊗
➲ *2m S of Ollerton off A614. (OS Map 120; ref SK 645646.)*
🚌 *Tel: 0115 924 0000.*

Rushton Triangular Lodge

✠ Rushton Triangular Lodge

NORTHAMPTONSHIRE
(p. 214, 9L)

Extraordinary building built by the Roman Catholic Sir Thomas Tresham on his return from imprisonment for his religious beliefs. Completed in 1597, it symbolizes the Holy Trinity – it has three sides, three floors, trefoil windows and three triangular gables on each side. Other buildings with Tresham connections can be explored on the 'Tresham Trail'.

Open *1 April–1 Nov: daily, 10am–6pm (6pm/dusk in Oct).*
Entry *£1.30/£1.00/70p.*
☎ *01536 710761*
🌐 📷
➲ *1m W of Rushton, on unclassified road 3m from Desborough on A6. (OS Map 141; ref SP 830831.)*
🚌 *Tel: 01604 20077.*
🚉 *Kettering 5m.*

☺ ➲ Sibsey Trader Windmill

LINCOLNSHIRE
(pp. 214/219, 11M)

An impressive tower mill built in 1877, with its machinery and six sails intact. Flour milled on the spot can be bought there.

Sibsey Trader Windmill

Open *Open for Milling Sundays on 29 March; 19 April; 10, 31 May; 14, 28 June; 12, 26 July; 9, 23 Aug; 13 Sept: 11am–5pm. (Site managed by Mr & Mrs Bent.)*
Entry *£1.70/£1.20/90p.*
☎ *01205 820065*
♀♂ 🅿 ♿ *(exterior only)* ⊗ 🍴
➲ *½m W of village of Sibsey, off A16 5m N of Boston. (OS Map 122; ref TF 345511.)*
🚌 *Tel: 01522 553135.*
🚉 *Boston 5m.*

♡ ⊕ Sutton Scarsdale Hall

DERBYSHIRE
(pp. 214/217, 11K)

The dramatic hilltop shell of a great early 18th-century baroque mansion.

Open *10am–6pm/dusk, whichever is earlier.*

Entry *Free.*

🅿 ♿ 🐾

➲ *Between Chesterfield and Bolsover, 1½m S of Arkwright Town.*
(OS Map 120; ref SK 441690.)
🚌 *Tel: 01332 292200.*
🚉 *Chesterfield 5m.*

✚ Tattershall College
LINCOLNSHIRE
(p. 214, 11M)

Remains of a grammar school for church choristers, built in the mid-15th century by Ralph, Lord Cromwell, the builder of nearby Tattershall Castle.

Open *Any reasonable time. (Site managed by Heritage Lincolnshire.)*
Entry *Free.*
✖

➲ *In Tattershall (off Market Place) 14m NE of Sleaford on A153.*

Sutton Scarsdale Hall

Wingfield Manor

(OS Map 122; ref TF 213577.)
🚌 *Tel: 01522 553135.*
🚉 *Ruskington 10m.*

♡❷✚ Wingfield Manor
DERBYSHIRE
(pp. 214/217, 11J)

Huge, ruined country mansion built in the mid-15th century. Mary Queen of Scots was imprisoned here in 1569. Although unoccupied since the 1770s, the manor's late-Gothic Great Hall and the 'High Tower' are fine testaments to Wingfield Manor in its heyday.

Open all year round.
📹 **The manor has been used as a film location for** Peak Practice **and** Zeffirelli's Jane Eyre.

Open *1 April–1 Nov: Wed–Sun, 12–5pm (5pm/dusk in Oct). 2 Nov–31 March: Sat–Sun, 10am–4pm (closed 24–26 Dec). Closed 1–2pm in winter. The manor incorporates a private working farm. Visitors are requested to respect the privacy of the owners and refrain from visiting outside official opening hours.*
Entry *£2.95/£2.20/£1.50.*
🎧 🗎 🗎 ✖ ♿ *(Great Hall and grounds, steep approach 600 metres.* 🅿 *available by prior arrangement only.)*
Orientation leaflet available.
☎ *01773 832060*
➲ *17m N of Derby, 11m S of Chesterfield on B5035 ½m S of South Wingfield. From M1 – J28, W on A38, A615 (Matlock Road) at Alfreton and turn onto B5035 after 1½m.*
(OS Map 119; ref SK 374548.)
🚌 *Tel: 01332 292200.*
🚉 *Alfreton 4m.*

WEST MIDLANDS

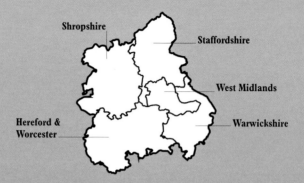

Shropshire

Staffordshire

West Midlands

Warwickshire

Hereford & Worcester

THE WEST MIDLANDS are home to Kenilworth, the largest castle ruin in England, and Witley Court, one of the most spectacular country-house ruins in England. At Boscobel House, discover the secret rooms and the Royal Oak in which King Charles II hid from Cromwell's troops. Stokesay Castle in the beautiful Welsh Marches is one of this country's finest fortified manor houses. And heritage from a more recent age can be seen at Iron Bridge in Shropshire – the birthplace of the Industrial Revolution, and the centrepiece of a World Heritage Site.

Discover your heritage at Wenlock Priory

132

⬤○ Acton Burnell Castle

SHROPSHIRE (p. 217, 9G)

The warm red sandstone shell of a fortified 13th-century manor house.

Open *Any reasonable time.*
Entry *Free.*
  ♿ 🐕
➲ *In Acton Burnell, on unclassified road 8m S of Shrewsbury. (OS Map 126; ref SJ 534019.)* 🚌 *Tel: 0345 056 785.* 🚉 *Shrewsbury or Church Stretton, both 8m.*

⬤ Arthur's Stone

Dorstone, HEREFORD & WORCESTER (p. 217, 7F)

Impressive prehistoric burial chamber formed of large blocks of stone.

Open *Any reasonable time.*
Entry *Free.*
🐕
➲ *7m E of Hay-on-Wye off B4348 near Dorstone. (OS Map 148; ref SO 319431.)* 🚌 *Tel: 01633 266336.*

⬤❀ Boscobel House and the Royal Oak

SHROPSHIRE (p. 217, 9H)

Fully refurnished and restored, the panelled rooms, secret hiding places and pretty gardens lend this 17th-century timber-framed hunting lodge a truly romantic character. King Charles II hid in the house and the nearby Royal Oak after the Battle of Worcester in 1651 to avoid detection by Cromwell's troops. Today there is a farmhouse with dairy, farmyard and smithy, and an exhibition in the house.

Open all year round.
• **See the Royal Oak and the secret places inside the house where Charles II hid.**
• **Free Children's Activity Sheet available.**
Open *1 April–1 Nov: daily, 10am–6pm (6pm/dusk in Oct). Last admission 5.30pm.*

Boscobel House: portrait of Charles II

2 Nov–31 Dec, 1 Feb–31 March: Wed–Sun, 10am–4pm (closed 24–26 Dec, 1–31 Jan). Last admission 3.30pm. Entry to house by guided tour only.
Entry *£3.95/£3.00/£2.00.*
📞 *01902 850244*
🅴 🏠 👫 🅿 ♿ *(gardens only)*
🍴 *('Boscobel House Tearoom'; April–Sept, Tues–Sun; Oct, Sundays only.)* ☕ ⊗
➲ *On minor road from A41 to A5, 8m NW of Wolverhampton. (OS Map 127; ref SJ 837083.)* 🚉 *Cosford 3m.*

Royal Oak with Boscobel House in the background

Boscobel House (left) and the White Room (above)

Buildwas Abbey from the west

✚ Buildwas Abbey

SHROPSHIRE (p. 217, 9G)

Set beside the River Severn, against a backdrop of wooded grounds, are extensive remains of this Cistercian abbey begun in 1135.

Open *1 April–1 Nov: daily, 10am–6pm (6pm/dusk in Oct).*
Entry £1.75/£1.30/90p.
✆ *01952 433274*
♿ 🐕 ⌂ Ⓟ
➲ *On S bank of River Severn on A4169, 2m W of Ironbridge.*

Clun Castle

(OS Map 127; ref SJ 642044.)
🚌 *Tel: 0345 056 785.*
🚉 *Telford Central 6m.*

◓ Cantlop Bridge

SHROPSHIRE (p. 217, 9G)

Single-span cast-iron road bridge over the Cound Brook, designed by the great engineer Thomas Telford.

Open *Any reasonable time.*
Entry *Free.*
🐕

➲ *¾m SW of Berrington on unclassified road off A458. (OS Map 126; ref SJ 517062.)*
🚉 *Shrewsbury 5m.*

◐◑◒ Clun Castle

SHROPSHIRE (p. 217, 8F)

The remains of a four-storey keep and other buildings of this border castle.

Open *Any reasonable time.*
Entry *Free.*
🐕 🦽
➲ *In Clun, off A488, 18m W of Ludlow. (OS Map 137; ref SO 299809.)*
🚌 *Tel: 0345 056 785.*
🚉 *Hopton Heath 6½m; Knighton 6½m.*

✚ Croxden Abbey

STAFFORDSHIRE
(pp. 214/217, 10J)

Remains of a Cistercian abbey founded in 1176.

Open *10am–6pm/dusk, whichever is earlier.*
Entry *Free.*
🐕
➲ *5m NW of Uttoxeter off A522. (OS Map 128; ref SK 065397.)*
🚉 *Uttoxeter 6m.*

✚ Edvin Loach Old Church

HEREFORD & WORCESTER
(p. 217, 8G)

Peaceful and isolated 11th-century church remains.

Open *Any reasonable time.*
Entry *Free.*

🅿 🚶

➲ *4m N of Bromyard on unclassified road off B4203. (OS Map 149; ref SO 663585.)*

✪ ○ Goodrich Castle
HEREFORD & WORCESTER (p. 217, 7G)

Remarkably complete, magnificent red sandstone castle with 12th-century keep and extensive remains from the 13th and 14th centuries.

Open all year round.
• Free Children's Activity Sheet available.
Open *1 April–1 Nov: daily, 10am–6pm (6pm/dusk in Oct). 2 Nov–31 March:*

Halesowen Abbey

daily, 10am–4pm (closed 24–26 Dec).
Entry *£2.95/£2.20/£1.50.*
✆ **01600 890538**

🚻 🅿 ⊗ 🎧 *(also available for the visually impaired and those with learning difficulties)* ▯ ▯

➲ *5m S of Ross-on-Wye off A40.*
(OS Map 162; ref SO 579199.)
🚌 *Tel: 0345 125 436.*

✛ Halesowen Abbey
WEST MIDLANDS (p. 217, 8H)

Remains of an abbey founded by King John in the 13th century, now incorporated into a 19th-century farm.

Open *July–August: weekends only, 10am–6pm.*
Entry *£1.30/£1.00/70p.*
🅿 ⊗ ♿ *(rough grass between church and infirmary)*
➲ *Off A456 Kidderminster road, 6m W of Birmingham city centre.*
(OS Map 139; ref SO 975828.)
🚌 *Tel: 0121 200 2700.*
🚂 *Old Hill 2½m.*

Goodrich Castle

Iron Bridge

✠ Haughmond Abbey
SHROPSHIRE (p. 217, 9G)

The extensive remains of this 12th-century Augustinian abbey include the Chapter House, which retains its late-medieval timber ceiling, and some fine medieval sculpture.

Open *1 April–1 Nov: daily, 10am–6pm (6pm/dusk in Oct).*
Entry *£1.75/£1.30/90p.*
℮ 01743 709661
🅿 ♿ 🐕 🏬 🎧

Haughmond Abbey: the Abbot's Chamber

➲ *3m NE of Shrewsbury off B5062.*
(OS Map 126; ref SJ 542152.)
🚌 *Tel: 0345 056 785.*
🚋 *Shrewsbury 3½m.*

◉ Iron Bridge
SHROPSHIRE (p. 217, 9G)

The world's first iron bridge and Britain's best-known industrial monument is now a World Heritage Site. Cast by local ironmaster Abraham Darby, it was erected across the River Severn in 1779.

Open *Any reasonable time.*
Entry *Free.*
⊗
➲ *In Ironbridge, adjacent to A4169.*
(OS Map 127; ref SJ 672034.)
🚌 *Tel: 0345 056 785.*
🚋 *Telford Central 5m.*

◐❂ Kenilworth Castle
WARWICKSHIRE (p. 217, 8J)
See pp. 138–9 for full details.

✠ Langley Chapel
SHROPSHIRE (p. 217, 9G)

This small chapel, standing alone in a field, contains a complete set of early 17th-century wooden fittings and furniture.

Open *Any reasonable time (closed 24–26 Dec).*
Entry *Free.*
⊗
➲ *1½m S of Acton Burnell, on unclassified road off A49, 9½m S of Shrewsbury.*
(OS Map 126; ref SJ 538001.)
🚌 *Tel: 0345 056 785.*
🚋 *Shrewsbury 7½m.*

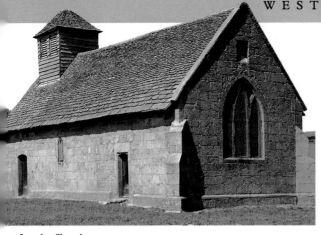

Langley Chapel

Leigh Court Barn

⊕⊘ Leigh Court Barn
HEREFORD & WORCESTER
(p. 217, 8H)

Magnificent 14th-century timber-framed barn, built for the monks of Pershore Abbey. It is the largest of its kind in Britain.

Open *1 April–30 Sept: Thurs–Sun, 10am–6pm.*

Entry *Free.*

⊗

➲ *5m W of Worcester on unclassified road off A4103. (OS Map 150; ref 784534.)* 🚌 *Tel: 0345 125 436.* 🚋 *Worcester Foregate St 5m.*

⊕ Lilleshall Abbey
SHROPSHIRE (p. 217, 9H)

Extensive and evocative ruins of an abbey of Augustinian canons, including remains of the 12th- and 13th-century church and the cloister buildings, surrounded by green lawns and ancient yew trees.

Open *1 April–1 Nov: Sat–Sun and Bank Holidays only, 12–5pm (5pm/dusk in Oct).*
Entry *£1.30/£1.00/70p.*
℃ *01604 730320 (regional office)*
🚩 📖 🏪
➲ *On unclassified road off A518, 4m N of Oakengates. (OS Map 127; ref SJ 738142.)* 🚌 *Tel: 0345 056 785.*

Lilleshall Abbey: the West Front

KENILWORTH CASTLE

♡ Ⓜ WARWICKSHIRE (p. 217, 8J)

Queen Elizabeth I *did* sleep here. The massive, red sandstone castle, which seems positively to glow in the early morning and evening light, was the Warwickshire power base of the best beloved of all her courtiers, Robert Dudley, Earl of Leicester. Among the buildings that remain are those that he built or rebuilt to entertain his queen. Other parts of Kenilworth date back to the 12th century. Kenilworth Castle has been intimately linked with some of the most important names in English history. Today, with its Tudor gardens, its impressive Norman 'keep' and John of Gaunt's Great Hall, it is the largest castle ruin in England.

A Civil War pikeman

The first castle at Kenilworth was built about 50 years after the Norman conquest. Henry II took over the castle 50 years later, to counter an attack from his son's rebel army. It was then radically extended by King John, who also transformed the mere (great lake) into one of its most glorious features.

Kenilworth stayed in royal hands until 1253, when it was given to Simon de Montfort by Henry III. The de Montforts turned against the Crown in the Barons' War in 1266, and the castle was besieged. Well-stocked with food, it managed to hold out for almost nine months before disease took its toll and surrender came.

Later, in a coup, Edward II was briefly imprisoned here, before being taken to Berkeley Castle and hideously murdered in 1326. Henry V retired there after winning the Battle of Agincourt a

Entrance to the keep

The castle from the south at sunset

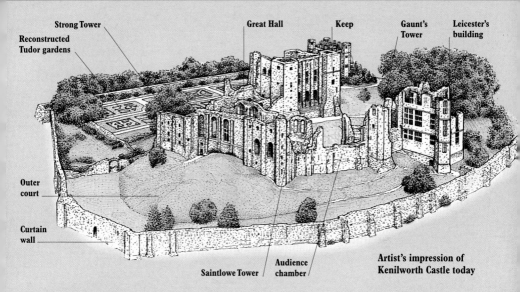

Strong Tower

Reconstructed
Tudor gardens

Great Hall

Keep

Gaunt's
Tower

Leicester's
building

Outer
court

Curtain
wall

Saintlowe Tower

Audience
chamber

Artist's impression of
Kenilworth Castle today

century later. He built himself a banqueting house, The Pleasuance, on the other side of the lake.

The castle took centre stage again in the 16th century, when it was acquired by the Dudley family. John Dudley, Duke of Northumberland and effectively ruler of England in the reign of the boy-king Edward VI, was executed for trying to place his daughter-in-law, Lady Jane Grey, on the throne in 1553. His son, Robert, was a great favourite of Elizabeth I. Kenilworth was given back to him and he transformed it into a place fit for her to visit.

Tales woven by Sir Walter Scott, in his novel *Kenilworth* (1821), around Dudley, his wife (who died in mysterious circumstances) and the Virgin Queen still give extra glamour to the castle.

Kenilworth never saw such glories again. After the Battle of Edgehill in the Civil War it was partially demolished by Parliamentary troops. Over the years it was allowed to fall further into ruin, and the lake drained away. The castle was saved for the nation in 1938. It remains a powerful reminder of great men, their glories, pleasures and rebellions, and

Visitors by Leicester's Barn

offers glorious views over a countryside now at peace.

Open all year round.
♿ New exhibition and
tearoom opening in
Leicester's Barn.
• Family Discovery Pack
and Free Children's
Activity Sheet available.
Open 1 April–1 Nov: daily,
10am–6pm (6pm/dusk in
Oct). 2 Nov–31 March: daily,
10am–4pm (closed 24–26 Dec).
Entry £3.10/£2.30/£1.60.
✆ 01926 852078
🅿 🚻 ♿ 🎧 *(also available for*
the visually impaired and those
with learning difficulties and in
French, German and Japanese)
♿ ⊗ 💻 📱 📷 🍴
➲ *In Kenilworth.*
(OS Map 140; ref SP 278723.)
Local Tourist Information:
Kenilworth (tel: 01926 852595).
🚌 *Tel: 01926 414140.*
🚂 *Warwick 5m.*

Longtown Castle

⊕♡⊘ Longtown Castle

HEREFORD & WORCESTER
(p. 217, 7F)

An unusual cylindrical keep built *c.*1200, with walls 4.5 metres (15 feet) thick. There are magnificent views to the Black Mountains.

Open *Any reasonable time.*
Entry *Free.*
🐕
➲ *4m WSW of Abbey Dore.*
(OS Map 161; ref SO 321291.)

⊕⊘ Mitchell's Fold Stone Circle

SHROPSHIRE (p. 217, 9F)

An air of mystery surrounds this Bronze Age stone circle, set on dramatic moorland and consisting of some 30 stones, of which 15 are visible.

Open *Any reasonable time. (Site managed by Shropshire County Council.)*
Entry *Free.*
⊗
➲ *16m SW of Shrewsbury, W of A488.*
(OS Map 137; ref SO 306984.)
🚌 *Tel: 0345 056 785.*
🚉 *Welshpool 10m.*

♡⊕⊘ Moreton Corbet Castle

SHROPSHIRE
(p. 217, 10G)

A ruined medieval castle with the substantial remains of a splendid Elizabethan mansion.

Open *Any reasonable time.*
Entry *Free.*
🅿 ♿ 🐕
➲ *In Moreton Corbet off B5063,*

Mortimer's Cross Water Mill

7m NE of Shrewsbury.
(OS Map 126; ref SJ 562232.)
🚌 *Tel: 0345 056 785.*
🚉 *Yorton 4m.*

⊘⊕ Mortimer's Cross Water Mill

HEREFORD & WORCESTER
(p. 217, 8G)

Intriguing 18th-century mill, still in working order, showing the process of corn milling.

Open *1 April–30 Sept: Thurs, Sun & Bank Holidays, 2pm–5.30pm.*
Entry *£2.00/£1.50/50p.*
☎ **01568 708820**
♿ *(exterior & ground floor only)*
⊗
➲ *7m NW of Leominster on B4362.*
(OS Map 148; ref SO 426637.)
🚉 *Leominster 7½m.*

STOKESAY CASTLE

♥ Ⓜ ✿ SHROPSHIRE (p. 217, 8G)

A gatehouse carved head

The finest and best-preserved 13th-century fortified manor house in England, Stokesay Castle nestles in peaceful countryside near the Welsh border in a picturesque group with its timber-framed Jacobean gatehouse and the parish church. The audio tour helps you imagine it as the centre of medieval life: feasts for the whole village in the Great Hall, the courtyard filled with farm animals or being defended against attack. Nowadays you can also stroll through the delightful cottage-style gardens. Stokesay offers a unique glimpse into a distant age when strength and elegance combined.

Stokesay from the east in winter

The Great Hall, almost untouched since medieval times, contains its original staircase, an open octagonal hearth and an innovative timber roof. Across the courtyard the delightful gatehouse, built in 1620, has carved animal heads decorating its gateposts.

The 17th-century gatehouse (below)

Open all year round.
♿ New shop opening Spring 1998.
Open 1 April–1 Nov: daily, 10am–6pm (6pm/dusk in Oct). 2 Nov–31 March: Wed–Sun, 10am–4pm (closed 24–26 Dec). Closed 1–2pm in winter.
Entry £2.95/£2.20/£1.50.
✆ 01588 672544
🚻 🅿 ♿ (gardens & Great Hall only) ✗ 🎧 🛍 ☕ (Refreshments, summer season only.)
➲ 7m NW of Ludlow off A49. (OS Map 137; ref SO 436817.)
Local Tourist Information:
Ludlow (tel: 01584 875053).
🚌 Tel: 0345 056 785.
🚂 Craven Arms 1m.

⬠ Old Oswestry Hill Fort

SHROPSHIRE (p. 217, 10F)

An impressive Iron Age fort of 68 acres defended by a series of five ramparts, with an elaborate western entrance and unusual earthwork cisterns.

Open *Any reasonable time.*
Entry *Free.*

🐕

➲ *1m N of Oswestry, accessible from unclassified road off A483.*
(OS Map 126; ref SJ 295310.)
🚐 *Tel: 0345 056 785.*
🚌 *Gobowen 2m.*

⊕ Rotherwas Chapel

HEREFORD & WORCESTER (p. 217, 7G)

This Roman Catholic chapel dates from the 14th and 16th centuries and features an interesting mid-Victorian side chapel and High Altar.

Open *Any reasonable time. Keykeeper at nearby filling station.*
Entry *Free.*
🅿 ♿ *(kissing gate)* ✸
➲ *1½m SE of Hereford on B4399.*
(OS Map 149; ref SO 537383.)
🚐 *Tel: 0345 125 436.*
🚌 *Hereford 3½m.*

♡ ✪ ❋ Stokesay Castle

SHROPSHIRE (p. 217, 8G)
See p. 141 for full details.

✿ Wall Roman Site (Letocetum)

STAFFORDSHIRE (pp. 214/217, 9J)

The remains of a staging post, alongside Watling Street. Foundations of an inn and bath house can be seen, and there is a display of finds in the site museum.

Open *1 April–1 Nov: daily, 10am–6pm (6pm/dusk in Oct).*
Entry *£1.75/£1.30/90p. National Trust members admitted free, but small charge on English Heritage Special Events Days. (Site maintained and managed by English Heritage, and owned by the National Trust.)*
☎ **01543 480768**
🍴 🛍 🎧 *(£1 for National Trust members)* 🐕 Ⓟ 🛒
➲ *Off A5 at Wall near Lichfield. (OS Map 139; ref SK099067.)*
🚌 *Shenstone 1½m.*

Rotherwas Chapel

Wall Roman Site: the bath house (bottom) with tiles from the museum (below)

WITLEY COURT

♡ 🏠 ⌇ HEREFORD & WORCESTER (p. 217, 8H)

The spectacular ruins of this once-great house are surrounded by magnificent landscaped gardens. You can step back in time with a personal audio tour to relive the house's Victorian heyday and hear stories of the extravagant parties and the 'upstairs, downstairs' lifestyle – perhaps you will even find yourself waltzing romantically across the ballroom! The landscaped grounds, fountains and woodlands are currently being restored to their former glory.

An early Jacobean manor house, Witley Court was converted in the 19th century into a vast Italianate mansion with porticoes by John Nash. The elaborate gardens, William Nesfield's 'Monster Work', still contain immense

The Perseus and Andromeda Fountain (above)

stone fountains. The largest, the Perseus and Andromeda Fountain, once shot water 120 feet skywards, with 'the noise of an express train'.

Open all year round.
⚘ *Stroll along the woodland walks.*

A pavilion in the grounds (above)

The magnificent facade (below)

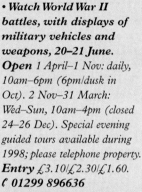

• *Watch World War II battles, with displays of military vehicles and weapons, 20–21 June.*
***Open** 1 April–1 Nov: daily, 10am–6pm (6pm/dusk in Oct). 2 Nov–31 March: Wed–Sun, 10am–4pm (closed 24–26 Dec). Special evening guided tours available during 1998; please telephone property.*
***Entry** £3.10/£2.30/£1.60.*
☎ **01299 896636**
🅿 ♿ 🍴 ☕ *(not managed by English Heritage)* ⚐ *(exterior & grounds only, poor access up long, rough drive)* 🎧
➲ *10m NW of Worcester on A443.*
(OS Map 150; ref 769649.)
***Local Tourist Information:** Droitwich Spa (tel: 01905 774312).*
🚌 *Tel: 0345 125 436*
🚆 *Droitwich Spa 8½m.*

✛ ✲ Wenlock Priory
SHROPSHIRE (p. 217, 9G)

The ruins of a large Cluniac priory in an attractive garden setting featuring delightful topiary. There are substantial remains of the early 13th-century church and Norman chapter house.

Open all year round.
Open *1 April–1 Nov: daily, 10am–6pm (6pm/dusk in Oct). 2 Nov–31 March: Wed–Sun, 10am–4pm (closed 24–26 Dec). Closed 1–2pm in winter.*
Entry *£2.30/£1.70/£1.20.*
(01952 727466
🅿 🎧 *(also available for the*

A carved panel from Wenlock Priory

visually impaired, those with learning difficulties, and in French, German and Japanese)
🛉 🍴 🏠
➜ *In Much Wenlock.*

(OS Map 127; ref SJ 625001.)
🚌 *Tel: 0345 056 785.*
🚇 *Telford Central 9m.*

✛ White Ladies Priory
SHROPSHIRE (p. 217, 9H)

The ruins of the late 12th-century church of a small priory of Augustinian canonesses.

Open *Any reasonable time.*
Entry *Free.*
🕱
➜ *1m SW of Boscobel House off unclassified road between A41 and A5, 8m NW of Wolverhampton.*
(OS Map 127; ref SJ 826076.)
🚇 *Cosford 2½m.*

Wenlock Priory

Wroxeter Roman City

Open all year round.
Museum with displays
and interactive computer
screen.
• From the Romans to the
Normans, see armoured
warriors on parade and
in combat, 3–4 May.
• Free Children's Activity
Sheet available.
Open 1 April–1 Nov: daily,
10am–6pm (6pm/dusk in
Oct). 2 Nov–31 March: Wed–
Sun, 10am–4pm (closed 24–26
Dec). Closed 1–2pm in winter.
Entry £2.95/£2.20/£1.50.
(01743 761330
🄴 🏠 🅿 ♿ ❌ 🅿 ♦ 🎧
➔ At Wroxeter, 5m E of
Shrewsbury on B4380.
(OS Map 126; ref
SJ 568088.)
🚌 Tel: 0345 056 785.
🚆 Shrewsbury 5½m;
Wellington Telford West 6m.

⊙ Wigmore Castle
HEREFORD &
WORCESTER (p. 217, 8G)

Fortified since the 1060s,
the present ruins date
from the 13th and 14th
centuries. The castle was
dismantled during the
Civil War, and remains
very much as it was
left then.

Open The castle is
undergoing major building
works and is not currently
open to the public. Access
arrangements will be
announced in the members'
magazine, Heritage Today,
and the local press. For
further details, contact
Customer Services on
0171 973 3434.

○❖ Witley Court
HEREFORD &
WORCESTER (p. 217, 8H)
See p.143 for full details.

⊘ Wroxeter Roman City
SHROPSHIRE (p. 217, 9G)

The excavated centre
of the fourth largest
city in Roman Britain,
with impressive remains
of the 2nd-century
municipal baths.

A reconstruction of Wroxeter Roman City

YORKSHIRE & THE HUMBER

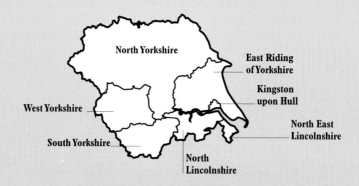

North Yorkshire

East Riding of Yorkshire

Kingston upon Hull

West Yorkshire

North East Lincolnshire

South Yorkshire

North Lincolnshire

WHEREVER YOU ARE in this vast area you will never be far from an English Heritage property. Most glorious of all is Rievaulx Abbey, in the beautiful and tranquil River Rye valley. A trip eastwards will take you to Whitby, where the ruins of the famous abbey tower over the fishing village. If instead you are touring the Moors and Dales, you'll have the chance to explore the magnificent castles at Richmond and Middleham. Further south is Brodsworth Hall, a grand Victorian house on a large scale with a stunningly restored garden.

Enjoy the peace and tranquillity of Rievaulx Abbey

Aldborough Roman Town mosaic

⊘ Aldborough Roman Town

NORTH YORKSHIRE
(p. 219, 14K)

The principal town of the Brigantes, the largest tribe in Roman Britain. The delightfully located remains include parts of the Roman defences and two mosaic pavements. The museum displays Roman finds from the town.

⌂ *New for 1998 –*
refurbished museum.
Open 1 April–1 Nov: daily,
10am–6pm (6pm/dusk in Oct).
Closed 1–2pm.
Entry £1.70/£1.30/90p.
Winter: grounds only,
admission free.
☏ *01423 322768*
⚥ *(summer only)* ⚒ ☉ ⓦ
➲ *¾m SE of Boroughbridge, on*
minor road off B6265 within 1m
of junction of A1 and A6055.
(OS Map 99; ref SE 405661.)
🚌 *Tel: 01423 566061.*

✚ Barton-upon-Humber, St Peter's Church

See St Peter's Church, p. 159.

⊕ ✿ Brodsworth Hall and Gardens

SOUTH YORKSHIRE
(p. 214, 12K)
See pp. 148–51 for full details.

⊙ Burton Agnes Manor House

EAST RIDING OF
YORKSHIRE (p. 219, 14L)

Rare example of a Norman house, altered and encased in brick in the 17th and 18th centuries.

Open 1 April–31 Oct: daily,
10am–6pm (6pm/dusk in Oct).
1 Nov–31 March: daily, 10am–
4pm. (The nearby Burton Agnes
Hall and Gardens are privately
owned and occupied, and not
managed by English Heritage.)
Entry Free.
☈
➲ *In Burton Agnes village, 5m*
SW of Bridlington on A166.

(OS Map 101; ref TA 103633.)
🚌 *Tel: 01482 327146.*
🚉 *Nafferton 5m.*

⊕ Byland Abbey

NORTH YORKSHIRE
(p. 219, 14K)

A hauntingly lovely ruin set in peaceful meadows in the shadow of the Hambleton Hills. It illustrates the later development of Cistercian churches, including the beautiful floor tiles.

Open 1 April–1 Nov: daily,
10am–6pm (6pm/dusk in
Oct). Closed 1–2pm.
Entry £1.50/£1.10/80p.
☏ *01347 868614*
🅿 ⚥ ⌂ *(including toilets)*
⚒ ☈ ⓦ
➲ *2m S of A170 between*
Thirsk and Helmsley, near
Coxwold village.
(OS Map 100; ref SE 549789.)

Byland Abbey (below) with the arch at the West Front (right)

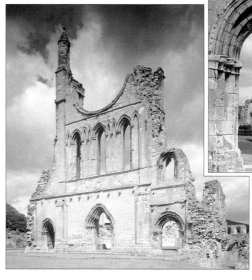

147

BRODSWORTH HALL AND GARDENS
🏛 ✤ SOUTH YORKSHIRE (p. 214, 12K)

One of England's most beautiful Victorian country houses, Brodsworth Hall has survived almost completely intact since the 1860s – an extraordinary time warp of richly marbled walls, Axminster carpets and family portraits. Opened for the first time in 1995, Brodsworth Hall and gardens offer visitors a breathtaking journey through the passage of time. When bequeathed to English

Charles Thellusson's father and grandmother, painted 1804

Heritage, conservation policy was aimed at preserving the Hall's faded grandeur. In the long-abandoned kitchen, visitors can readily picture how meals were really made in the age of Mrs Beeton. And deep in the cluttered remains of the servants' wing, it is easy to imagine life below stairs, with all the benefits and drawbacks that such an insular Victorian existence brought.

When Charles Thellusson acquired Brodsworth in the early 1860s he immediately commissioned Chevalier

Casentini, whom he had met in Italy, to build him a suitably impressive house. The result is formal, Italianate, four-square and lacks any fanciful detail. Casentini's designs were executed by a little-known English architect, Philip Wilkinson. It is said that Casentini never came to

Yorkshire to view what he had designed, fearing the cold and a setting wholly different from the pastoral landscape and blue skies he had drawn.

At the same time, a new garden incorporating both formal and informal features was created, all contained within magnificent parkland.

Marble greyhounds flank the steps down from the south front of the house (left)

Watercolour of the south front of Brodsworth showing only minor differences from the house as it was built (below)

WINNER OF THE GOLD
NPI AWARD 1997

The flower garden with its symmetrical beds cut into the turf

If the exterior of the house seems a little pompous, the interior is Brodsworth's chief glory. The entrance hall, with its gold, red and marbled walls, is a prelude to the splendours of the inner halls and reception rooms.

The colours provide a dramatic backdrop to another of the house's remarkable features, the succession of white marble statues with typically Victorian themes. Casentini created a grand processional route through the house from the entrance hall, via the soaring height of the top-lit staircase, to the pillared south hall. The ceremonial feel is emphasized by the poise of the statues. Of all the sculptures, Argenti's *Sleeping Venus* is particularly memorable, lying beneath the huge painted-glass internal window at the end of the hall, which was inserted by Wilkinson in order to lighten what would otherwise have been the impenetrable gloom of Casentini's original design. With its colourful garlands and playful cherubs, it provides a busy foil to the statue's lines.

Rich decorative schemes appear everywhere in the house: in the grand reception rooms, bedrooms and private quarters. The drawing room, with a dividing screen of Corinthian columns, red silk damask on the walls, chandeliers and gilding, is a grand monument to Thellusson's ambitions. The dining room, intended as much for show as for eating, contains some of the finest paintings in the house. Away from the finery of the reception rooms are the more intimate spaces of the library and morning room. Each has original wallpaper, a hand-painted pattern of roses and trellises resembling leather wallcoverings.

Urns line the paths around Brodsworth's lawns (left)

One of the follies hidden in Brodsworth's gardens (right)

'Nymph going to Bathe' (left) by Giuseppe Lazzarini in the South Hall (above)

When Brodsworth was first built and occupied, it amply fulfilled its role as a grand residence. Parties were conducted in sumptuous style; and in the evenings the gentlemen would relax in the billiard room, which has survived remarkably intact. By the mid-19th century a billiard room was considered an essential part of a country house, and Brodsworth retains its original massive table, along with the leather-bound book in which scores have been recorded since the 1880s.

The bedrooms have always been identified by a simple numbering system. Although much of their original decoration has

The dining room with many family portraits

been lost through frequent refurbishment, many pieces of mahogany furniture provided by Lapworths remain, including beds, marble-topped washstands, chests of drawers and armchairs.

The servants were housed in a wing abutting the house's main block. From the 1860s until about 1918 there were about ten female servants and several male. Their domain, the Victorian kitchen, is one of the most delightful features. Its 'Eagle Range' by Farr and Sons of Doncaster and its grained dressers still contain a vast range of cooking utensils.

Gradually, after World War I, with spiralling costs, parts of the house were shut away and, almost inadvertently, house and contents were preserved for the future. The kitchen too was gradually abandoned,

Library with the 1725 picture of Peter Thellusson's mother

although many of its original contents remain and can still be seen today. Brodsworth's history is written everywhere in its decoration: in the carpets in the library, laid one upon the other as each wore out; the High Victorian taste; the grandeur; the marbling; the painted decorative effects; and the sculptures. The gardens are still being coaxed from their overgrown state. They include croquet lawns and

The drawing room (above) with many of the original furnishings from Lapworths

The billiard room

a large formal flower garden; a quarry garden and a formal rose garden. The house itself has emerged from its slumber. Brodsworth, the grand Victorian sleeping beauty, has now awakened.

Open all year round.
• Winner of the NPI National Heritage Awards 1997 for best overall property.
• Free Children's Activity Sheet available.

• Voted by visitors as their favourite English Heritage property.
• Exhibitions at Brodsworth include 'Family Life', 'Serving the House' and 'The Gardens'.
Open *1 April–1 Nov: Tues–Sun & Bank Holidays, 1pm–6pm (6pm/dusk in Oct). Last admission 5pm. Gardens and tearoom open 12 noon. 7 Nov–28 March: Sat–Sun:*

11am–4pm (gardens, shop & tearooms only). Guided tours are available from 10am for pre-booked parties.
Entry *£4.50/£3.40/£2.30. Gardens only £2.50/£1.90/ £1.00; gardens only winter £1.50/£1.00/free.*
✆ 01302 722598
🅿 ♿ 🐕 ♿ (house and formal gardens) ⍾ ('Brodsworth Hall Tearoom') ▢ (colour)
▢ 🅔 ⊗ 🍴 Pushchairs, prams and back carriers for babies are regrettably not permitted in the fragile interiors of the house.
➲ In Brodsworth, 5m NW of Doncaster off A635 Barnsley Road, from junction 37 of A1(M). (OS Map 111; ref SE 507071.)
Local Tourist Information: *Doncaster (tel: 01302 734309).*
🚎 Tel: 01709 515151.
🚌 Doncaster 5½m.

The kitchen, abandoned since 1919, showing a part of the large collection of pots and pans

151

◉ Clifford's Tower
CITY OF YORK (p. 219,13K)
See p. 153 for full details.

◉ Conisbrough Castle
SOUTH YORKSHIRE
(pp. 214/219, 12K)

The spectacular 12th-century white circular keep is the oldest in England. It has recently been restored with a roof, two floors and interpretive features. There is also a visitor centre with gift shop, displays, information and an audio-visual presentation.

Open *1 April–30 Sept: daily, 10am–5pm (6pm weekends). 1 Oct–31 March: daily, 10am–4pm (5pm weekends, closed 24–25 Dec). Last admission 40 minutes before*

closing. *(Castle managed by the Ivanhoe Trust.)*
Entry
£2.75/£1.75/£1.25. English Heritage members admitted free. Concessionary rates for group bookings of over 20 people. Guided tours available. Castle available for private hire and special events outside general opening hours.
℡ *01709 863329*
🅿 ♿ *(limited access)* ✗
➲ *NE of Conisbrough town centre off A630, 4½m SW of Doncaster. (OS Map 111; ref SK 515989.)*
🚌 *Tel: 01709 515151.*
🚉 *Conisbrough ½m.*

⊕ Easby Abbey
NORTH YORKSHIRE
(pp. 218/220, 15J)

Substantial remains of the medieval abbey buildings stand in a beautiful setting by the River Swale near Richmond. The abbey can be reached by a pleasant riverside walk from Richmond Castle.

Open *1 April–1 Nov: daily, 10am–6pm (6pm/dusk in Oct).*
Entry *£1.50/£1.10/80p. Please telephone 0191 261 1585 for further details.*
🅿 ♿ ✗

Easby Abbey

➲ *1m SE of Richmond off B6271. (OS Map 92; ref NZ 185003.)*
🚌 *Tel: 0345 124 125.*

◉◉ Gainsthorpe Medieval Village
NORTH LINCOLNSHIRE
(pp. 214/219, 12L)

Originally discovered and still best seen from the air, this hidden village comprises earthworks of peasant houses, gardens and streets.

Open *Any reasonable time.*
Entry *Free.*
🐾
➲ *On minor road W of A15 S of Hibaldstow 5m SW of Brigg (no directional signs). (OS Map 112; ref SK 955012.)*
🚉 *Kirton Lindsey 3m.*

Conisbrough Castle

CLIFFORD'S TOWER

Ⓜ CITY OF YORK (p. 219, 13K)

Standing high on its mound, Clifford's Tower is one of the few vestiges of the pair of castles built by William the Conqueror in the city of York. William needed to establish his control in the North and York's castles were the stepping stones for the Normans to terrorize the northern counties. York was often the seat of government in the 13th and 14th centuries, so the castle would have been magnificently appointed. Today, the tower stands as a proud symbol of the might of the medieval English kings.

The original wooden keep was burnt down in 1190, when members of the Jewish community were sheltering there from a violent mob.

The present tower, a rare design of interlocking circles, was started in the mid-13th century by Henry III, but not completed until the early 14th century. It is thought to take its name from Roger Clifford, the Lancastrian leader defeated in 1322 at Boroughbridge, who was hung in chains from the keep. The tower survived intact until the Civil War, since when it has remained a shell.

Part of a Viking sword found in York (above left) and the south face and entrance of Clifford's Tower (above)

Clifford's Tower was built in 1069–70 on an ingenious mound of gravel, clay, stone and timber to overcome the problems of waterlogged land.

Open all year round.
↻ *New shop for 1998.*
• *Tactile model with Braille text.*
Open 1 April–1 Nov: daily, 10am–6pm (July–Aug, 9.30am–7pm. Closes 6pm/dusk in Oct). 2 Nov–31 March: daily, 10am–4pm (closed 24–26 Dec).
Entry £1.70/£1.30/90p.
✆ *01904 646940*
🅿 (council; fee charged) ✖ 🗋 🗍
➋ *In Tower St, York.*
(OS Map 105; ref SE 605515.)
Local Tourist Information:
York (tel: 01904 621756 or 01904 620557).
🚌 Tel: 01904 435637.
🚆 York 1m.

A reconstruction of how Clifford's Tower may have looked in the late 13th century

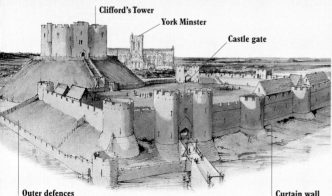

Clifford's Tower
York Minster
Castle gate
Outer defences
Curtain wall

The River Ouse (above) divided the sites of York's two castles

MIDDLEHAM CASTLE

 NORTH YORKSHIRE (p. 218, 14J)

The childhood home of Richard III, Middleham Castle controls the upper reaches of Wensleydale and Coverdale. Built in the 12th century, its central keep, one of the largest in England, has magnificent views of the surrounding countryside from the battlements. Middleham, though, was in its heyday three centuries later when the future Richard III lived there in the care of the Earl of Warwick. On Warwick's death in 1471 the castle was granted to Richard by his brother, Edward IV, in turn being seized on Richard's death by Henry VII. It then remained in royal hands until it was sold by James I in 1604.

Middleham Castle stands on the site of an 11th-century motte and bailey castle probably established by Alan, Lord of Richmond. The massive stone keep, with its 4-metre (12-foot) thick outer walls, was built in the following century, with an outer stone curtain wall being added in about 1300.

By 1450, the castle had been transformed into a comfortable residence by Ralph Neville, Earl of Westmoreland. The Nevilles were a powerful family who first came into possession of Middleham in 1270. Over the next 200 years they grew into the most influential family in the northern counties. In 1410

Henry IV was entertained there and from 1460–71 it was the home of Richard Neville, Earl of Warwick, who held Edward IV captive while trying to rule England in the King's name. In 1472 Richard III took over his childhood home and it remained in royal hands for over 130 years until it was

The castle as it stands today

The castle as it was in 1300, with Middleham village nearby

sold and fell into ruin. Today there is a new stairway and viewing platform, so that visitors can stand in the Great Hall and imagine the scene when it was playing host to some of the major figures in Britain's history.

A child (above) explores the castle using the new walkway (left)

Open all year round.
♿ *New viewing gallery.*
♿ *New introductory exhibition opens in 1998.*
♿ *See a replica of the fabulous medieval pendant, the Middleham Jewel.*
🏰 **James Herriot's Yorkshire** *was filmed at Middleham.*
Open 1 April–1 Nov: daily, 10am–6pm (6pm/dusk in Oct). 2 Nov–31 March: Wed–Sun, 10am–4pm (closed 24–26 Dec). Closed 1–2pm in winter.
Entry £2.20/£1.70/£1.10.
📞 *01969 623899*

🚗 ♿ *(except tower)* 🚻 *(in town centre)* 🛍 🚻
➔ *At Middleham, 2m S of Leyburn on A6108.*
(OS Map 99; ref SE 128875.)
Local Tourist Information: *Richmond (tel: 01748 850252).*

◎ Helmsley Castle

NORTH YORKSHIRE
(p. 219, 14K)

Spectacular earthworks surround the great ruined keep of this 12th-century castle. There is an exhibition on the history of the castle in Elizabethan buildings.

Open all year round.
Open *1 April–1 Nov: daily, 10am–6pm (6pm/dusk in Oct). 2 Nov–31 March: Wed–Sun, 10am–4pm (closed 24–26 Dec). Closed 1–2pm.*
Entry *£2.20/£1.70/£1.10.*
☎ *01439 770442*
🅿 *(large car park N of castle; charge payable)* ☼ 🛍 ⛩ *(in car park and in town centre)*
➔ *Near town centre.*
(OS Map 100; ref SE 611836.)
🚌 *Tel: 01723 375463 or 01347 838990.*

⊕ Howden Minster

EAST RIDING OF YORKSHIRE (p. 219, 13L)

A large, cathedral-like church dating from the 14th century. The chancel and octagonal chapter house are managed by Howden Minster Parochial Church Council and may be viewed from the outside only.

Open *Any reasonable time (closed 24–26 Dec).*
Entry *Free.*
🅿 *(street parking nearby)*
➔ *In Howden, 23m W of Kingston Upon Hull, 25m SE of York, near junction of A63 & A614.*

Helmsley Castle

(OS Map 106; ref SE 748283.)
🚌 *Tel: 01432 327146.*
🚌 *Howden 1½m.*

⊕ Kirkham Priory

NORTH YORKSHIRE
(p. 219, 14K)

The ruins of an Augustinian priory, set in a peaceful valley by the River Derwent.

Open *1 April–30 Sept: daily, 12pm–5pm.*
Entry *£1.50/£1.10/80p.*
☎ *01653 618768*
🅿 ⛩ 🛍 ⛩
➔ *5m SW of Malton on minor road off A64.*
(OS Map 100; ref SE 735657.)
🚌 *Tel: 01653 692556.*
🚌 *Malton 6m.*

◎ Marmion Tower

NORTH YORKSHIRE
(p. 219, 14J)

A medieval gatehouse with a fine oriel window.

Open *Any reasonable time (closed 24–26 Dec).*
Entry *Free.*
⛩
➔ *N of Ripon on A6108 in West Tanfield.*
(OS Map 99; ref SE 267787.)
🚌 *Thirsk 10m.*

◎ Middleham Castle

NORTH YORKSHIRE
(p. 218, 14J)
See pp. 154/5 for full details.

⊕ Monk Bretton Priory

SOUTH YORKSHIRE
(pp. 214/219, 12K)

Sandstone ruins of a Cluniac monastery founded in 1153 with extensive remains of the fully restored 14th-century gatehouse.

Open *1 April–31 Oct: daily, 10am–6pm (6pm/dusk in Oct). 1 Nov–31 March: daily, 10am–4pm.*
Entry *Free.*
🅿 ⛩ 🛍 ⛩
➔ *1m E of Barnsley town centre off A633.*
(OS Map 111; ref SE 373065.)
🚌 *Tel: 01709 515151.*
🚌 *Barnsley 2½m.*

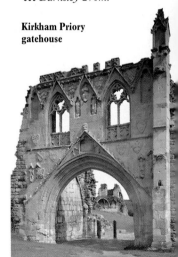

Kirkham Priory gatehouse

MOUNT GRACE PRIORY

✚ ♡ NORTH YORKSHIRE (pp. 219/220, 15K)

Mount Grace Priory is the best-preserved Carthusian monastery in Britain. Founded in 1398, it is beautifully situated amongst attractive woodlands. The monks lived as virtual hermits in their own cells, only congregating for services in the monastery's small church. Today, you can see what life must have been like there in the 15th century by viewing the specially reconstructed cell and wandering through the remains of the Great Cloister, outer court, as well as the extensive gardens.

Mount Grace, with its individual two-storey cells, is practically unique. The reconstructed cell gives a fascinating insight into the monks' solitary but highly ordered lives, and contains replica furniture. Today, the monastery is a vivid reminder of the extreme lifestyle of the Carthusians in medieval England, while the gardens are a perfect spot to relax and enjoy the beautiful surrounding countryside.

Open all year round.
• Picnic spot of exceptional beauty. Nature trail.
• Free Children's Activity Sheet and nature trail leaflet available.
Open 1 April–1 Nov: daily, 10am–6pm (6pm/dusk in Oct). Last admission 5.30pm. 2 Nov–31 March: Wed–Sun, 10am–4pm. Last admission 3.30pm. Closed 1–2pm in winter.
Entry £2.70/£2.00/£1.40. National Trust members admitted free. (Site owned by the

National Trust, maintained and managed by English Heritage.)
℘ 01609 883494
🚹🅿️♿🚫📷📖📱🖨️
➲ *12m N of Thirsk, 7m NE of Northallerton on A19.*
(OS Map 99; ref SE 453982.)
Local Tourist Information:
Northallerton (tel: 01609 776864).
🚌 *Tel: 0345 124 125.*
🚆 *Northallerton 6m.*

The living room of a reconstructed monk's cell (above)

Reconstructed monk's cell

Aerial view of the priory complex

Priory church

Inner court

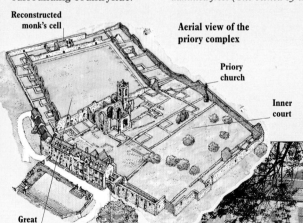

Great cloister

Guest house

The Manor House and the monk's fish pond (right)

✛ Mount Grace Priory

NORTH YORKSHIRE
(pp. 219/220, 15K)
See p. 157 for full details.

⊕ Pickering Castle

NORTH YORKSHIRE
(p. 219, 14L)

A splendid motte and bailey castle, once a royal hunting lodge. It is well preserved, with much of the original walls, towers and keep, and spectacular views over the surrounding countryside. There is an exhibition on the castle's history.

Open all year round.
• Free Children's Activity Sheet available.
Open *1 April–1 Nov: daily, 10am–6pm (6pm/dusk in Oct). 2 Nov–31 March: Wed–Sun, 10am–4pm (closed 24–26 Dec). Closed 1–2pm.*
Entry *£2.20/£1.70/£1.10.*
(01751 474989
🅿 ♀♂ ☂ ♿ *(except motte)*
🄴 ⌂ ◻ ⬦
➲ *In Pickering 15m SW of Scarborough.*

Pickering Castle: Colemans Tower, the motte and keep (left) and an aerial view (below)

(OS Map 100; ref SE 800845.)
🚌 *Tel: 01653 692556 or 01723 375463.*
🚆 *Malton 9m; Pickering (N.York Moors Rly) ¼m.*

⊘ Piercebridge Roman Bridge

NORTH YORKSHIRE
(pp. 218/220, 15J)

Remains of the stone piers and abutment of a Roman timber bridge over the River Tees.

Open *Any reasonable time.*
Entry *Free.*
☂
➲ *At Piercebridge, 4m W of Darlington on B6275. (OS Map 93; ref NZ 214154.)*
🚌 *Tel: 01325 468771.*
🚆 *Darlington 5m.*

⊘ Richmond Castle

NORTH YORKSHIRE
(pp. 218/220, 15J)

Hugely dramatic Norman fortress, built by William the Conqueror in his quest to quell the rebellious North. William's close ally,

Richmond Castle

Alan of Brittany, chose the site for his principal castle and residence. The 11th-century remains of the curtain wall and domestic buildings are combined with the 30-metre (100-foot) high keep with its hugely thick walls, added in the 12th century. There are magnificent views over the River Swale from the keep and there is a delightful riverside walk to Easby Abbey.

Open all year round.
• Free Children's Activity Sheet available.
Open *1 April–1 Nov: daily, 10am–6pm (6pm/dusk in Oct). 2 Nov–31 March: daily, 10am–4pm (closed 24–26 Dec). Closed 1–2pm in winter.*
Entry *£2.20/£1.70/£1.10.*
(01748 822493
♀♂ ⬦ ◻ ☂ ◻
➲ *In Richmond. (OS Map 92; ref NZ 174006.)*
🚌 *Tel: 01325 468771.*

✛ ♡ Rievaulx Abbey

NORTH YORKSHIRE
(p. 219, 14K)
See pp. 160–61 for full details.

Roche Abbey seen from
the air

✠ Roche Abbey
SOUTH YORKSHIRE
(pp. 214/219, 11K)

A Cistercian monastery,
founded in 1147, which is
set in an enchanting valley
landscaped by Capability
Brown. Excavation has
revealed the complete
layout of the abbey.

Open *1 April–1 Nov: daily,
10am–6pm (6pm/dusk in Oct).*
Entry *£1.50/£1.10/80p.*
☏ *01709 812739*

🚶 🅿 ♿ 🐕 ⓦ 🍴
➜ *1½ m S of Maltby off A634.
(OS Map 111; ref
SK 544898.)*
🚌 *Tel: 01709 515151.*
🚌 *Conisbrough 7m.*

✠ St Mary's Church
Studley Royal, NORTH
YORKSHIRE (p. 219, 14J)

Magnificent Victorian
church, designed by
William Burges in the
1870s, with a highly
decorated interior.
Coloured marble, stained
glass, gilded and painted
figures and a splendid
organ remain in their
original glory.

Open *22 March–30 Sept:
daily, 1–5pm. (English
Heritage property managed by
the National Trust as part
of Studley Royal estate.)*
Entry *Free.*
☏ *01765 608888*

Richmond Castle from the River Swale

St Mary's Church

🅿 *(free at visitor centre)* ♿ 🐕
➜ *2½ m W of Ripon off
B6265, in grounds of
Studley Royal estate.
(OS Map 99; ref SE 278703.)*
🚌 *Tel: 01423 566061 or
0345 124 125.*

✠ St Peter's Church
Barton-upon-Humber,
NORTH LINCOLNSHIRE
(p. 219, 12L)

A fine 15th-century
former parish church,
with an Anglo-Saxon
tower and baptistry.

Open *Daily, 2–4pm
(closed 24–26 Dec).*
Entry *Free.*
☏ *01652 632516*
♿
➜ *In Barton-upon-Humber.
(OS Map 112; ref
TA 034220.)*
🚌 *Tel: 01724 297444.*
🚌 *Barton-upon-Humber ½ m.*

RIEVAULX ABBEY

✠ ♡ NORTH YORKSHIRE (p. 219, 14K)

'Everywhere peace, everywhere serenity, and a marvellous freedom from the tumult of the world.' Those words could describe Rievaulx today, for it is one of the most atmospheric of all the ruined abbeys of the North. In fact, they were written over eight centuries ago by St Aelred, the monastery's third abbot. Although much of what was built by the monks is in ruins, most of the spectacular presbytery, the great eastern part of the abbey church, stands virtually to its full height. Built in the 13th century, its soaring beauty conveys the glory and splendour that Rievaulx once possessed.

Rievaulx was founded directly by the holy St Bernard of Clairvaux, as part of the missionary effort to bring Christianity to western Europe. Twelve Clairvaux monks came to Rievaulx in 1132, and from these modest beginnings sprang one of the wealthiest monasteries of medieval England and the first Cistercian monastery in the North.

A medieval carving depicting the abbey's mill

In the Middle Ages, wealthy families vied with each other in founding churches. Rievaulx enjoyed the protection and endowment of Walter Espec, who provided much of the abbey's land. The monks of Byland Abbey, over the river, cooperated with the Cistercians in agreeing to divert the course of the River Rye. You can still make out traces of the old river, and the channels dug by the monks.

A steady stream of monks came to Aelred, author and preacher, who was regarded then, and since, as a wise and saintly man. After his death in 1167 the monks sought his canonization and, in the 1220s, rebuilt the east part of their church in a much more elaborate style for his tomb. Rievaulx was still a vibrant community when Henry VIII dissolved it in 1538. Its new owner, Thomas Manners, first Earl of Rutland, swiftly began the systematic destruction of the buildings. What he left was one of the most eloquent of all monastic sites, free 'from the tumult of the world', as Aelred once said.

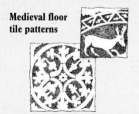

Medieval floor tile patterns

The incomparable setting of Rievaulx Abbey (below)

The new shop (above)

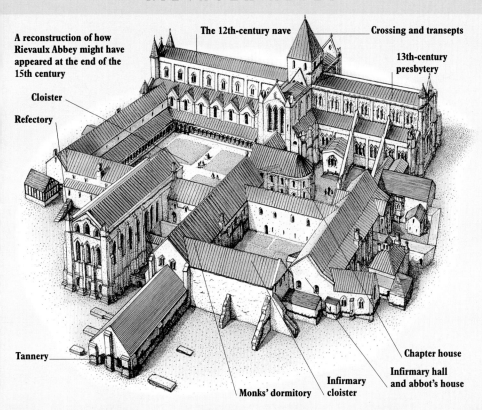

A reconstruction of how Rievaulx Abbey might have appeared at the end of the 15th century

The 12th-century nave

Crossing and transepts

13th-century presbytery

Cloister

Refectory

Tannery

Monks' dormitory

Infirmary cloister

Chapter house

Infirmary hall and abbot's house

Open all year round.
⛥ *New shop now open.*
🎬 *The ITV film,* James Herriot's Yorkshire, *was filmed at Rievaulx Abbey.*
Open 1 April–30 June: daily, 10am–6pm. 1 July–31 Aug, 9.30am–7pm. 1 Sept–1 Nov: 10am–6pm (6pm/dusk in Oct). 2 Nov–31 March: daily, 10am–4pm (closed 24–26 Dec).
Entry £2.90/£2.20/£1.50.
☎ *01439 798228*
🅿 ♿ 🐕 🔒 ⛥ ♿ 📷 (also available for the visually impaired, those with learning difficulties and in French, Swedish and Japanese)*
➡ *In Rievaulx, 2¼ m W of Helmsley on minor road off B1257.*
(OS Map 100; ref SE 577849.)
Local Tourist Information:
Helmsley (tel: 01439 770773).
🚌 Tel: 01723 375463 or 01347 838990.

Ruins of the monastic buildings (left)

A view through the arcades of the abbey church (right)

The deserted medieval village at Wharram Percy

Scarborough Castle

NORTH YORKSHIRE
(p. 219, 14L)

There are spectacular coastal views from the buttressed walls of this enormous 12th-century castle. The remains of the great rectangular stone keep still stand to over three storeys high. There is also the site of a 4th-century Roman signal station.

Open all year round.
♿ New gift shop.
♿ New first-floor viewing gallery.
• Thrilling action as the Cavaliers re-enact the 1648 Assault on Scarborough Castle with musket, pike and cannon, 15–16 August.
• Free audio tour.

• Free Children's Activity Sheet available.
Open 1 April–1 Nov: daily, 10am–6pm (6pm/dusk in Oct). 2 Nov–31 March: Wed–Sun, 10am–4pm (closed 24–26 Dec). Closed 1–2pm in winter.
Entry £2.20/£1.70/£1.10.
℡ 01723 372451
⋔ 🐕 🎧 *(also available for the visually impaired and those with learning difficulties)*
⛪ *(except keep)* 🛍 🎫 💻 🎁
➲ *Castle Rd, E of town centre. (OS Map 101; ref TA 050893.)*
🚌 *Tel: 01723 375463.*
🚉 *Scarborough 1m.*

Skipsea Castle

EAST RIDING OF YORKSHIRE (p. 219, 13M)

The remaining earthworks of a Norman motte and bailey castle.

Open Any reasonable time.
Entry Free.
🐕
➲ *8m S of Bridlington, W of Skipsea village.*

Scarborough Castle and a decorated 16th-century slipware plate found there

(OS Map 107; ref TA 163551.)
🚉 *Bridlington 9m.*

Spofforth Castle

NORTH YORKSHIRE
(p. 219, 13J)

This manor house has some fascinating features including an undercroft built into the rock. It was once owned by the Percy family.

Open 1 April–30 Sept: daily, 10am–6pm. 1 Oct–31 March: daily, 10am–4pm (closed 24–26 Dec). Keykeeper. (Site managed by Spofforth-with-Stockeld Parish Council.)
Entry Free.
🐕
➲ *3½m SE of Harrogate, off A661 at Spofforth. (OS Map 104; ref SE 360511.)*
🚌 *Tel: 01423 566061.*
🚉 *Pannal 4m.*

Stanwick Iron Age Fortifications

NORTH YORKSHIRE
(pp. 218/220, 15J)

The tribal stronghold of

Thornton Abbey

the Brigantes, whose vast earthworks cover some 850 acres. Today you can see an excavated section of the ditch, cut into the rock, and the rampart.

Open *Any reasonable time.*
Entry *Free.*
🏕
➲ *On minor road off A6274 at Forcett Village.*
(OS Map 92; ref NZ 178124.)
🚂 *Tel: 0191 383 3337.*
🚉 *Darlington 10m.*

✪ Steeton Hall Gateway
NORTH YORKSHIRE
(p. 219, 13K)

A fine example of a small, well-preserved 14th-century gateway.

Open *Daily, 10am–5pm (exterior only).*
Entry *Free.*
✆ *Regional Office 0191 261 1585*
🚻 🏕
➲ *4m NE of Castleford, on minor road off A162 at South Milford.*
(OS Map 105; ref SE 484314.)
🚉 *South Milford 1m.*

✪ Thornton Abbey and Gatehouse
NORTH LINCOLNSHIRE
(p. 219, 12M)

Ruined Augustinian priory with magnificent brick gatehouse.

Open *Abbey grounds, any reasonable time. Gatehouse, 1 April–30 Sept: 1st & 3rd Sun, 12–6pm. 1 Oct–31 March: 3rd Sun, 12–4pm.*
Entry *Free.*
🅿 🚻 *(except interior of gatehouse and part of chapter house ruins)* 🚻 🥪
➲ *18m NE of Scunthorpe on minor road N of A160; 7m SE of Humber Bridge on minor road E off A1077.*
(OS Map 113; ref TA 115190.)
🚉 *Thornton Abbey ¼m.*

✪ Wharram Percy Deserted Medieval Village
NORTH YORKSHIRE
(p. 219, 14L)

One of over 3,000 deserted villages to have been identified from faint outlines of walls and foundations. The remains of the medieval church still stand.

Open *Any reasonable time.*
Entry *Free.*
🅿 *(at Bella Farm, ¾m walk to site)* 🏕 🥪
➲ *6m SE of Malton, on minor road from B1248 ½m S of Wharram le Street.*
(OS Map 100; ref SE 859645.)
🚉 *Malton 8m.*

✪ Wheeldale Roman Road
NORTH YORKSHIRE
(p. 219, 15L)

This mile-long stretch of Roman road, still with its hardcore and drainage ditches, runs across isolated moorland.

Open *Any reasonable time. (Site managed by North York Moors National Park.)*
Entry *Free.*
🏕
➲ *S of Goathland, W of A169, 7m S of Whitby.*
(OS Map 94; ref SE 805975.)
🚉 *Goathland (N York Moors Rly) 4m.*

✪○ Whitby Abbey
NORTH YORKSHIRE
(p. 219, 15L)
See pp. 164–5 for full details.

WHITBY ABBEY

✠ ♡ NORTH YORKSHIRE (p. 219, 15L)

Set high on a North Yorkshire clifftop, the remains of Whitby Abbey overlook a picturesque town and harbour with associations ranging from Victorian jewellery and whaling to Count Dracula. Whitby Abbey is a magnificent reminder of the early church's power and dedication; it contained the shrine of St Hilda, the foundress who died in 680,

Pilgrim's badge

and it symbolized the continuing Christian tradition in the North.

Destroyed by Viking invaders, rebuilt by Normans, embellished by later generations and dismantled by Henry VIII, the abbey is today a gaunt and moving ruin. Those who choose to approach it up the 199 steps from Whitby town also know the meaning of dedication.

St Hilda brought nuns and monks, including the poet Caedmon, to found a religious house on the coastal headland in 657. Because of her reputation, the Synod of 664 was held there and the two branches of early English Christianity, the Celtic and Roman Churches, buried many differences in practice and doctrine. The matter that had principally divided them was the date of Easter, and the Synod decided in favour of the Roman tradition. When the Vikings

invaded Northumbria in 867, the abbey was destroyed and its wealth pillaged. A Norman invader, Reinfrid, revived Whitby Abbey in the late 1070s; he also resettled

Jarrow, home of Bede, whose writings had kept alive the memory of the early holy places, and refounded Whitby. The Norman church proved inadequate under the

The towering mass of the largely standing east end

The abbey and parish church, perched above the town and harbour

pressure of pilgrims, and in the 1220s rebuilding commenced. Since its dissolution in 1538, Whitby's dramatic location has attracted 18th-century painters and engravers. They helped begin the appreciation of the grandeur of these ruins, which has led to their continued preservation.

Open all year round.
📺 The Abbey has been used as the setting for the popular TV series, Heartbeat.
📺 The Riddlers, *a children's drama series, was filmed here*.

• *Activity book for children available.*
Open *1 April–1 Nov: daily, 10am–6pm (6pm/dusk in Oct). 2 Nov–31 March: daily, 10am–4pm (closed 24–26 Dec).*
Entry *£1.70/£1.30/90p.*
☎ 01947 603568
👪 🚻 🅿 *(both local*

council; charge payable) 🎫 🏪
(We regret access unsuitable for wheelchairs.) ♿
➡ *On cliff top E of Whitby. (OS Map 94; ref NZ 904115.)*
Local Tourist Information:
Whitby (tel: 01947 602674).
🚌 *Tel: 01947 602146.*
🚂 *Whitby ½m.*

Plan of existing remains at Whitby, showing the underlying 12th-century apsed east end

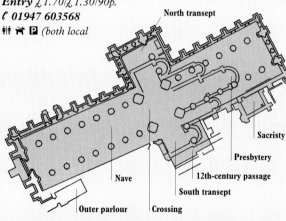

North transept

Sacristy

Presbytery

12th-century passage

Nave

South transept

Outer parlour

Crossing

The abbey ruins in 1789

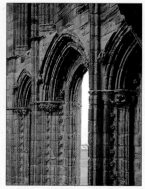

Sculpted decoration around the north transept windows (above)

NORTH WEST

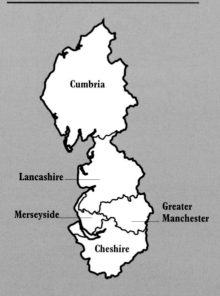

Cumbria

Lancashire

Merseyside

Greater Manchester

Cheshire

ROM BOTH THE HILL-TOP fortress of Beeston and the massive keep of Carlisle Castle you can almost believe you are seeing the whole of this region, as the countryside stretches away in every direction. Reminders of the times of conflict with Scotland are not only at Carlisle but also at Brougham Castle, on the banks of the beautiful River Eamont. Alternatively, why not enter the age of the Industrial Revolution at Stott Park Bobbin Mill, a working mill and museum, where you can see bobbins being made before taking one home as a souvenir.

A warm welcome to visitors at Beeston Castle

⊘⊜ Ambleside Roman Fort

CUMBRIA (pp. 218/220, 15G)

The remains of this 1st- and 2nd-century fort were built to guard the Roman road from Brougham to Ravenglass.

Open *Any reasonable time. (Site managed by the National Trust.)*
Entry *Free.*
🏹
➲ *200 yds W of Waterhead car park, Ambleside. (OS Map 90; ref NY 376033.)*
🚌 *Tel: 01946 63222.*
🚉 *Windermere 5m.*

⊜ Arthur's Round Table

CUMBRIA (pp. 218/220, 15G)

A prehistoric circular earthwork bounded by a ditch and an outer bank.

Open *Any reasonable time.*
Entry *Free.*
♿ 🏹
➲ *At Eamont Bridge, 1m S of Penrith. (OS Map 90; ref NY 523284.)*
🚉 *Penrith 1½m.*

⊙ Baguley Hall

GREATER MANCHESTER (pp. 217/218, 11H)

A medieval timber-framed hall house dating from the 14th century, with 18th- and 19th-century additions. An extensive programme of repair is being carried out, with access on advertised open days only.

Brough Castle

Open *Please telephone 0191 261 1585 for details.*
Entry *Free.*
➲ *6m S of Manchester, in Hall Lane, Baguley, near Wythenshawe (E of Junction 3 of M56, off A560). (OS Map 109; ref SJ 815893.)*
🚌 *Tel: 0161 228 7811.*
🚉 *Gatley 2½m.*

⊙♡ Beeston Castle

CHESHIRE (pp. 217/218, 11G)
See p. 168 for full details.

⊙➲ Bow Bridge

Barrow-in-Furness, CUMBRIA (p. 218, 14F)

Late medieval stone bridge across Mill Beck, carrying a route to nearby Furness Abbey (see p. 170).

Open *Any reasonable time.*
Entry *Free.*
🏹
➲ *½m N of Barrow-in-Furness, on minor road off A590 near Furness Abbey. (OS Map 96; ref SD 224715.)*
🚌 *Tel: 01946 63222.*
🚉 *Barrow-in-Furness 1½m.*

Brough Castle from the air

⊙ Brough Castle

CUMBRIA (p. 218/220, 15H)

Dating from Roman times, the 12th-century keep replaced an earlier stronghold destroyed by the Scots in 1174. It was restored by Lady Anne Clifford in the 17th century.

Open *1 April–31 Oct: daily, 10am–6pm (6pm/dusk in Oct). 1 Nov–31 March: daily, 10am–4pm.*
Entry *Free.*
🏹 🅿
➲ *8m SE of Appleby S of A66. (OS Map 91; ref NY 791141.)*
🚌 *Tel: 01228 606000.*
🚉 *Kirkby Stephen 6m.*

BEESTON CASTLE

ⓗ ♡ CHESHIRE (pp. 217/218, 11G)

Standing majestically on sheer, rocky crags which fall sharply away from the castle walls, Beeston has possibly the most stunning views of any castle in England. Its history stretches back over 4,000 years, to when it was a Bronze Age hill fort. The huge castle was built from 1226 and soon became a royal stronghold, only falling centuries later during the English Civil War.

A new exhibition, 'The Castle of the Rock', outlines the history of this strategic site from prehistoric times, through the Middle Ages to the Civil War. It is illustrated with finds from Beeston.

Beeston Castle (bottom) and Lord Tollemache's Gatehouse (below)

Open all year round.
⚘ Learn about Beeston's history by visiting the new exhibition, 'The Castle of the Rock'.
⚘ New gift shop.
⚔ Robin Hood, starring Patrick Bergin and Uma Thurman was filmed at Beeston.
• Free Children's Activity Sheet available.
Open 1 April–1 Nov: daily, 10am–6pm (6pm/dusk in Oct). 2 Nov–31 March: daily, 10am–4pm (closed 24–26 Dec).
Entry £2.70/£2.00/£1.40.

Children enjoying a day at Beeston

✆ 01829 260464
🅿 🚗 🍴 ⚓ 🛈 🎒 📷
➲ 11m SE of Chester on minor road off A49 or A41. (OS Map 117; ref SJ 537593.)
Local Tourist Information: Nantwich (tel: 01270 610983).
🚌 *Tel: 01244 602666.*
🚃 *Chester 10m.*

Brougham Castle

CUMBRIA (pp. 218/220, 15G)

These impressive ruins on the banks of the River Eamont include an early 13th-century keep and later buildings. Its one-time owner Lady Anne Clifford restored the castle in the 17th century. A new introductory exhibition includes carved stones from the nearby Roman fort.

New shop.

Open *1 April–1 Nov: daily, 10am–6pm (6pm/dusk in Oct).* **Entry** *£1.90/£1.40/£1.00.* **01768 862488**
P ††† **⚲** 🗋 **&** *(excluding keep)*
🗄
➲ *1½m SE of Penrith on minor road off A66. (OS Map 90; ref NY 537290.)*
🚌 *Penrith 2m.*

Carlisle Castle

CUMBRIA (pp. 218/220, 16G)
See pp. 170–71 for full details.

Castlerigg Stone Circle

CUMBRIA (pp. 218/220, 15F)

Possibly one of the earliest Neolithic stone circles in Britain, its 33 stones stand in a beautiful setting.

Open *Any reasonable time. (Site managed by the National Trust.)* **Entry** *Free.*
⚲
➲ *1½m E of Keswick. (OS Map 90; ref NY 293236.)*
🚌 *Tel: 01946 63222.*
🚌 *Penrith 16m.*

Chester Castle: Agricola Tower and Castle Walls

CHESHIRE (pp. 217/218, 11G)

Set in the angle of the city walls, this 12th-century tower contains a fine vaulted chapel.

Open *Castle walls open any reasonable time; cell block open 1 April–30 Sept: daily, 10am–6pm. 1 Oct–31 March: daily, 10am–4pm (closed 24–26 Dec).* **Entry** *Free.*
& *(parts)* ⚲
➲ *Access via Assizes Court car park on Grosvenor St. (OS Map 117; ref SJ 405658.)*
🚌 *Tel: 01244 602666.*
🚌 *Chester 1m.*

Castlerigg Stone Circle

Chester Roman Amphitheatre

CHESHIRE (pp. 217/218, 11G)

The largest Roman amphitheatre in Britain, partially excavated. It was used for entertainment and military training by the 20th Legion, based at the fortress of Deva.

Open *Any reasonable time.* **Entry** *Free.*
& *(no access to amphitheatre floor)* ⚲
➲ *On Vicars Lane beyond Newgate, Chester. (OS Map 117; ref SJ 404660.)*
🚌 *Tel: 01244 602666.*
🚌 *Chester ¾m.*

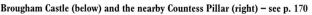

Brougham Castle (below) and the nearby Countess Pillar (right) – see p. 170

169

CARLISLE CASTLE

 CUMBRIA (pp. 218/220, 16G)

Sitting proudly on the highest point above the River Eden, Carlisle Castle has guarded the western end of the Anglo-Scottish border for over nine centuries. It was first built after William II relieved Carlisle of two centuries of Scottish domination in 1092. Since then it has often been the scene of turbulent conflict between the two nations, being fought over fairly constantly until the union of the crowns in 1603. It then fell into Scottish hands again during the Civil War and the Jacobite Rising 100 years later.

Henry I, who built the stone keep at Carlisle

Today, Carlisle Castle offers the visitor many insights into its violent past, including the legendary 'licking stones' in its dungeon, where parched Jacobite prisoners found enough moisture to stay alive, only to be barbarically executed on Gallow's Hill. The castle displays an exhibition about Bonnie Prince Charlie and the Jacobite Rising of 1745.

The views from the massive keep are magnificent, stretching from the Lakes to the Pennines, from the Solway Firth to the Grampians.

Carlisle Castle's heritage stretches back to the forging of the English and Scottish nations. Briefly the seat of royal government while Parliament met at Carlisle in 1306–7, it has played host to kings, been attacked by both Robert the Bruce and Bonnie Prince Charlie, and been a prison for Mary Queen of Scots following her abdication in 1568.

The outer gatehouse (right), built about 1167, altered 1378–83

A helmet (above) from the Civil War

The imposing Norman keep and curtain wall date from 1157, when Carlisle and its castle were handed back to Henry II by the Scots. The keep remains the nucleus of the castle to this day, while almost every other part has been remodelled, repaired or rebuilt. Throughout its long history, Carlisle has never

The outer gatehouse

Graffiti by medieval prisoners

&. (except interiors of buildings) 👫 🦽 🗋 ⊗ 🚌 🗋 Guided tours available at a small extra charge. Tours are daily, June–Oct; weekends in May. Please telephone for times.
➔ In Carlisle city centre. (OS Map 85; ref NY 397563.)

Local Tourist Information:
Carlisle (tel: 01228 512444).
🚌 Tel: 01228 606000.
🚆 Carlisle ½m.

lost its purpose as a fortress and today it remains the headquarters of the King's Own Royal Border Regiment and houses the Regimental Museum.

Entry £2.90/£2.20/£1.50.
☎ 01228 591922
🅿 (disabled only). Car parking in nearby city car parks (signposted).

Open all year round.
• Free Children's Activity Sheet available.
• Fine views from the keep and rampart walk.
Open 1 April–1 Nov: daily, 10am–6pm (opens 9.30am April–Sept, closes 6pm/dusk in Oct). 2 Nov–31 March: daily, 10am–4pm (closed 24–26 Dec).

The Warden's apartments furnished in 14th-century style

Clifton Hall

CUMBRIA (pp. 218/220, 15G)

The surviving tower block of a 15th-century manor house.

Open *Any reasonable time (closed 24–26 Dec).*
Entry *Free.*

➲ *In Clifton next to Clifton Hall Farm, 2m S of Penrith on A6.*
(OS Map 90; ref NY 530271.)
🚃 *Penrith 2½m.*

Countess Pillar

Brougham, CUMBRIA
(pp. 218/220, 15G)

An unusual monument, bearing sundials and family crests, erected in 1656 by Lady Anne Clifford to commemorate her parting with her mother in 1616.

Open *Any reasonable time.*
Entry *Free.*

➲ *1m SE of Brougham on A66.*
(OS Map 90; ref NY 546289.)
🚃 *Penrith 2½m.*

Furness Abbey

CUMBRIA (p. 218, 14F)

In a peaceful valley, the red sandstone remains of a wealthy abbey founded in 1123 by Stephen, later King of England, are at the end of an ancient route from Bow Bridge (see p. 167). The museum contains an exhibition and fine stone carvings.

Open all year round.
• Free audio tour.
Open *1 April–1 Nov: daily, 10am–6pm (6pm/dusk in Oct). 2 Nov–31 March: Wed–Sun, 10am–4pm (closed 24–26 Dec). Closed 1–2pm in winter.*
Entry *£2.50/£1.90/£1.30.*
☎ *01229 823420*
🚻 🅿 🎧 *(also available for the visually impaired and those with learning difficulties)*

➲ *1½m N of Barrow-in-Furness, on minor road off A590.*
(OS Map 96; ref SD 218717.)
🚉 *Tel: 01946 63222.*
🚃 *Barrow-in-Furness 2m.*

Goodshaw Chapel

LANCASHIRE (p. 218, 13H)

A restored 18th-century Baptist chapel with all its furnishings complete.

Open *Keykeeper. Tel: 0191 261 1585 for details.*
Entry *Free.*

➲ *In Crawshawbooth, 2m N of Rawtenstall, in Goodshaw Avenue off A682.*
(OS Map 103; ref SD 815263.)
🚉 *Tel: 01706 213677.*
🚃 *Burnley Manchester Road 4½m.*

Hadrian's Wall

(pp. 176–77)
See pp. 176–83 for details of sites along Hadrian's Wall.

Hardknott Roman Fort

CUMBRIA (pp. 218/220, 15F)

One of the most dramatic Roman sites in Britain, with stunning views across the Lakeland fells. The fort, built between AD120 and 138, controlled the road from Ravenglass to Ambleside. There are visible remains of granaries, the head-quarters building and the commandant's house, with

Furness Abbey

Lanercost Priory: the undercroft (above)
and tomb of Elizabeth Dacre Howard (left)

a bath house and parade
ground outside the fort.

Open *Any reasonable time.
Access may be hazardous in
winter. (Site managed by the
National Trust.)*

🅿 🐾

➲ *9m NE of Ravenglass, at
W end of Hardknott Pass.
(OS Map 96; ref NY 218015.)*
🚌 *Eskdale (Dalegarth)
(Ravenglass & Eskdale
Railway) 3m.*

⊕ Lanercost Priory

CUMBRIA (p. 220, 17G)

Augustinian priory founded
*c.*1166. The church's nave
contrasts with the ruined
chancel, transepts and
priory buildings.

👂 **Free audio tour.**
Open *1 April–1 Nov: daily,
10am–6pm (6pm/dusk in
Oct). (Parish church not
managed by English Heritage.)*
Entry *£1.90/£1.40/£1.00.*
✆ **01697 73030**
🅿 🐾 🎧 🏠 🛍 ♿

➲ *Off minor road S of
Lanercost, 2m NE of Brampton.
(OS Map 86; ref NY 556637.)*

🚌 *Tel: 01946 63222.*
🚌 *Brampton 3m.*

⛰ Mayburgh Earthwork

CUMBRIA (pp. 218/220, 16G)

An impressive prehistoric
circular earthwork, with
banks up to 4.5 metres
(15 feet) high, enclosing a
central area of one and a
half acres containing a
single large stone.

Open *Any reasonable time.*
Entry *Free.*
🐾

➲ *At Eamont Bridge,
1m S of Penrith off A6.
(OS Map 90; ref NY 519285.)*
🚌 *Penrith 1½m.*

⊖ Penrith Castle

CUMBRIA (pp. 218/220, 16G)

A 14th-century castle
set in a park on the edge
of the town.

Open *Park: summer,
7.30am–9pm; winter,
7.30am–4.30pm.*
Entry *Free.*
🐾 🚻

➲ *Opposite Penrith railway
station.
(OS Map 90; ref NY 513299.)*
🚌 *Penrith, adjacent.*

●○ Piel Castle

CUMBRIA (p. 218, 14F)

The ruins of a 14th-
century castle, accessible by
boat from Roa Island, with
the massive keep, inner and
outer baileys, and curtain
walls and towers.

Open *Any reasonable time.
Access by small boat from
Roa Island during summer,
subject to tides and weather.
For information tel: 01229
833609 or 870156.*
Entry *Free.*
🐾

➲ *On Piel Island, 3¼m
SE of Barrow.
(OS Map 96; ref SD 233636.)*
🚌 *Tel: 01946 63222.*
🚌 *Barrow-in-Furness 4m
to Roa Island.*

⊘ Ravenglass Roman Bath House

CUMBRIA (p. 218, 15F)

The walls of the bath
house are among the
most complete Roman
remains in Britain.

Open *Any reasonable time.
(Site managed by Lake District
National Park Authority.)*
Entry *Free.*
🐾

➲ *¼m E of Ravenglass, off
minor road leading to A595.
(OS Map 96; ref NY 088961.)*
🚌 *Ravenglass, adjacent.*

✪ Salley Abbey

LANCASHIRE (p. 218, 13H)

The remains of a Cistercian abbey founded in 1147.

Open *1 April–31 Oct: daily, 10am–6pm (6pm/dusk in Oct). 1 Nov–31 March: daily, 10am–4pm. (Site managed by Heritage Trust for the North West.)*
Entry *Free.*
& ⚑
➲ *At Sawley 3½m N of Clitheroe off A59.*
(OS Map 103; ref SD 776464.)
🚌 *Clitheroe 4m.*

✪ Sandbach Crosses

CHESHIRE (pp. 217/218, 11H)

Rare Saxon stone crosses from the 9th century, carved with animals, dragons and biblical scenes, in the centre of the market square.

Open *Any reasonable time.*
Entry *Free.*
& ⚑
➲ *Market square, Sandbach.*
(OS Map 118; ref SJ 758608.)
📞 *Tel: 01244 602666.*
🚌 *Sandbach 1½m.*

✪ Shap Abbey

CUMBRIA (pp. 218/220, 15G)

The striking tower and other remains of this Premonstratensian abbey stand in a remote and isolated location.

Open *Any reasonable time.*
Entry *Free.*
🅿 & ⚑
➲ *1½m W of Shap on bank of River Lowther.*
(OS Map 90; ref NY 548153.)
📞 *Tel: 01946 63222.*
🚌 *Penrith 10m.*

✪ Stott Park Bobbin Mill

CUMBRIA (p. 218, 14G)
See p. 175 for full details.

✪ Warton Old Rectory

LANCASHIRE (p. 218, 14G)

Rare medieval stone house with remains of the hall, chambers and domestic offices.

Open *1 April–31 Oct: daily, 10am–6pm (6pm/dusk in Oct). 1 Nov–31 March: daily, 10am–4pm (closed 24–26 Dec). (Site managed by Heritage Trust for the North West.)*
Entry *Free.*
⚑ &
➲ *At Warton, 1m N of Carnforth on minor road off A6.*

(OS Map 97; ref SD 499723.)
📞 *Tel: 01772 886633.*
🚌 *Carnforth 1m.*

✪ Wetheral Priory Gatehouse

CUMBRIA (pp. 218/220, 16G)

A Benedictine priory gatehouse, preserved after the Dissolution by serving as the vicarage for the parish church.

Open *1 April–31 Oct: daily, 10am–6pm (6pm/dusk in Oct). 1 Nov–31 March: daily, 10am–4pm (closed 24–26 Dec).*
Entry *Free.*
⚑
➲ *On minor road in Wetheral village, 6m E of Carlisle on B6263.*
(OS Map 86; ref NY 469542.)
📞 *Tel: 01946 63222.*
🚌 *Wetherall ½m.*

✪ Whalley Abbey Gatehouse

LANCASHIRE (p. 218, 13H)

The outer gatehouse of the nearby Cistercian abbey. There was originally a chapel on the first floor.

Open *Any reasonable time. (Site managed by Heritage Trust for the North West.)*
Entry *Free.*
⚑ &
➲ *In Whalley, 6m NE of Blackburn on minor road off A59.*
(OS Map 103; ref SD 730360.)
📞 *Tel: 01254 681120.*
🚌 *Whalley ½m. Rishton 5½m.*

Sandbach Crosses

STOTT PARK BOBBIN MILL

◉ CUMBRIA (p. 218, 14G)

A working mill built in 1835, Stott Park created the wooden bobbins vital to the spinning and weaving industries of Lancashire. Typical of mills across the Lake District, today you can see industry from a bygone age and watch as bobbins are made using the mill's original machinery. Although Stott Park worked continuously until 1971 it remains almost identical to its Victorian appearance of 100 years ago, making it a unique and important monument.

With its Victorian machinery originally powered by a waterwheel and steam engine, Stott Park used birch, ash and sycamore to make wooden tool handles as well as bobbins. The mass of belts which fills the building still drives the cutting, boring and finishing machines that turn long thin poles into bobbins. Today you can watch a bobbin being made before taking it home as a souvenir.

See a real working Victorian bobbin mill.
• See the steam engine operating on Tues, Weds and Thurs every week.
• Bobbins for sale.
Open *1 April–1 Nov: daily, 10am–6pm (6pm/dusk in Oct). Guided tours lasting 45 minutes included in admission charge, last tour starts 1 hour before closure.*
Entry *£2.90/£2.20/£1.50.*
℆ 01539 531087
P ♯♯ & *(ground floor only)*

The mill in action

🛍 ⊗ 📄 🍴
➲ ½m N of Finsthwaite near Newby Bridge.
(OS Map 96; ref SD 373883.)
Local Tourist Information:
Hawkshead (tel: 01539 436525).
🚌 *Tel: 01946 63222.*

Bobbins for sale (below) at Stott Park Bobbin Mill (left)

HADRIAN'S WALL

⊘ CUMBRIA & NORTHUMBERLAND

Stretching across northern England from the Solway Firth in the west to the Tyne in the east, Hadrian's Wall divided the 'civilized' world of the Romans from the northern tribes beyond. Emperor Hadrian, who came to Britain in AD122, was unusual in that he believed consolidation to be more glorious than new conquest. The Wall was the manifestation of his strategy, a defensive barrier linking the existing system of forts and watchtowers along the

Head of Hadrian, emperor from AD117 to 138

Stanegate road. Fortified lines once marked many of the Roman Empire's boundaries – along the Rhine and the Danube, on North Africa's desert edge, and in the Middle East. These, along with Hadrian's Wall and the Antonine Wall in Britain, were the outposts of the empire. Of them all, Hadrian's Wall, a World Heritage Site, is by far the best-preserved and being there still invokes a sense of standing on the edge of the world.

The original Wall was built from AD122–23. From coast to coast 73 miles (80 Roman miles), it was punctuated by small forts a mile apart ('milecastles') with turrets positioned between them. In front of the Wall was a deep ditch running in parallel and, behind it, a great earthwork or Vallum stretching along its entire length.

➲ *West of Hexham, the Wall runs roughly parallel to the A69 Carlisle–Newcastle-Upon-Tyne road, lying between 1–4 miles north of it, close to the B6318.*
Local Tourist Information: *Hexham (tel: 01434 605225) or Carlisle (tel: 01228 512444).* 🚌 *Tel 0191 232 5325 or 0191 212 3000 or 01670 533128.* 🚆 *Carlisle–Newcastle line has stations at Hexham, Haydon*

Bridge, Bardon Mill, Haltwhistle and Brampton. For all public transport information: in Northumberland tel. 01670 533128 and in Cumbria tel. 01228 606000.

Building tools found at Corbridge

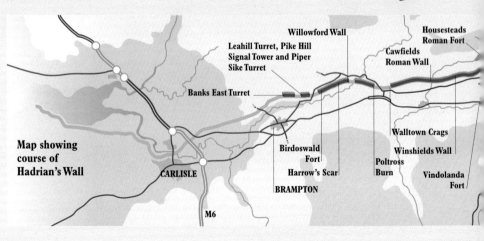

Map showing course of Hadrian's Wall

Willowford Wall
Leahill Turret, Pike Hill Signal Tower and Piper Sike Turret
Housesteads Roman Fort
Cawfields Roman Wall
Banks East Turret
Walltown Crags
Birdoswald Fort
Winshields Wall
Poltross Burn
CARLISLE
Harrow's Scar
Vindolanda Fort
BRAMPTON
M6

Banks East Turret
Well-preserved turret with adjoining stretches of Wall.

(Site managed by Cumbria County Council.)

P

➲ *On minor road E of Banks village, 3½m NE of Brampton. (OS Map 86; ref NY 575647.)*

Illustration of a typical milecastle

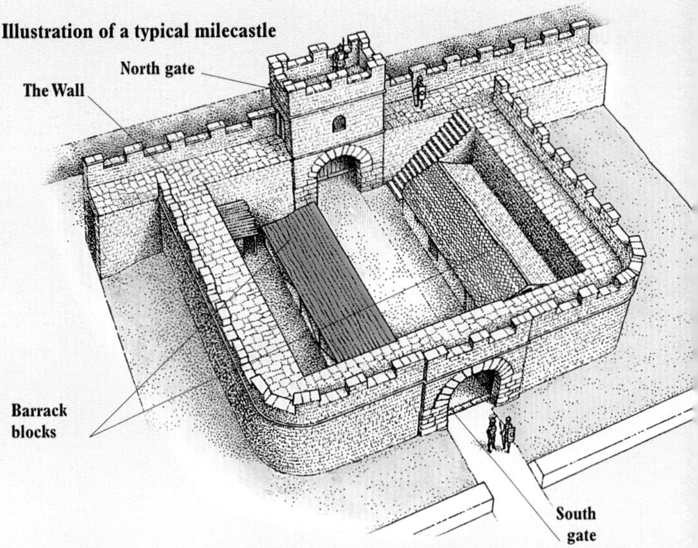
North gate
The Wall
Barrack blocks
South gate

Benwell Roman Temple and Vallum Crossing
Remains of small temple, and the sole remaining stone-built causeway across the Vallum earthwork.

➲ *Immediately S off A69 at Benwell in Broomridge Ave. (OS Map 88; ref NZ 217646.)*

Birdoswald Fort
Almost on the edge of the Irthing escarpment, remains survive of granaries and the east gate, which is among the best preserved on the Wall.

Open *1 April–30 Oct: daily 10am–5.30pm. Winter season, exterior only. (Site managed by Cumbria County Council on behalf of English Heritage.)*

Entry *£1.95/£1.45/£1.00.*

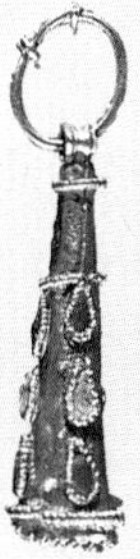

Earring found at Birdoswald

✆ **01697 747602**

➲ *2¾m W of Greenhead, on minor road off B6318. (OS Map 86; ref NY 615663).*

Black Carts Turret
A 460-metre (500-yard) length of Wall and turret.

➲ *2m W of Chollerford on B6318. (OS Map 87; ref NY 884712.)*

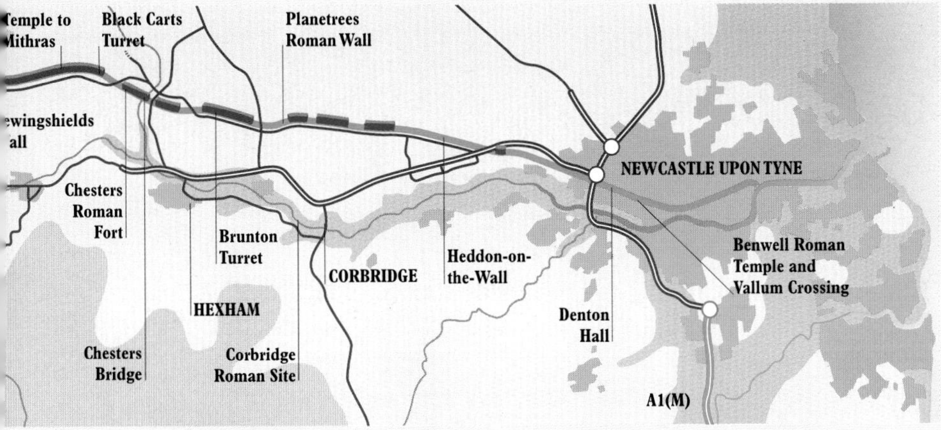
Temple to Mithras
Black Carts Turret
Planetrees Roman Wall
Sewingshields Wall
Chesters Roman Fort
Brunton Turret
CORBRIDGE
Heddon-on-the-Wall
NEWCASTLE UPON TYNE
Benwell Roman Temple and Vallum Crossing
HEXHAM
Denton Hall
Chesters Bridge
Corbridge Roman Site
A1(M)

Chesters Roman Fort

Across the Empire, Roman forts were built to a very similar pattern. Chesters, located between the 27th and 28th milecastles, is one of the best-preserved examples. Laid out in a rectangle but with rounded corners, it had two gates on the shorter sides, with a main road running between them, and two gates in each of the longer sides. Administrative buildings were placed in the centre, including the headquarters of the legion or garrison and the commanding officer's house. The complete plan is not exposed at

Bath-house statue of Neptune

A roman grain measure (above)

An artist's reconstruction of Chesters Roman Fort (below)

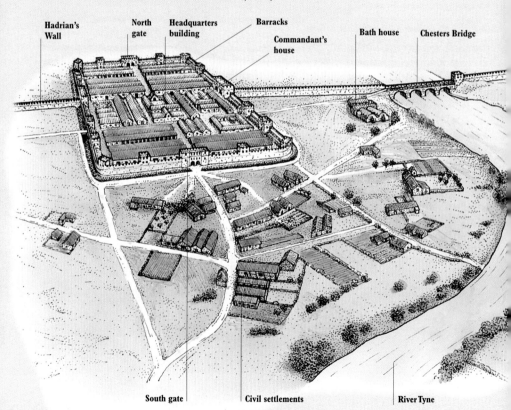

Hadrian's Wall

North gate

Headquarters building

Barracks

Commandant's house

Bath house

Chesters Bridge

South gate

Civil settlements

River Tyne

Chesters Roman Fort

Chesters, but many parts are visible: the four principal gates, the headquarters building, commandant's house and barracks for the troops. The Wall's line ran through the fort and down to cross the River Tyne. The finely preserved bath house is sited between the fort and the river. Originally, an aqueduct brought water from the river to serve both fort and baths. Large changing rooms led to a welcoming sequence of hot, steam, warm (and cold) baths. An altar to the goddess Fortuna (Luck), found in the bath house, suggests that gambling and bathing co-existed.

So much is known about this early fort because of the pioneering archaeological work of John Clayton, who inherited the local estate in 1832. The museum, which was built in 1896 soon after his death, houses many of the important finds from the site, and still contains its original displays.

Open all year round.
• Watch superb military displays by the Imperial Roman Army, 31 August.
Open 1 April–30 Sept: daily, 9.30am–6pm. 1 Oct–1 Nov: daily, 10am–6pm (6pm/dusk in Oct). 2 Nov–31 March: daily, 10am–4pm (closed 24–26 Dec).
***Entry** £2.70/£2.00/£1.40.*
☏ 01434 681379
⌂ ♦♦ P & ⊕ ⑰ ⬛ (not managed by English Heritage)
➲ 1½ m W of Chollerford on B6318.
(OS Map 87; ref NY 913701.)
Local Tourist Information:
Hexham (tel: 01434 605225).
▦ Tel: 01670 533128.
🚂 Hexham 5½ m.

Cawfields Milecastle

Brunton Turret
Well-preserved 2.5-metre (8-foot) turret with a stretch of Wall.

P
➲ ¼ m S of Low Brunton on A6079.
(OS Map 87; ref NY 922698.)

Cawfields Roman Wall
Camps, turrets, a fortlet, and Milecastle 42 – along with a fine, consolidated stretch of the Wall.

P ♦♦
➲ 1¼ m N of Haltwhistle off B6318.
(OS Map 87; ref NY 716667.)

Chesters Bridge
Fragments of the bridge that carried Hadrian's Wall across the North Tyne are visible on both banks. The most impressive remains are on the east side.

➲ ¼ m S of Low Brunton on A6079.
(OS Map 87; ref NY 922698.)

Corbridge Roman Site

Originally the site of a fort on the former patrol road, Corbridge evolved into a principal town of the Roman era, flourishing until the 5th century. The large granaries, with their ingenious ventilation system, are among its most impressive remains. Corbridge is an excellent starting point to explore the Wall.

Corbridge Roman site

Open all year round.
• *Children's Activity Book available.*
Open *1 April–1 Nov: daily, 10am–6pm (6pm/dusk in Oct). 2 Nov–31 March:*

Wed–Sun, 10am–4pm (closed 24–26 Dec). (Closed 1–2pm in winter.)
Entry £2.70/£2.00/£1.40.
℄ 01434 632349
⬚ � 🅿 ♿ ⓢ ⓦ ∩ *(also available for the visually impaired and those with learning difficulties)*

➍ *½m NW of Corbridge on minor road, signed Corbridge Roman Site. (OS Map 87; ref NY 983649.)*
Local Tourist Information: *Hexham (tel: 01434 605225).* 🚌 *Tel: 0191 212 3000.* 🚆 *Corbridge 1¼m*

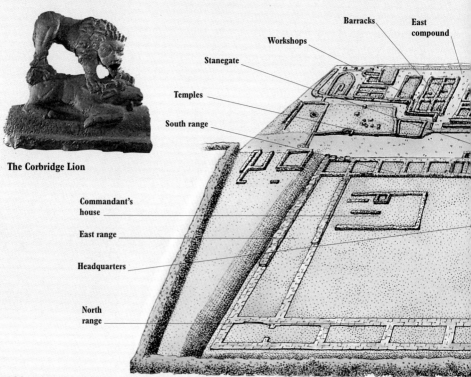

The Corbridge Lion

Stanegate

Temples

South range

Workshops

Barracks

East compound

Commandant's house

East range

Headquarters

North range

Denton Hall Turret

The foundations of a turret and 65-metre (70-yard) section of Wall.

➲ *4m W of Newcastle city centre on A69.*
(OS Map 88; ref NZ 195656.)

Hare Hill

A short length of Wall standing nine feet high.

(Site managed by Cumbria County Council.)
➲ *¾m NE of Lanercost, off minor road.*
(OS Map 86; ref NY 562646.)

Harrow's Scar Milecastle

The most instructive mile section on the whole length of Hadrian's Wall linked to Birdoswald Fort.

(Site managed by Cumbria County Council.)
➲ *¼m E of Birdoswald, on minor road off B6318.*
(OS Map 86; ref NY 621664.)

Heddon-on-the-Wall

A stretch of Wall up to 3 metres (10 feet) thick.

➲ *Immediately E of Heddon village, S of A69.*
(OS Map 88; ref NZ 136669.)

Leahill Turret and Piper Sike Turret

Turrets west of Birdoswald.

(Site managed by Cumbria County Council.)
➲ *On minor road 2m W of Birdoswald Fort.*
(OS Map 86; ref NY 585653.)

Pike Hill Signal Tower

Remains of a signal tower joined to the Wall at an angle of 45 degrees.

(Site managed by Cumbria County Council.)
➲ *On minor road E of Banks village.*
(OS Map 86; ref NY 597648.)

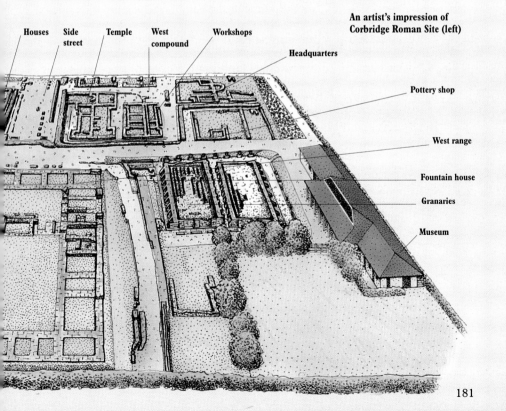

Houses Side street Temple West compound Workshops Headquarters

An artist's impression of Corbridge Roman Site (left)

Pottery shop

West range

Fountain house

Granaries

Museum

Housesteads Roman Fort

Housesteads occupies a commanding position on the cliffs of the Whin Sill. One of the twelve permanent forts built by Hadrian *c.* AD124, between Milecastles 36 and 37, Housesteads is the most complete example of a Roman fort in Britain. Its visible remains include four gates, with towers between them, and their curtain walls, as well as the principal buildings from within an auxiliary fort: military headquarters, commandant's house, barracks, granaries, hospital and latrines. There are also remains of the civilian settlement that clustered

An artist's reconstruction of the Housesteads latrines

Sculpture of Victory which once adorned the east gate at Housesteads and is now in Chesters Museum

at Housesteads' gates, while standing sections of Wall run to the east.

From the archaeological record of Housesteads, we can glimpse the people who lived at the edge of the Empire. We know that cavalry from the modern Netherlands were stationed here in the 3rd century – flat-bottomed pottery and larger cooking pots found at the site are Frisian in origin. A child's shoe was also found in the wet ground alongside. Carved deities from a shrine wear the hooded cape raingear, *byrrus Britannicus*, that was one of the famed exports of

Roman Britain and an important garment for life on Hadrian's Wall.

Some of the Wall has been partially reconstructed, to give one of the most vivid pictures of the Romans and their works in Britain.

Open all year round.
• Children's Activity Book available.
Open 1 April–1 Nov: daily, 10am–6pm (6pm/dusk in Oct). 1 Nov–31 March: daily, 10am–4pm (closed 24–26 Dec).
Entry £2.70/£2.00/£1.40. National Trust members admitted free. (Site owned by the National Trust, and maintained and managed by English Heritage.)
(01434 344363
▟▐ ▐ (both on main road, ½m walk to S, parking charge payable to National Park)
⟐ (car park at site; enquire at information centre on main road) ⟐ ⟐ ⟐
➲ 2¾m NE of Bardon Mill on B6318.
(OS Map 87; ref NY 790687.)
Local Tourist Information: Hexham (tel: 01434 605225).
▭▭ ▭ see p. 176.

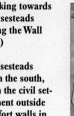

Looking towards Housesteads along the Wall (left)

Housesteads from the south, with the civil settlement outside the fort walls in the foreground (right)

Planetrees Roman Wall
A 15-metre (50-foot) length of narrow Wall on broad foundations.

➲ *1m SE of Chollerford on B6318.*
(OS Map 87; ref NY 928696.)

Poltross Burn Milecastle
One of the best-preserved milecastles with a flight of steps and remains of gates.

(Site managed by Cumbria County Council.)
🅿 *(near Station Hotel)*
➲ *Immediately SW of Gilsland village by old railway station.*
(OS Map 86; ref NY 634662.)

Sewingshields Wall
Largely unexcavated section of Wall, with remains of a milecastle.

➲ *N of B6318, 1½m E of Housesteads Fort.*
(OS Map 87; ref NY 813702.)

Temple of Mithras, Carrawburgh
A 3rd-century temple with facsimiles of altars found during excavation.

🅿
➲ *3¾m W of Chollerford on B6318.*
(OS Map 87; ref NY 869713.)

Vindolanda Fort
A fort and well-excavated civil settlement. A museum there contains many unusual artefacts from everyday Roman life.

Open April and Sept: daily, 10am–5.30pm. May and June: daily, 10am–6pm. July and Aug: daily, 10am–6.30pm. March and Oct: daily, 10am–5pm. Nov–Feb: daily, 10am–4pm (closed 25 Dec) (usually site open at reduced charge and museum closed during this period). Site owned and managed by Vindolanda Trust.
Entry £3.50/£2.75/£2.25. (10% discount for English Heritage members and groups of 15 or more.)
☎ **01434 344277**
ⓜ ⴕ 🅿 ⊗
➲ *1¼m SE of Twice Brewed, on minor road off B6318.*
(OS Map 87; ref NY 771664.)
🚌 🚆 *see p. 176.*

see p. 176.

Walltown Crags
One of the best-preserved sections of the Wall, snaking over the crags to the turret on its summit.

🅿 *(nearby)*
➲ *1m NE of Greenhead*

Walltown Crags

Bronze terrier found at Coventina's Well near the Temple of Mithras

off B6318.
(OS Map 87; ref NY 674664.)

Willowford Wall, Turrets and Bridge
1,000 yards of Wall, including two turrets.

Open Access to bridge controlled by Willowford Farm; small charge levied.
➲ *W of minor road ¾m W of Gilsland.*
(OS Map 86; ref NY 629664.)

Winshields Wall
Rugged section of the Wall, including its highest point.

➲ *W of Steel Rigg car park, on minor road off B6318.*
(OS Map 87; ref NY 745676.)

NORTH EAST

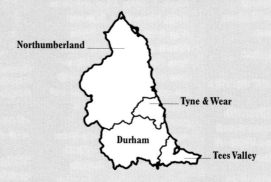

Northumberland

Tyne & Wear

Durham

Tees Valley

THE WILDNESS OF the medieval North is reflected in the strength and vitality of the English Heritage properties in Northumberland and County Durham. Along the coast are the magnificent castles of Berwick, Warkworth and Tynemouth, as well as the spectacular ruins of Lindisfarne Priory, situated on Holy Island. Along Hadrian's Wall, one of our World Heritage Sites, stand the forts of Chesters, Corbridge and Housesteads – the highlights of this extraordinary landmark. Further north at Belsay Hall you can roam through more than 30 acres of beautiful gardens.

Lindisfarne Priory never fails to capture the imagination

⊙ Auckland Castle Deer House

Bishop Auckland, COUNTY DURHAM (pp. 218/220, 16J)

A charming building erected in 1760 in the park of the Bishops of Durham so that deer could shelter and find food.

Open *Park opening times 1 April–30 Sept: daily, 10am–6pm. 1 Oct–31 March: daily, 10am–4pm (closed 24–26 Dec). (Site managed by the Church Commissioners for England.)* **Entry** *Free. Castle not managed by English Heritage; separate charge for members.*
🐕
➲ *In Auckland Park, Bishop Auckland, N of town centre on A68.*
(OS Map 93; ref NZ 216305.)
🚌 *Tel: 0191 383 3337.*
🚆 *Bishop Auckland 1m.*

❶❍ Aydon Castle

NORTHUMBERLAND (p. 220, 17H)

One of the finest fortified manor houses in England, built in the late 13th century. Situated in a position of great natural beauty, its remarkably intact state is due to its conversion to a farmhouse in the 17th century.

🎬 *Both* **Ivanhoe** *and the new release,* **Elizabeth I,** *were filmed at Aydon.* **Open** *1 April–1 Nov: daily, 10am–6pm (6pm/dusk in Oct).* **Entry** *£1.90/£1.40/£1.00.*
(01434 632450

👫 🅿 ♿ *(ground floor)* ⊗ 🚪 💺 🍴
➲ *1m NE of Corbridge, on minor road off B6321 or A68.*
(OS Map 87; ref NZ 002663.)
🚌 *Corbridge 4m – approach by bridle-path from W side of Aydon Road, immediately N of Corbridge bypass.*

❶ Barnard Castle

COUNTY DURHAM (pp. 218/220, 15H)

Substantial remains of this large castle stand on a rugged escarpment overlooking the River Tees. You can see parts of the 14th-century Great Hall and the cylindrical 12th-century tower.

Open all year round.
• Free audio tour.
Open *1 April–1 Nov: daily, 10am–6pm (6pm/dusk in Oct).*

Barnard Castle

Aydon Castle

2 Nov–31 March: Wed–Sun, 10am–4pm (closed 24–26 Dec). Closed 1–2pm. **Entry** *£2.20/£1.70/£1.10.*
(01833 638212
♿ 🐕 👫 *(in town)* 🚪 🎧 🍴
➲ *In Barnard Castle.*
(OS Map 92; ref NZ 049165.)
🚌 *Tel: 0345 124125.*

🏛❶❀❍ Belsay Hall and Gardens

NORTHUMBERLAND (p. 220, 17J)

See pp. 186–7 for full details.

BELSAY HALL AND GARDENS

🏠 🖼 ✳ ♥ NORTHUMBERLAND (p. 220, 17J)

The beautiful honey-coloured stone from which Belsay Hall is built came from its own quarries in the grounds. Those quarries have since become the unusual setting for one of a series of spectacular gardens. They are the property's finest feature, deservedly listed Grade I in the Register of Gardens. The house itself was innovative, when built between 1810 and 1817 in a style derived directly from Ancient Greece.

The thirty acres of magnificent landscaped grounds and gardens are Belsay's particular glory. The quarry gardens and the Cragwood Walk are the most special features. Sir Charles Monck, who built the present hall, saw their potential and introduced many rare and fine specimens into them to make a garden.

The south side of Belsay Hall

Succeeding generations extended the quarry and added to its planting. They made a green gorge, its sheer walls hung with exotic plants and the floor dotted with ferns. It is an adventure in itself to explore its paths and shady corners. Rhododendrons are among Belsay's great delights; many beautiful

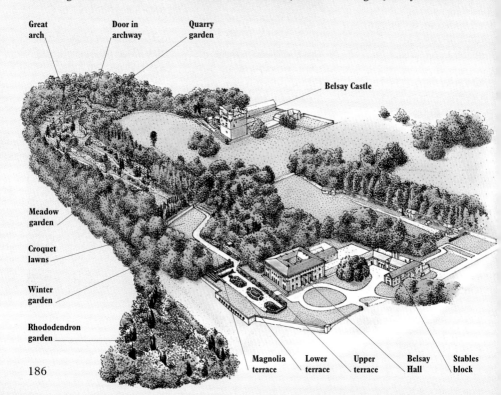

Great arch

Door in archway

Quarry garden

Belsay Castle

Meadow garden

Croquet lawns

Winter garden

Rhododendron garden

Magnolia terrace

Lower terrace

Upper terrace

Belsay Hall

Stables block

examples grow in the quarry, as well as in the woodland and rhododendron gardens created later in the 19th century. These wilder areas are separated from the more formal terraces at the front of the Hall, with their beds of roses, lilies, lavender and other fragrant and brightly coloured plants. English Heritage has made great efforts to return Belsay's gardens, which suffered from neglect after World War II, to their former state, to complement the great house.

Sir Charles Monck built the Hall to his own designs in 1810 after studying Greek architecture. Inside and out, Belsay Hall has a severity that is softened by its garden setting. It resembles a Greek temple, raised on a podium with giant columns at the entrance and pilasters on the walls.

The castle preceded the house. Originally built in the 14th century, with a new range attached in 1614, its L-shaped plan provided special protection to the entrance staircase and it was crowned with prominent defensive towers and battlements. The castle was abandoned in 1817 when the new Hall was built.

Belsay has much to offer: the splendour of the ancient castle, an important house in the Greek Revival of the 19th century, and the glorious gardens. Plants are on sale in summer.

The pure Greek Classicism of the present Hall

Open all year round.
🎬 *Catherine Cookson's* **The Cinderpath** *was filmed at Belsay.*
• *Come to the NCCPG Annual Plant Sale for unusual plants, 14 June.*
Open 1 April–1 Nov: daily, 10am–6pm (6pm/dusk in Oct). 2 Nov–31 March: daily, 10am–4pm (closed 24–26 Dec). *Entry* £3.60/£2.70/£1.80.
✆ *01661 881636*
🅿 ⊗ ♀♂ ⬇ ♿ *(grounds, tearoom and ground floor only; toilets)* ⬜ ⬜ Ⓔ 🛍 ¶ *('Belsay Hall Tearoom'; normally open summer only.)*
➲ *In Belsay, 14m NW of Newcastle on A696. (OS Map 88; ref NZ 088785.)*
Local Tourist Information: Morpeth (tel: 01670 511323).
🚌 *Tel: 01670 533128 or any National Express agent.*
🚆 *Morpeth 10m.*

The quarry garden in spring

Berwick Barracks:
Ravensdown (above)
and the exhibition
(right)

❶ Berwick-upon-Tweed Barracks

NORTHUMBERLAND
(p. 220, 19H)

Among the earliest purpose-built barracks, these have changed very little since 1717. The barracks house 'By Beat of Drum', an exhibition which re-creates scenes from the life of the British infantryman, the Museum of the King's Own Scottish Borderers, the Borough Museum with its imaginative exhibitions and part of the Burrell Collection.

Open all year round.
⚘ *Visit the Gymnasium Art Gallery.*
• *A lively exhibition, 'By Beat of Drum'.*
• *Imaginative and colourful display at Borough Museum.*
Open *1 April–1 Nov: daily, 10am–6pm (6pm/dusk in Oct). 2 Nov–31 March: Wed–Sun, 10am–4pm (closed 24–26 Dec). Closed 1–2pm in* winter. *(Museum of King's Own Scottish Borderers open Mon–Sat, 10am–4pm.)*
Entry *£2.50/£1.90/£1.30.*
✆ *01289 304493*
🚻 🅿 *(in town)* ♿ 🚌 🄴 ☐
➲ *On the Parade, off Church St, Berwick town centre. (OS Map 75; ref NT 994535.)*
🚌 *Tel: 01670 533128.*
🚉 *Berwick-upon-Tweed ¼m.*

❻ Berwick-upon-Tweed Castle

NORTHUMBERLAND
(p. 220, 19H)

Remains of 12th-century castle.

Open *Any reasonable time.*
Entry *Free.*
🐾
➲ *Adjacent to Berwick railway station, W of town centre, accessible also from river bank. (OS Map 75; ref NT 994535.)*
🚌 🚉 *see*
Berwick-upon-Tweed Barracks.

❺ Berwick-upon-Tweed Main Guard

NORTHUMBERLAND
(p. 220, 19H)

Georgian Guard House near the quay. 'The Story of a Border Garrison Town' is a permanent display of the history of the town and its fortifications.

Open *10–13 April, 2–4 May, 23–25 May, 1 June–30 Sept: daily, 1pm–5pm (closed Wed). (Site managed by Berwick Civic Society.)*
Entry *Free.*
♿
➲ *Surrounding Berwick town centre on N bank of River Tweed.*

Berwick Ramparts

(OS Map 75; ref NT 994535.)
🚌 🚉 *see* **Berwick-upon-Tweed Barracks**.

🆔 ○ Berwick-upon-Tweed Ramparts
NORTHUMBERLAND
(p. 220, 19H)

Remarkably complete, 16th-century town fortifications, with gateways and projecting bastions.

Open *Any reasonable time.*
Entry *Free.*
&. (🚻 & 🅿 *in town centre*) 🐕
➲ *Surrounding Berwick town centre on N bank of River Tweed.*
(OS Map 75; ref NT 994535.)
🚌 🚉 *see* **Berwick-upon-Tweed Barracks**.

🆔 Bessie Surtees House
TYNE & WEAR
(pp. 219/220, 16J)

Two 16th- and 17th-century merchants' houses. One is a remarkable and rare example of Jacobean domestic architecture. An exhibition about these buildings is on the first floor.

Open *Weekdays only 10am–4pm (closed Bank Holidays).*
Entry *Free.*
☎ *0191 261 1585*
🚻 ⊗
➲ *41–44 Sandhill, Newcastle.*
(OS Map 88; ref NZ 252639.)
🚌 *Tel: 0191 232 5325.*
🚉 *Newcastle ½m.*
Metro *Central Station ½m.*

Bessie Surtees House

🆔 Bishop Auckland Deer House
See Auckland Castle Deer House.

🆔🆔 Black Middens Bastle House
NORTHUMBERLAND
(p. 220, 17H)

A 16th-century two-storey defended farmhouse, set in splendid walking country.

Open *Any reasonable time.*
Entry *Free.*
🅿 ⅊ 🐕
➲ *200 yards N of minor road 7m NW of Bellingham; access also along minor road from A68.*
(OS Map 80; ref NY 774900.)

🆔🆔 Bowes Castle
COUNTY DURHAM
(p. 218, 15H)

Massive ruins of Henry II's tower keep, three storeys high and set within the earthworks of a Roman fort.

Open *Any reasonable time.*
Entry *Free.*
🐕
➲ *In Bowes Village just off A66, 4m W of Barnard Castle.*
(OS Map 92; ref NY 992135.)
🚌 *Tel: 0191 383 3337.*

⊕ Brinkburn Priory
NORTHUMBERLAND
(p. 220, 17J)

This late 12th-century church is a fine example of early Gothic architecture, almost perfectly preserved, and is set in a lovely spot beside the River Coquet.

Open *1 April–1 Nov: daily, 10am–6pm (6pm/dusk in Oct).*
Entry *£1.50/£1.10/80p.*
☎ *01665 570628*
🅿 ❂ ⅊ *(400 yards from* 🅿*)*
➲ *4½m SE of Rothbury off B6344.*
(OS Map 81; ref NZ 116984.)
🚌 *Tel: 01670 533128.*
🚉 *Acklington 10m.*

Brinkburn Priory

◉ Derwentcote Steel Furnace

COUNTY DURHAM
(pp. 218/220, 16J)

Built in the 18th century, the earliest and most complete steel-making furnace to have survived. Closed in the 1870s, it has now been restored and opened to the public.

Open *1 April–30 Sept: 1st & 3rd Sunday of every month, 1pm–5pm.*
Entry *Free.*
(*01207 562573*
🅿 ⊗
➲ *10m SW of Newcastle on A694 between Rowland's Gill and Hamsterley. (OS Map 88; ref NZ 131566.)* 🚌 *Tel: 0191 232 5325.* 🚃 *Blaydon 7m.*

◉◯ Dunstanburgh Castle

NORTHUMBERLAND
(p. 220, 18J)

An easy 1½-mile coastal walk leads to the eerie skeleton of this wonderful 14th-century castle, which is sited on a basalt crag more than 30 metres (100 feet) high. Dunstanburgh is noted for its seabirds, wildlife and flowers. The surviving ruins include the large gatehouse, which later became the keep, and curtain walls.

Open all year round.
Open *1 April–1 Nov: daily, 10am–6pm (6pm/dusk in*

Dunstanburgh Castle

Oct). 2 Nov–31 March: Wed–Sun, 10am–4pm (closed 24–26 Dec).
Entry *£1.70/£1.30/90p. National Trust members admitted free. (Property owned by the National Trust, maintained and managed by English Heritage.)*
(*01665 576231*
🍴 ⛵ 🅿 *(in Craster village – charge payable)*
➲ *8m NE of Alnwick, on foot-paths from Craster or Embleton. (OS Map 75; ref NU 258220.)* 🚌 *Tel: 01670 533128.* 🚃 *Chathill 7m, Alnmouth 8m.*

◉ Edlingham Castle

NORTHUMBERLAND
(p. 220, 18J)

Set in a beautiful valley, this complex ruin has defensive features spanning the 13th–15th centuries.

Open *Any reasonable time. (Site managed by the*

Parochial Church Council St John the Baptist, Edlingham with Bolton Castle.)
Entry *Free.*
⛵
➲ *At E end of Edlingham village, on minor road off B6341 6m SW of Alnwick (OS Map 81; ref NU 115092.)* 🚃 *Alnmouth 9m.*

⊕ Egglestone Abbey

COUNTY DURHAM
(pp. 218/220, 15J)

Picturesque remains of a 12th-century abbey. Substantial parts of the church and abbey buildings remain.

Open *Any reasonable time.*
Entry *Free.*
🅿 ♿ 🍴 ⛵
➲ *1m S of Barnard Castle on minor road off B6277. (OS Map 92; ref NZ 062151.)* 🚌 *Tel: 0345 124 125.*

⊕ Etal Castle

NORTHUMBERLAND
(p. 220, 19H)

A 14th-century border castle located in the picturesque village of Etal. There is a major award-winning exhibition about the castle, border warfare and the Battle of Flodden, which took place nearby in 1513.

A free personal stereo tour guides you through this dramatic exhibition.
Open *1 April–1 Nov: daily, 10am–6pm (6pm/dusk in Oct).*
Entry *£2.50/£1.90/£1.30.*
(01890 820332
P ♦♦♦ *(in village)* ∩ ☺ ♨
➲ *In Etal village, 10m SW of Berwick.*
(OS Map 75; ref NT 925394.)
▭▭▭ *Tel: 01670 533128.*
⇶ *Berwick-upon-Tweed 10½m.*

⊕ Finchale Priory

COUNTY DURHAM
(pp. 219/220, 16J)

These beautiful priory ruins, dating from the 13th century, are in a wooded setting beside the River Wear.

Open *1 April–30 Sept: daily, 12–5pm.*
Entry *£1.20/90p/60p.*
(0191 386 3828
P *(on south side of river, charge payable)* ⚘
➲ *3m NE of Durham, on minor road off A167.*
(OS Map 88; ref NZ 29471.)

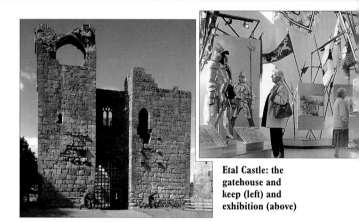

Etal Castle: the gatehouse and keep (left) and exhibition (above)

▭▭▭ *Tel: 0345 124 125.*
⇶ *Durham 5m.*

⊕ Gisborough Priory

REDCAR & CLEVELAND
(pp. 219/220, 15K)

An Augustinian priory. The remains also include the gatehouse and the east end of an early 14th-century church.

Open all year round.
Open *1 April–30 Oct: daily,*
9am–5pm. 1 Nov–31 March: Tues–Sun, 9am–5pm (closed 24 Dec–1 Jan). (Property managed by Langbaurgh Borough Council.)
Entry *80p/60p/40p.*
(01287 633801
♿ ♨ ♦♦♦ *(in town)* ⚘
➲ *In Guisborough town, next to parish church.*
(OS Map 94; ref NZ 618163.)
▭▭▭ *Tel: 0345 124 125.*
⇶ *Marske 4½m.*

Finchale Priory

LINDISFARNE PRIORY

✚ ♡ NORTHUMBERLAND (p. 220, 19J)

One of the holiest sites of Anglo-Saxon England, Lindisfarne was renowned as the original burial place of St Cuthbert, and for being founded by St Aidan, who came from Iona, the centre of Christianity in Scotland.

The island of Lindisfarne, with its wealthy monastery, was easy prey for Viking raiders from the end of the 8th century. Only in the 12th century did monks from Durham, Cuthbert's final resting place, re-establish a religious house on Lindisfarne, now usually known as Holy Island. The priory was a victim of the dissolution of the monasteries in 1537 and seems to have been disused by the early 18th century.

Lindisfarne, with its ancient associations, is still a holy site and place of pilgrimage. Today, going to visit Lindisfarne requires prior knowledge of the tide tables (see ➊ opposite). At high tide the causeway linking Holy Island to the Northumberland coast is submerged under water and the island is cut off from the mainland.

St Aidan founded Lindisfarne in 635. Austerity was the watchword of the community – a few monks and a simple wooden church. It was, however, to become a shrine when the corpse of the former bishop St Cuthbert was dug up 11 years after his burial in 698 and found undecayed. Cuthbert was an

The priory ruins with Lindisfarne Castle in the distance

A modern sculpture of St Aidan, founder of Lindisfarne (below)

exceedingly holy man who earlier withdrew to be a hermit on the lonely Farne Islands and later returned there to die. His relics survive in Durham Cathedral, taken there after the monks fled the plundering Vikings at the end of the 8th century. Lindisfarne

Grave-marker (c. 900) with a procession of armed soldiers

The priory's 'Rainbow Arch'

was a treasure house of jewels and manuscripts, including incomparable illuminated Gospels (now in the British Library).

A modern version of Lindisfarne's Madonna and Child

Today, in the award-winning museum, Anglo-Saxon carvings are displayed in a lively, atmospheric exhibition. The dramatic ruins of the medieval priory express its lasting power and beauty.

Open all year round.
📹 Oliver's Travels, starring Alan Bates, was filmed at Lindisfarne.
• Free Children's Activity Sheet available.
Open 1 April–1 Nov: daily, 10am–6pm (6pm/dusk in Oct). 2 Nov–31 March: daily, 10am–4pm (closed 24–26 Dec). Entry £2.70/£2.00/£1.40.
✆ 01289 389200
🗋 👬 🐕 🗋 🚾
➲ On Holy Island, only reached at low tide across

causeway (tide tables at each end or details from Berwick Tourist Information Centre).
(OS Map 75; ref NU 126418.)
Local Tourist Information:
Berwick-upon-Tweed (tel: 01289 330733).
🚌 *Tel: 01670 533128.*
🚌 *Berwick-upon-Tweed 14m via causeway.*

Lindisfarne Museum

⊘ Hadrian's Wall

(pp. 176–77)

See pp. 176–83 for details on sites along Hadrian's Wall.

⊘ Hylton Castle

TYNE & WEAR

(pp. 219/220, 16J)

A 15th-century keep-gatehouse, with a fine display of medieval heraldry adorning the facades.

Open *Any reasonable time (access to grounds only). (Property managed by Sunderland City Council.)*
Entry *Free.*
🅿 ♿ *(grounds only)* ❧
➲ *3¾m W of Sunderland. (OS Map 88; ref NZ 358588.)*
🚃 *Tel: 0191 232 5325.*
🚌 *Seaburn 2½m.*

⊕ ♡ Lindisfarne Priory

NORTHUMBERLAND

(p. 220, 19J)

See pp. 192–93 for full details.

Norham Castle

⊕ ⊘ Norham Castle

NORTHUMBERLAND

(p. 220, 19H)

Set on a promontory in a curve of the River Tweed, this was one of the strongest of the border castles, built *c.*1160.

⊙ *Free audio tour.*
Open *1 April–1 Nov: daily, 10am–6pm (6pm/dusk in Oct).*
Entry *£1.70/£1.30/90p.*
☎ *01289 382329*
❧ ♿ *(excluding keep)* 🎧 🛍 🖨
➲ *Norham village, 6½m SW of*

Berwick-upon-Tweed on minor road off B6470 (from A698). (OS Map 75; ref NT 907476.)
🚃 *Tel: 01670 533128.*
🚌 *Berwick-upon-Tweed 7½m.*

⊙ Prudhoe Castle

NORTHUMBERLAND

(pp. 218/220, 16J)

Set on a wooded hillside overlooking the River Tyne are the extensive remains of a 12th-century castle, with gatehouse, curtain wall and keep. There is a small exhibition and video presentation.

• *Picnic spot.*
• *Brass rubbing.*
Open *1 April–1 Nov: daily, 10am–6pm (6pm/dusk in Oct).*
Entry *£1.70/£1.30/90p.*
☎ *01661 833459*
🅿 🚻 ⊙ 🛍 🄴 🖨
➲ *In Prudhoe, on minor road off A695. (OS Map 88; ref NZ 092634.)*
🚃 *Tel: 01670 533128.*
🚌 *Prudhoe ¼m.*

Prudhoe Castle

✠ St Paul's Monastery and Bede's World Museum

Jarrow, TYNE & WEAR
(p. 220, 16J)

The home of the Venerable Bede, partly surviving as the chancel of the parish church. The monastery has become one of the best-understood Anglo-Saxon monastic sites. The museum tells the story of St Paul's Monastery and displays excavated finds. There is an Anglo-Saxon landscape with fields, crops, animals and timber buildings on land next to the museum. Phase One of the new museum building is now open.

Open all year round.
Open *Monastery ruins, any reasonable time. Museum, 1 April–31 Oct: Tues–Sat and Bank Holidays, 10am–5.30pm. Sun, 2.30–5.30pm (opens 12pm May–Sept); 1 Nov–31 March: Tues–Sat 10am–4.30pm, Sun 1.30–4.30pm (for Christmas*

and New Year, ring for details). (Property managed by Jarrow 700AD Ltd.)
Entry *£3.00/£1.50/£1.50, family ticket £7.20. Free to monastery ruins.*
☎ **0191 489 2106**
♿ ⅋ ♟ & ▢ ✉ ☯ *(only guide dogs allowed in museum)* Ⓜ
➲ *In Jarrow, on minor road N of A185.*
(OS Map 88; ref NZ 339652.)
🚌 *Tel: 0191 460 5144.*
🚆 *Brockley Whins 2½m.*
Metro *Bede ¼m, Jarrow ¼m.*

✠ Tynemouth Priory and Castle

TYNE & WEAR (p. 220, 17J)

The castle walls and gatehouse enclose the substantial remains of a Benedictine priory founded *c.*1090 on a Saxon monastic site.

Open all year round.
🎬 **The History Detective** *was filmed here.*
• ***Explore underground chambers beneath the World War I gun batteries.***

• ***Witness the fury of the Norsemen – Living History and ferocious military action, 24–25 May.***
Open *1 April–1 Nov: daily, 10am–6pm (6pm/dusk in Oct). 2 Nov–31 March: Wed–Sun, 10am–4pm (closed 24–26 Dec). Closed 1–2pm in winter. Gun battery April–Sept: Sat–Sun and Bank Holidays 10am–6pm.*
Entry *£1.70/£1.30/90p.*
☎ **0191 257 1090**
▢ ♟ *(nearby; local council)*
♿ *(priory)* ✉ 🐾
➲ *In Tynemouth, near North Pier.*
(OS Map 88; ref NZ 374695.)
🚌 *Tel: 0191 232 5325.*
Metro *Tynemouth ½m.*

♡ ☯ ⊕ Warkworth Castle and Hermitage

NORTHUMBERLAND
(p. 220, 18J)
See pp. 196–97 for full details.

Tynemouth Castle Barbican (below) and Priory (bottom)

WARKWORTH CASTLE AND HERMITAGE

○ ✖ Ⓜ NORTHUMBERLAND (p. 220, 18J)

The magnificent eight-towered keep of Warkworth Castle stands on its hill above the River Coquet, dominating all around it. A large and complex stronghold, it was home to the Percy family who at times wielded more power in the North than the King himself. Most famous of them all was

The keep from the south

Harry Hotspur (Sir Henry Percy), immortalized in Northumbrian ballads and Shakespeare's *Henry IV*, several scenes of which were set at Warkworth. He dominated the Borders in the 15th century with his father, the Earl of Northumberland, and fought off the Scots on behalf of the King before being instrumental in the removal of Richard II from the throne.

As headquarters and home to the region's most powerful family, Warkworth needed to be an impressive castle and it remains so to this day.

Warkworth is one of the most outstanding examples of an aristocratic fortified residence. It was not only a mighty defence against the sieges and attacks prevalent in medieval England but also the home of the most powerful family in the vicinity, the Percys. Along with their castle at Alnwick, some eight miles away, Warkworth allowed them to influence the entire region. As the largest landowners in an area far from London, local society revolved around the Percy family and Warkworth was a regional court quite as much as it was a military stronghold.

The huge defences that make up the original castle

were begun in the 12th century, when the area was regained from the Scots. But it was the granting of the castle to the Percy family in the early

A medieval dance re-enacted

The Lion Tower and the remains of the Great Hall

Aerial view of the castle complex

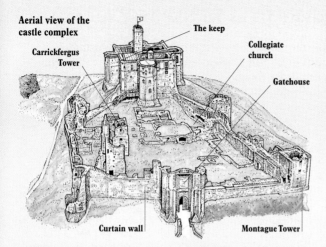

Carrickfergus Tower

The keep

Collegiate church

Gatehouse

Curtain wall

Montague Tower

Open all year round.
⚒ *New shop for 1998.*
🎬 **Elizabeth I,** *starring Geoffrey Rush, shot here.*
• *Many chambers, passageways and dark staircases to explore.*
• *Free Children's Activity Sheet available.*
Open Castle: 1 April–1 Nov: daily, 10am–6pm (6pm/dusk in Oct). 2 Nov–31 March: daily, 10am–4pm (closed 24–26 Dec). Closed 1–2pm in winter. Hermitage: 1 April–30 Sept: Wed, Sun & Bank Holidays, 11am–5pm.
Entry Castle £2.70/£2.00/£1.40. Hermitage £1.50/£1.10/80p.
☎ **01665 711423**
🚻 🅿 *(at castle)* 🐕 ♿ *(castle, excluding keep)* 🕐 🛍
➲ *In Warkworth, 7½m S of Alnwick on A1068. (OS Map 81; Castle ref NU 247057, Hermitage ref NU 242060.)*
Local Tourist Information: *Alnwick (tel: 01665 510665).*
🚌 *Tel: 01670 533128.*
🚉 *Alnmouth 3½m.*

14th century that ensured its stature. Their power built a castle strong enough to withstand the mightiest enemy, protected by a huge curtain wall surmounted with towers at each corner which dominate the

The entrance hall in the keep

surrounding countryside to this day. Like many castles it was built piece by piece and adapted as time and money permitted. The curtain wall with its gatehouse enclosed the outer bailey and included

the living quarters for the garrison as well as for the Percys and their retinue.

The great keep was added in the late 14th century, and this more than anything indicates the family's power. It was in effect a second castle, built to a single plan, as the new residence for a family who could justify their permanence and importance in the locality. Today you can still get lost in its maze of passages and rooms.

The Hermitage is cut into the rock of the river cliff, hidden away underneath the wooded bank, a short walk upstream from the castle. It remains very much as a 14th-century recluse would remember it. Visit by taking a short ferry trip across the river after the walk from the village.

Steps leading to the Hermitage

OTHER HISTORIC SITES TO SEE IN ENGLAND

As well as giving you free entry to our own properties, becoming a member of English Heritage allows you to enjoy half- or reduced-price admission to numerous other historic attractions across the country, including the Weald and Downland Museum, Pendle Heritage Centre and the six historic attractions in the care of Sussex Past. These benefits are only available to members of English Heritage.

More information about sites and prices is available from the relevant organization.

 Sussex Past,
Bull House,
92 High Street,
Lewes, East Sussex,
BN7 1XH.
Tel: 01273 486260.
English Heritage members receive 50% off full adult & child tickets.

Anne of Cleves House Museum

LEWES (p. 211, 3M)
Picturesque timber-framed house with wide-ranging collections of Sussex interest and a small, formal garden.
Open 25 Mar–8 Nov: daily, 10am–5.30pm (Sun, opens 12pm). 9 Nov–24 Mar: Tues, Thur & Sat, 10am–5.30pm.
Entry £2.20/£1.10, joint ticket with Lewes Castle: £4.50/£2.50.
(01273 474610. ♦♦♦ 🗋 🗌 ⓦ ⊗
➥ *In Southover High Street, Lewes, off A27.*
(OS Map 198; ref TQ 412097.)

Lewes Castle

Fishbourne Roman Palace

CHICHESTER (p. 210, 3L)
The remains of the largest Roman residence yet discovered north of the Alps, featuring some of the finest mosaics in northern Europe.
Open 8 Feb–13 Dec: daily, 10am–5pm (6pm in Aug, 4pm in Feb, Nov & Dec). 14 Dec–7 Feb: Sunday only, 10am–4pm.
Entry £4.00/£2.20.
(01243 785859.
🅿 ♿ ♦♦♦ 🗋 🗌 E ⓦ ¶◄ ⊗
➥ *In Fishbourne village, 1½m W of Chichester, off A27/A259.*
(OS Map 197; ref SZ 839048.)

Lewes Castle

LEWES (p. 211, 4M)
Splendid Norman castle with superb views across Sussex. The adjacent Barbican House is home to the Museum of Sussex Archaeology.
Open All year: Mon–Sat, 10am–5.30pm, Sun & Bank Holidays, 11am–5.30pm.
(Closed 25–26 Dec.)
Entry £3.40/£1.80, joint ticket with Anne of Cleves House: £4.50/£2.50.
(01273 486290.
♦♦♦ 🗋 🗌 ⌂ E ⓦ ⊗
➥ *In Lewes town centre, off A27, A26 and A275.*
(OS Map 198; ref TQ 413102.)

Marlipins Museum

SHOREHAM (p. 210, 3M)
Dedicated to the history of Shoreham, with its long

maritime tradition, the building dates back to Norman times.
Open 1 May–30 Sept: Tues–Sat, 10am–4.30pm (closed 1–2pm), Sun, 2pm–4.30pm.
Entry £1.50/75p.
(01273 462994. 🗋 🗌 ⊗
➥ *In town centre of Shoreham-by-Sea on A259 and off A27.*
(OS Map 198; ref TQ 214051.)

Michelham Priory

HAILSHAM (p. 211, 3N)
A moated Elizabethan country house among spacious gardens. The house incorporates parts of the medieval priory.
Open 15 March–31 July: Wed–Sun, 10.30am–5pm (11am–4pm in March). 1–31 Aug: daily, 10.30am–5.30pm. 1 Sep–31 Oct: Wed–Sun, 10.30am–5pm (11am–4pm in Oct).
Entry £4.00/£2.20.
(01323 844224.
🅿 ♿ ♦♦♦ 🗋 🗌 E ⓦ ¶◄ ⊗
➥ *Nr Hailsham, off A22/A27.*
(OS Map 198; ref TQ 558093.)

Priest House

WEST HOATHLY (p. 211, 4M)
A 15th-century timber-framed house, containing a fine collection of 17th- and 18th-century furniture.
Open 1 Mar–31 Oct: daily, 11am–5.30pm (Sun, opens 2pm).
Entry £2.20/£1.10.
(01342 810479. 🗋 🗌 ⓦ ⊗
➥ *West Hoathly, 4 miles W of Wych Cross off A22.*
(OS Map 187; ref TQ 810479.)

Weald & Downland Open Air Museum

Singleton, Chichester,
West Sussex, PO18 0EU.
Tel: 01243 811348.
WEST SUSSEX (p. 210, 4L)
A museum of historic buildings rescued from destruction and re-built on a beautiful 40-acre site in the South Downs.
🅿 ♟ ⛵ 🏹 ♿ *(limited facilities)*
🏠 🍽 🎁 🅴 ⓦ 🍴
➲ *In Singleton, 6 miles N of Chichester off A286.*
(OS map 197, ref SU 875128.)

Flag Fen Excavations

Fourth Drove,
Fengate, Peterborough,
PE1 5UR.
Tel: 01733 313414.
CAMBRIDGESHIRE (p. 214, 9M)
One of Europe's most important ongoing archaeological sites. The Bronze Age museum contains the earliest wheel in England. See also 3,000-year-old timbers, a re-created fen landscape and primitive breeds of pig and sheep.
⚘ *Award-winning exhibition and Bronze Age farm.*
Open *All year: daily, 10am–5pm (last entry 4pm). Closed 25–26 Dec.*

Jorvik Viking Centre

Registered charity 295116.
ⓦ ♟ ♿ *(toilets)* ⊗ 🏠 🍴 🎁 ▬ 🅿
➲ *Signposted from A47 and A1139, 2m from Peterborough city centre.*

 ## Pendle Heritage Centre

Park Hill,
Barrowford, Nelson,
Lancashire, BB9 6JQ.
Tel. 01282 695366.
LANCASHIRE (p. 218, 13H)
A group of historic farm buildings, with walled garden. Displays about the Pendle area.
Open *All year: daily, 10am–5pm.*
Entry *£2.75/£1.50 (50% discount to English Heritage members).*
♟ ♿ *(toilets)* 🅿 🎁 ⓦ 🍴 ⊗ ▬
➲ *In Barrowford at junction of A682 and B6247.*

 ## Jorvik Viking Centre

Coppergate,
York, YO1 1NT.
Tel: 01904 643211.
YORK (p. 219, 13K)
The famous time-car journey back 1,000 years to a bustling street in Jorvik – Viking-age York – reconstructed on the site of extensive excavations in the heart of the city.
Open *1 April–31 Oct: daily, 9am–5.30pm (last admission). 1 Nov–31 March: daily, 9am–3.30pm (last admission).*
Entry *10% discount to English Heritage members. Discount not applicable on Timed, Family or PASTport tickets or any other promotions. Jorvik Viking Centre is a project of the York Archaeological Trust, registered charity 509060.*
⚘ ♟ ♿ *(toilets)* 🏠 🎧 🎁 ⓦ ⊗
♩ *Information Hotline 01904 653000.*
➲ *In Coppergate, York city centre.*

 ## The Archaeological Resource Centre (ARC)

St Saviour's Church,
St Saviourgate, York,
YO1 2NN.
Tel: 01904 654324.
YORK (p. 219, 13K)
Visit the ARC and touch the past – award-winning hands-on archaeology for all ages.
Open *All year: Mon–Fri, 10am–4pm, Sat, 1–4pm (last admission 3.30pm). Closed Suns and last 2 weeks of December.*
Entry *25% discount for English Heritage members. Discount not applicable on Family or PASTport tickets or any other promotions. The ARC is a project of the York Archaeological Trust, registered charity 509060.*
⚘ ♟ ♿ *(toilets provided)* ⊗ 🎁 ⓦ
♩ *Information Hotline 01904 653000.*

 ## Merchant Adventurers' Hall

Fossgate, York, YO1 2XD.
Tel: 01904 654818.
YORK (p. 219, 13K)
Finest remaining guild hall in Europe today, little altered since its 14th-century origin. It houses furniture, paintings, archives, silver and other objects used by the merchants of York.
Open *14 Mar–14 Nov: daily, 8.30am–5pm. 15 Nov–13 Mar: Mon–Sat, 8.30am–3.30pm (closed 24 Dec–2 Jan).*
Entry *£1.90/£1.60/60p.*
♟ ⓦ 🏹 🎁 🍴
➲ *In York, from Piccadilly near Clifford's Tower. (OS map 105, ref SE 605517.)*

FREE OR HALF-PRICE ADMISSION TO HISTORIC SITES THROUGHOUT BRITAIN

English Heritage members planning to spend some time across England's borders will benefit from our long-standing arrangement with our sister organizations in Scotland, Wales and the Isle of Man. Entry to these properties, totalling over 100 sites, is half-price in the first year of membership and free in the following years. These benefits are only available to members of English Heritage.

For further information about these sites, please contact our sister organizations:

Historic Scotland,
Longmore House,
Salisbury Place,
Edinburgh EH9 1SH.
Tel: 0131 668 8800.

Aberdour Castle
FIFE (p. 221, 20F)
A 14th-century castle, with splendid residential accommodation and a terraced garden.
☏ *01383 860519.*
➲ *In Aberdour.*

Arbroath Abbey
ANGUS (p. 221, 21G)
Founded by William the Lion in 1178, this was the scene of the Declaration of Arbroath of 1320, which asserted Scotland's independence from England.
☏ *01241 878756.*
➲ *In Arbroath.*

Balvenie Castle
GRAMPIAN (p. 221, 24G)
A castle of enclosure first owned by the Comyns with a 13th-century curtain wall.
☏ *01340 820121.*
➲ *At Dufftown.*

Bishop's and Earl's Palaces
ORKNEY (p. 221, 29G)
The Bishop's palace is a 12th-century hall-house, later much altered, with a round tower begun by Bishop Reid in

Black House

1541. A later addition was made by the notorious Patrick Stewart, Earl of Orkney, who built the adjacent Earl's Palace between 1600 and 1607 in a splendid Renaissance style.
☏ *01856 875461.*
➲ *In Kirkwall.*

Black House
Arnol, WESTERN ISLES
(p. 221, 27A)
A traditional Isle of Lewis thatched house, complete and furnished.
☏ *01851 710395.*
➲ *In Arnol village, Lewis.*

Blackness Castle
CENTRAL (p. 221, 20F)
Built in the 1440s, Blackness was an ammunition depot in the 1870s.

☏ *01506 834807.*
➲ *4m N of Linlithgow, on a promontory in the Forth estuary.*

Bonawe Iron Furnace
ARGYLL (p. 221, 21C)
Founded in 1753, this is the most complete charcoal-fuelled ironworks in Britain.
☏ *01866 822432.*
➲ *Close to the village of Taynuilt.*

Bothwell Castle
GREATER GLASGOW (p. 221, 19E)
The largest and finest 13th-century stone castle in Scotland.
☏ *01698 816894.*
➲ *In Bothwell, approached from Uddingston, off the B7071.*

Broch of Gurness
ORKNEY (p. 221, 30G)
Protected by three lines of ditch and rampart, the base of the broch is surrounded by a warren of Iron Age buildings.
☏ *01831 579478.*
➲ *At Aikerness, about 14m NW of Kirkwall.*

Caerlaverock Castle
DUMFRIES & GALLOWAY (p. 221, 17F)
One of the finest castles in Scotland, on a triangular site surrounded by moats.
☏ *01387 770244.*
➲ *8m SE of Dumfries.*

Cardoness Castle
DUMFRIES & GALLOWAY
(p. 221, 16D)
The well-preserved ruin of a
15th-century tower house.
(01557 814427.
➲ *1m SW of Gatehouse of Fleet.*

Castle Campbell
CENTRAL (p. 221, 20E)
The 'Castle of Gloom', the
oldest part is a well-preserved
15th-century tower.
(01259 742408.
➲ *At the head of Dollar Glen.*

Corgarff Castle
GRAMPIAN (p. 221, 23F)
A 16th-century tower house
converted into a barracks for
Hanoverian troops in 1748.
(01975 651460.
➲ *8m W of Strathdon village.*

Craigmillar Castle
EDINBURGH & LOTHIANS
(p. 221, 19F)
Expanded in the 15th and
16th centuries, this is a handsome ruin, and includes a
range of private rooms.
(0131 661 4445.
➲ *2½m SE of central Edinburgh,
E of Edinburgh–Dalkeith road.*

Craignethan Castle
GREATER GLASGOW
(p. 221, 19E)
The oldest part is a tower
house built by Sir James

Hamilton of Finnart in the
16th century.
(01555 860364.
➲ *5½m NW of Lanark.*

Crichton Castle
EDINBURGH & LOTHIANS
(p. 221, 19G)
A large and sophisticated
castle with a spectacular
range erected by the Earl of
Bothwell in 1581–91.
(01875 320017.
➲ *2½m SW of Pathhead.*

Crossraguel Abbey
GREATER GLASGOW
(p. 221, 18D)
13th-century remains, which
are remarkably complete and
of high quality.
(01655 883113.
➲ *2m S of Maybole.*

Dallas Dhu Distillery and Visitor Centre
GRAMPIAN (p. 220, 25F)
A perfectly preserved time
capsule of the distiller's art.
(01309 676548.
➲ *About 1m S of Forres off the
Grantown Road.*

Dirleton Castle and Gardens
EDINBURGH & LOTHIANS
(p. 221, 20G)
The oldest part of this
romantic castle dates from
the 13th century.

Caerlaverock Castle

(01620 850330.
➲ *In the village of Dirleton.*

Doune Castle
FIFE & CENTRAL (p. 221, 20E)
A late 14th-century courtyard
castle built for the Regent
Albany.
(01786 841742.
➲ *In Doune.*

Dryburgh Abbey
BORDERS (p. 221, 18G)
Both beautifully situated and
of intrinsic quality, the Abbey
ruins are remarkably complete.
(01835 822381.
➲ *5m SE of Melrose, near
St Boswells.*

Dumbarton Castle
GREATER GLASGOW
(p. 221, 20D)
Spectacularly sited on a vol-
canic rock, this was the site of
the ancient capital of Strathclyde.
(01389 732167.
➲ *At Dumbarton.*

Dundonald Castle
GREATER GLASGOW
(p. 221, 18D)
A fine 13th-century tower
built by Robert II as a summer
residence until his death.
(01563 850201.
➲ *In Dundonald, off the A759.*

Dirleton Castle and gardens

201

Dundrennan Abbey

DUMFRIES & GALLOWAY
(p. 221, 16E)
The beautiful ruins of a
Cistercian abbey founded
by David I.
☎ *01557 500262.*
➲ *6½m SE of Kirkcudbright.*

Dunfermline Abbey and Palace

FIFE (p. 221, 20F)
The remains of a Benedictine
abbey which was founded
by Queen Margaret in the
11th century.
☎ *01383 739026.*
➲ *In Dunfermline.*

Dunstaffnage Castle and Chapel

ARGYLL (p. 221, 21B)
A very fine 13th-century castle enclosure, built on a rock.
☎ *01631 562465.*
➲ *By Loch Etive, 3½m from Oban.*

Edinburgh Castle

EDINBURGH & LOTHIANS
(p. 221, 20F)
The most famous of
Scottish castles has a
complex history. The castle
houses the crown jewels
(Honours) of Scotland.
☎ *0131 225 9846.*
➲ *In the centre of Edinburgh.*

Fort George (above and right)

Edzell Castle and Garden

ANGUS (p. 221, 22G)
Very beautiful complex with a
late-medieval tower house
incorporated into a 16th-
century courtyard mansion.
☎ *01356 648631.*
➲ *At Edzell, 6m N of Brechin.*

Elgin Cathedral

GRAMPIAN (p. 221, 25F)
The superb ruin of what
many think was Scotland's
most beautiful cathedral.
☎ *01343 547171.* ➲ *In Elgin.*

Fort George

HIGHLANDS (p. 221, 25E)
A vast site and one of the
most outstanding artillery
fortifications in Europe.
☎ *01667 462777.*

➲ *11m NE of Inverness, by the village of Ardersier.*

Glenluce Abbey

DUMFRIES & GALLOWAY
(p. 221, 16C)
The remains include a
handsome early 16th-
century chapter house.
☎ *01581 300541.*
➲ *2m NW of Glenluce village.*

Hermitage Castle

BORDERS (p. 221, 17G)
A vast and eerie ruin. Mary
Queen of Scots made her
famous ride here to meet
the Earl of Bothwell.
☎ *013873 76222.*
➲ *In Liddesdale, 5½m NE of Newcastleton, off the B6399.*

Huntingtower Castle

PERTHSHIRE (p. 221, 21F)
Two fine and complete
towers, of the 15th and
16th centuries, now linked
by a 17th-century range.
☎ *01738 627231.*
➲ *3m NW of Perth.*

Edinburgh Castle

Huntly Castle

GRAMPIAN (p. 221, 24G)
A magnificent ruin consisting mainly of a palace block erected by the Gordon family.
☎ *01466 793191.*
➲ *In Huntly.*

Inchcolm Abbey

FIFE (p. 221, 20F)
The best-preserved group of monastic buildings in Scotland.
☎ *0131 331 4857.*
➲ *On an island on the Firth of Forth, opposite Aberdour. Ferries from South Queensferry and North Queensferry.*

Inchmahome Priory

CENTRAL (p. 221, 20D)
A beautifully situated Augustinian monastery founded in 1238.
☎ *01877 385294.*
➲ *On an island in the Lake of Menteith, approached by boat from Port of Menteith.*

Jarlshof Prehistoric and Norse Settlement

SHETLAND (p. 221, INSET)
A complex of ancient settlements. The oldest is a Bronze Age village. There is an Iron Age broch and an entire Viking settlement.
☎ *01950 460112.*
➲ *At Sumburgh Head, about 22m S of Lerwick.*

Jedburgh Abbey and Visitor Centre

BORDERS (p. 221, 18G)
The church is mostly in Romanesque and early Gothic styles and is remarkably complete.
☎ *01835 863925.* ➲ *In Jedburgh.*

Kildrummy Castle

GRAMPIAN (p. 221, 24G)
The best example in Scotland of a 13th-century castle, with a curtain wall, four round towers, hall and chapel.
☎ *01975 571331.*
➲ *10m W of Alford.*

Kinnaird Head Lighthouse

GRAMPIAN (p. 221, 25H)
Kinnaird Head was the first lighthouse built by the Northern Lighthouse Company.
☎ *01346 511022.*
➲ *On a promontory in Fraserburgh.*

Linlithgow Palace

EDINBURGH & LOTHIANS (p. 221, 20E)
Magnificent ruin of a great royal palace, set in its own park.
☎ *01506 842896.*
➲ *In Linlithgow.*

Lochleven Castle

PERTHSHIRE (p. 221, 21F)
Mary Queen of Scots was imprisoned here in 1567 and escaped in 1568.
☎ *01786 450000.*
➲ *On an island in Loch Leven, accessible by boat from Kinross.*

MacLellan's Castle

DUMFRIES & GALLOWAY (p. 221, 16E)
A castellated town house built by the then provost of Kirkcudbright.

Jedburgh Abbey

Kinnaird Head Lighthouse

☎ *01557 331856.*
➲ *In the centre of Kirkcudbright.*

Maes Howe Chambered Cairn

ORKNEY (p. 221, 29G)
The finest megalithic tomb in the British Isles, broken into during Viking times, with Viking runes carved on the walls.
☎ *01856 761606.*
➲ *About 9m W of Kirkwall.*

Meigle Sculptured Stone Museum

ANGUS (p. 221, 22F)
A magnificent collection of 25 sculptured monuments of the Celtic Christian period.
☎ *01828 640612.*
➲ *In Meigle.*

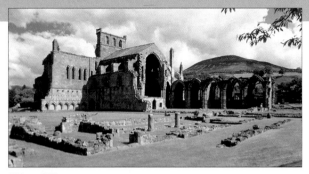

Melrose Abbey

Melrose Abbey

BORDERS (p. 221, 19G)
Probably the most famous
ruin in Scotland. The
surviving remains of the
church are of an elegance
unique in Scotland.
☎ *01896 822562.*
➲ *In Melrose.*

New Abbey Corn Mill

DUMFRIES & GALLOWAY
(p. 221, 17E)
A carefully renovated water-
powered oatmeal mill, in
working order.
☎ *01387 850260.*
➲ *In New Abbey village.*

Newark Castle

GREATER GLASGOW
(p. 221, 20D)
The oldest part of the castle is
a tower built soon after 1478.
☎ *01475 741858.*
➲ *In Port Glasgow.*

St Andrews Cathedral

Rothesay Castle

BUTE (p. 221, 20C)
A favourite residence of the
Stewart kings.
☎ *01700 502691.*
➲ *In Rothesay, Isle of Bute.*

St Andrews Castle and Visitor Centre

FIFE (p. 220, 21G)
Features include a 'bottle
dungeon', and mine and
counter-mine tunnelled
during the siege that followed
the murder of Cardinal
Beaton in 1546.
☎ *01334 477196.*
➲ *In St Andrews.*

St Andrews Cathedral

FIFE (p. 221, 21G)
Remains of the largest
cathedral in Scotland.
☎ *01334 472563.*
➲ *In St Andrews.*

Seton Collegiate Church

EDINBURGH & LOTHIANS
(p. 221, 20G)
The chancel and apse of this
lovely building date from the
15th century.
☎ *01875 813334.*
➲ *1m SE of Cockenzie
off Edinburgh–North
Berwick road.*

Skara Brae Prehistoric Village

ORKNEY (p. 221, 29F)
The best-preserved group

of Stone Age houses in
Western Europe.
☎ *01856 841815.*
➲ *19m NW of Kirkwall.*

Smailholm Tower

BORDERS (p. 221, 19G)
It houses costume figures
and tapestries relating to Sir
Walter Scott's 'Minstrelsy of
the Scottish Borders'.
☎ *01573 460365.*
➲ *Near Smailholm village,
6m W of Kelso.*

Spynie Palace

GRAMPIAN (p. 221, 25F)
Residence of the Bishops of
Moray from the 14th century
to 1686.
☎ *01343 546358.*
➲ *2m N of Elgin, off the A941.*

Stirling Castle

CENTRAL (p. 221, 20E)
The grandest of all Scottish
castles. The Great Hall of
James IV, the marvellous
Palace of James V, the
Chapel Royal remodelled
by James VI, are all of
outstanding interest.
☎ *01786 450000.*
➲ *In Stirling.*

Sweetheart Abbey

DUMFRIES & GALLOWAY
(p. 221, 17E)
Splendid ruin of a late
13th- and early 14th-century
Cistercian abbey.
☎ *01387 850397.*
➲ *In New Abbey village, 7m
S of Dumfries.*

Tantallon Castle

EDINBURGH & LOTHIANS
(p. 221, 20G)
Remarkable fortification
with a massive 14th-century
curtain wall with towers.
☎ *01620 892727.*
➲ *3m E of North Berwick.*

Urquhart Castle

Threave Castle

DUMFRIES & GALLOWAY
(p. 221, 17E)
Massive tower built in the late
14th century. Round its base
is an artillery fortification built
before 1455.
(*0831 168512.*
➲ *3m W of Castle Douglas.*

Tolquhon Castle

GRAMPIAN (p. 221, 24H)
Built for the Forbes family,
it is noted for its highly
ornamented gatehouse.
(*01651 851286.*
➲ *15m from Aberdeen off
the Pitmedden–Tarves road.*

Urquhart Castle

HIGHLANDS (p. 221, 24D)
Standing above Loch Ness,
this was one of the largest
castles in Scotland.
(*01456 450551.*
➲ *On Loch Ness, near
Drumnadrochit.*

Whithorn Priory and Museum

DUMFRIES & GALLOWAY
(p. 221, 16D)
Site of the first Christian
church in Scotland, founded
as 'Candida Casa' by St
Ninian in the early 5th
century.
(*01988 500508.*
➲ *In Whithorn.*

 Cadw:
Welsh Historic
Monuments,
Crown Building,
Cathays Park, Cardiff,
CF1 3NQ.
Tel: 01222 500200.

Beaumaris Castle

ANGLESEY (p. 216, 11D)
A partly restored moat
surrounds the formidable but
unfinished defences of the last
Edwardian castle in Wales.
(*01248 810361.*
➲ *In Beaumaris, off A545.*
*(OS Map 114; ref
SH 607762.)*

Blaenavon Ironworks

TORFAEN (pp. 213/217, 6F)
Substantial remains of five
early blast furnaces and
associated workers' housing,
dating in part from 1788–89.
➲ *6m N of Pontypool,
off A4043.*
(OS Map 161; ref SO 249092.)

Caerleon Roman Fortress

NEWPORT (pp. 213/217, 6F)
Impressive remains of the
Fortress Baths, amphitheatre,
barracks and fortress wall
dating from *c.* AD75.
(*01633 422518.*
➲ *B4596 to Caerleon, from M4.*
(OS Map 171; ref ST 337906.)

Caernarfon Castle

GWYNEDD (p. 216, 11D)
An immense fortress intended
by Edward I to be his seat of
government in north Wales.
(*01286 677617.*
➲ *In Caernarfon town centre.*
(OS Map 115; ref SH 477626.)

Caerphilly Castle

CAERPHILLY (pp. 213/216, 6F)
Largest medieval fortress in

Beaumaris Castle

Wales, begun in 1268.
Famous for its leaning tower.
(*01222 883143.*
➲ *In Caerphilly town centre.*
(OS Map 171; ref ST155870.)

Carreg Cennen Castle

CARMARTHENSHIRE
(p. 216, 7E)
The remains of a 13th- and
early 14th-century castle in a
magnificent cliff-top location.
(*01558 822291.*
➲ *Near Trapp, off A484, 4m
SE of Llandeilo.*
*(OS Map 159; ref
SH 668191.)*

Castell Coch

CARDIFF (pp. 213/216, 6F)
Late 19th-century 'fairy-tale'
castle designed by Burgess
and lavishly decorated in
Victorian Gothic style.
(*01222 810101.*
➲ *Near Tongwynlais, off A470,
5m NW of Cardiff.*
(OS Map 171; ref ST 131826.)

Caernarfon Castle

Kidwelly Castle

Chepstow Castle

MONMOUTHSHIRE
(pp. 213/217, 6G)
One of Britain's earliest stone castles. Modified through the Middle Ages and the Civil War.
(01291 624065. 🅿🏠
➲ *In Chepstow town centre, off A48 or M4.*
(OS Map 162; ref ST 533941.)

Cilgerran Castle

CEREDIGION (p. 216, 7C)
Picturesque remains dating from the early 13th century.
➲ *In Cilgerran, 3m S of Cardigan, off A478.*
(OS Map 145; ref SN 195431.)

Conwy Castle

CONWY (p. 216, 11E)
Outstanding example of medieval military architecture, built for Edward I between 1283 and 1287.
(01492 592358. 🏠🕴
➲ *In Conwy town centre.*
(OS Map 115; ref SH 783774.)

Conwy Castle

Criccieth Castle

GWYNEDD (p. 216, 10D)
Imposingly sited castle, still dominated by the twin-towered gatehouse built by Llywelyn the Great.
(01766 522227. 🕴
➲ *On coastal bluff, near Criccieth town centre.*
(OS Map 123/124; ref SH 500377.)

Cymer Abbey

GWYNEDD (p. 216, 10E)
Remains of a simple Cistercian abbey church founded in 1198 by Maredudd ap Cynan.
(01341 422854.
➲ *Near Llanelltyd, off A470, 1½m N of Dolgellau.*
(OS Map 124; ref SH 721195.)

Dolwyddelan Castle

CONWY (p. 216, 10E)
A 13th-century square, stone keep and ruined fortifications built by Llywelyn the Great.
(01690 750366.
➲ *1m W of Dolwyddelan on A470.*
(OS Map 115; ref SH 721523.)

Harlech Castle

GWYNEDD (p. 216, 10D)
Built for Edward I, the castle was seized by Owain Glyndwr and held for four years.
(01766 780552. 🅿🕴🏠
➲ *Harlech town centre.*
(OS Map 124; ref SH 581312.)

Kidwelly Castle

CARMARTHENSHIRE
(pp. 212/216, 6D)
Impressive remains of a stone castle on the site of a huge 12th-century earthwork.
(01554 890104. 🅿🕴🏠🎧
➲ *In centre of Kidwelly.*
(OS Map 159; ref SN 409701.)

Laugharne Castle

CARMARTHENSHIRE
(pp. 212/216, 6D)
There have been several transformations since the 12th-century to this 'castle within a garden within a castle'.
(01994 427906.
In Laugharne on A4066, 14m SW of Carmarthen.
(OS Map 159; ref SN 302107.)

Oxwich Castle

SWANSEA (pp. 212/216, 6D)
Remains of a sumptuous court-yard house built by the Mansel family during the 16th century.
(01792 390359. 🅿
➲ *In Oxwich, off A4118, Gower peninsula, 8m SW of Swansea.*
(OS Map 159; ref SS 497862.)

Plas Mawr

CONWY (p. 216, 11E)
Reputedly the best-preserved Elizabethan townhouse in Britain, its elaborately decorated plasterwork faithfully restored.
🎧🏠➲ *In High Street, Conwy.*
(OS Map 115, ref SH 781776.)

Raglan Castle

MONMOUTHSHIRE
(pp. 213/217, 6G)
Much remains of the impressive 15th-century castle despite demolition attempts during the Civil War.
(01291 690228. 🅿🕴
➲ *½m N of Raglan, 7m SW of Monmouth, off A40.*
(OS Map 161; ref S414083.)

Raglan Castle

Rhuddlan Castle

DENBIGHSHIRE (p. 216, 11F)
Begun in 1277, this concentrically planned castle was the second of Edward I's great Welsh fortifications.
(01745 590777. 🅿 ⅲ
➲ In Rhuddlan, 3m S of Rhyl.
(OS Map 116; ref SJ 026777.)

Rug Chapel and Llangar Church

DENBIGHSHIRE (p. 216, 7B)
17th-century Rug has a gloriously decorated wooden interior. Llangar's wall paintings (14th–18th-century) are of immense importance.
(01490 412025. 🅿 ⅲ
➲ W of Corwen, off A5(T).
(OS Map 125; ref SJ 055442.)

St Davids Bishop's Palace

PEMBROKESHIRE (p. 216, 7B)
Imposing palace within the defences of the cathedral precincts dating mainly from the 14th-century.
(01437 720517.
➲ Near centre of St Davids.
(OS Map 157; ref SM 750254.)

Strata Florida Abbey

CEREDIGION (p. 216, 8E)
Present buildings erected for the Cistercian order in 12th-century under the patronage of Lord Rhys.
(01974 831261.
➲ 1¼m SE of Pontrhydfendigaid, off B4343,

14m SE of Aberystwyth.
(OS Map 135; ref SN 746657.)

Talley Abbey

CARMARTHENSHIRE (p. 216, 7D)
Parts of the abbey church survive in this Premonstratensian house founded in the 1180s.
➲ In Talley, on B4302, 6m N of Llandeilo.
(OS Map 146; ref JN 632327.)

Tintern Abbey

MONMOUTHSHIRE
(pp. 213/217, 6G)
Founded in 1131, this beautifully located Cistercian abbey has a remarkably complete abbey church.
(01291 689251. 🅿 ⅲ 🛍 🎧
➲ In Tintern, on A466, 5m N of Chepstow.
(OS Map 162; ref SO 533000.)

Tretower Castle

POWYS (p. 217, 7F)
12th-century keep and 13th-century round tower on the site of a motte and bailey castle.
(01874 730279. 🅿 ⅲ 🎧
➲ In Tretower, off A40, 3m NW of Crickhowell.
(OS Map 161; ref SO 185212.)

Tretower Court

POWYS (p. 217, 7F)
Restored courtyard house with origins in the 15th century. Re-created late medieval pleasure garden.
(01874 730279. 🅿 ⅲ 🎧
➲ In Tretower, off A40, 3m NW of Crickhowell.
(OS Map 161; ref SO 185212.)

Valle Crucis Abbey

DENBIGHSHIRE (p. 217, 10F)
Extensive remains of a Cistercian abbey founded in 1201. The church dates from the 13th century.
(01978 860326. 🅿 ⅲ
➲ 1½m NW of Llangollen, on A542.
(OS Map 117; ref SJ 205442.)

Weobley Castle

SWANSEA (pp. 212/216, 6D)
Medieval fortified manor house with substantial remains dating principally from the later 13th and 14th centuries.
(01792 390012. 🅿
➲ 2m W of Llanrhidian, off B4271, 11m W of Swansea.
(OS Map 159; ref SS 478927.)

White Castle

MONMOUTHSHIRE (p. 217, 7G)
Imposing moated remains of a 12th-century castle, substantially remodelled in the later 13th century.
(01600 780380.
➲ 6m NE of Abergavenny, off B4233.
(OS Map 161; ref SO 379167.)

Valle Crucis Abbey

'The Story of Mann' is an award-winning concept which brings together all aspects of the Isle of Man's heritage sites under one organization: Manx National Heritage, The Manx Museum, Douglas, Isle of of Man.

The Manx Museum, Douglas, Isle of Man, IM1 3LY. Tel: 01624 648000.

Castle Rushen

Castletown (p. 216, INSET)
Situated in the Island's ancient capital, Castletown, this is regarded as one of the most complete castles in the British Isles. The interior has exciting displays re-creating life in the medieval period.
℄ 01624 648000.
➲ *In Castletown.*

Cregneash Village Folk Museum

Creagneash (p. 216, INSET)
In breathtaking landscape, Cregneash farm and village is a unique interpretation of a 19th-century Manx upland crofting community with distinctive whitewashed and thatched cottages, a number of which have regular demonstrations of traditional village life.
℄ 01624 648000.
➲ *Near Port St Mary, Cregneash.*

Grove Museum

Ramsey (p. 216, INSET)
Step back in time in this perfectly preserved Victorian house. The grounds, house and furniture all reflect life as it was in a bygone era when used as a summer residence of the Gibb family from Liverpool.
℄ 01624 648000.
➲ *In Ramsey.*

The Great Laxey Wheel

The Great Laxey Wheel and Mines Trail

Laxey (p. 216, INSET)
Visit the world's largest working waterwheel, built to drain the mine in 1854. Today a visit can include a trip into a section of the mine as well as a stroll around the picturesque glen and gardens.
℄ 01624 648000. ➲ *In Laxey.*

House of Manannan

Peel (p. 216, INSET)
Opened in 1997, this £6 million centre is an unforgettable experience, with interactive displays using state-of-the-art technology. A visit leaves the visitor in awe of Manx heritage and eager to learn more.
℄ 01624 648000. ➲ *In Peel.*

The Manx Museum

Douglas (p. 216, INSET)
Free entry into the Island's treasure house combines education with fun in an award-winning complex which provides an introduction to the 'Story of Mann' and the uniqueness of Manx life of yesterday and today.
℄ 01624 648000. ➲ *In Douglas.*

Nautical Museum

Castletown (p. 216, INSET)
In 1935 *The Peggy*, an 18th-century armed yacht, was discovered in her original boathouse. Built in 1791, she is now the centrepiece of a display of memorabilia of life and trade at sea many years ago.
℄ 01624 648000.
➲ *In Castletown.*

Old Grammar School

Castletown (p. 216, INSET)
Built in the 12th century, the Island's first church, St Mary's, has had a significant role in Manx education. The school dates back to 1570 and evokes memories of school life in the Victorian era.
℄ 01624 648000.
➲ *In Castletown.*

Peel Castle

Peel (p. 216, INSET)
Situated on St Patrick's Isle, the former ruling seat of the Norse kingdom of Mann and the Isles includes ruins from the 11th century.
℄ 01624 648000. ➲ *In Peel.*

House of Manannan

A guide to maps

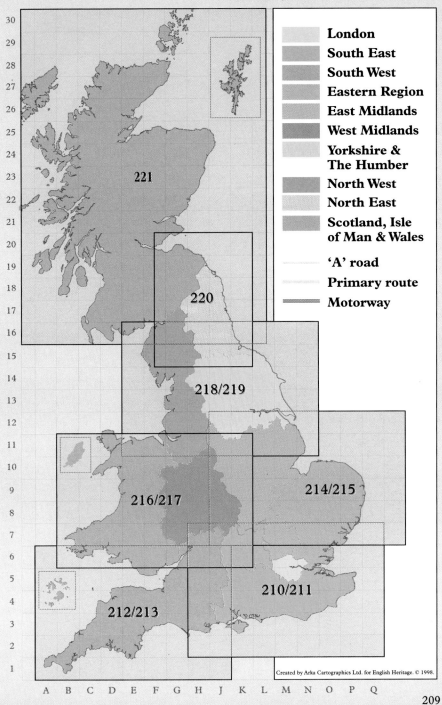

London
South East
South West
Eastern Region
East Midlands
West Midlands
Yorkshire &
The Humber
North West
North East
Scotland, Isle
of Man & Wales

'A' road
Primary route
Motorway

221

220

218/219

216/217

214/215

210/211

212/213

Created by Arka Cartographics Ltd. for English Heritage. © 1998.

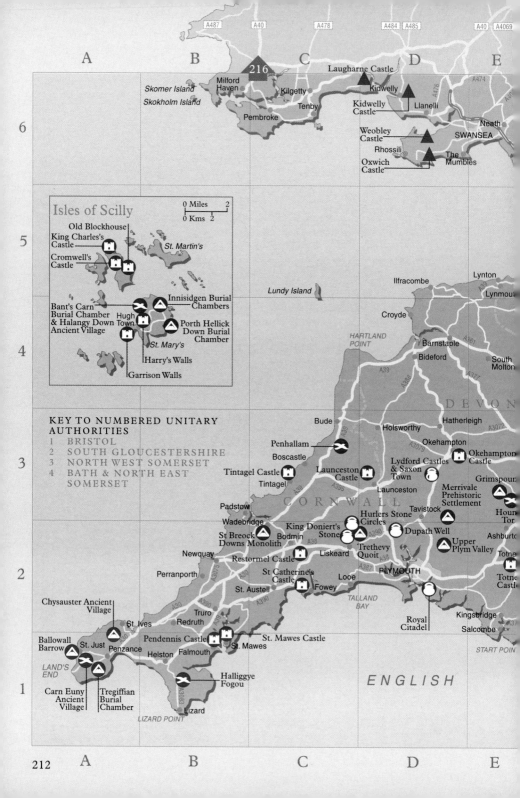

KEY TO NUMBERED UNITARY AUTHORITIES
5 NORTH EAST LINCOLNSHIRE
6 NORTH LINCOLNSHIRE

Scale

| 0 Miles | 20 |
| 0 Kms | 30 |

12

NORTH SEA

11

10

Creake Abbey
Blakeney Guildhall
Wells-next-the-Sea
Sheringham
Cromer
Hunstanton
Holt
Binham Wayside Cross
Binham Priory
Baconsthorpe Castle
North Walsham
Aylsham
Castle Rising Castle
Fakenham
Castle Acre Bailey Gate
Castle Acre Castle
North Elmham Chapel
Castle Acre Priory
East Dereham
Hemsby
Cow Tower
Caister Roman Site
Great Yarmouth
NORWICH
Berney Arms Windmill
Swaffham
N O R F O L K
Wymondham
Loddon
Row 111 Houses, Old Merchant's House & Greyfriar's Cloister
Attleborough
St. Olave's Priory
Burgh Castle
Grime's Graves
Weeting Castle
LOWESTOFT
Thetford Warren Lodge
Bungay
Brandon
Thetford
Beccles
Kessingland
Thetford Priory
Diss
Church of the Holy Sepulchre
Halesworth
Southwold
Isleham Priory Church
Framlingham Castle
Newmarket
Bury St. Edmunds
Saxtead Green Post Mill
Leiston Abbey
Moulton Packhorse Bridge
Bury St. Edmunds Abbey
Stowmarket
Aldeburgh
S U F F O L K
Woodbridge
Orford Castle
Orford
Haverhill
St. James's Chapel
IPSWICH
Sudbury
Mistley Towers
Felixstowe
E S S E X
St. Botolph's Priory
Landguard Fort
Halstead
Harwich
Lexden Earthworks
St. John's Abbey Gate
Braintree
COLCHESTER
Walton-on-the-Naze
Witham
Tiptree
West Mersea
Frinton-on-Sea
Clacton-on-Sea
CHELMSFORD

Key to symbols

- ✠ Christian heritage
- 🏰 Castle/Fort
- 🏛 Historic house
- Romantic ruin
- Humps & bumps
- Roman
- Garden/Park
- Industrial monument
- Pot luck
- Far from the crowd
- Great antiquity
- ▲ Other historic sites

Created by Arka Cartographics Ltd. for English Heritage. © 1998.

9

8

7

211

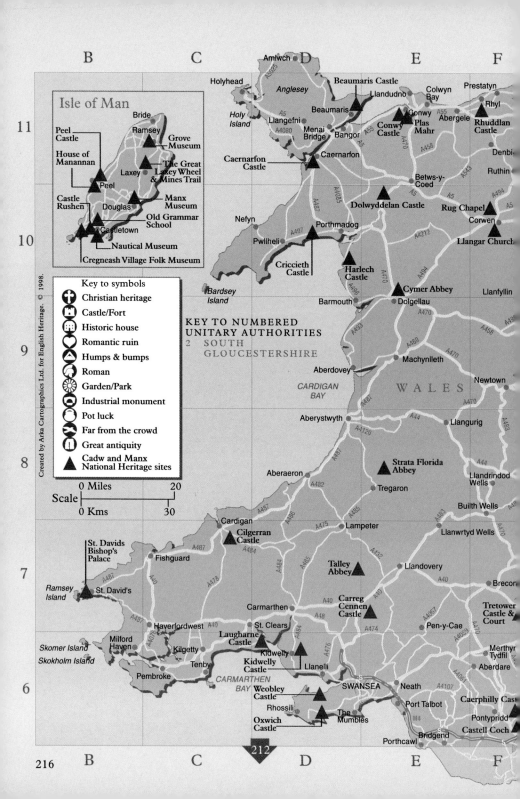

Isle of Man

Bride

Peel
Castle
Ramsey
Grove
Museum

House of
Manannan

Laxey
The Great
Laxey Wheel
& Mines Trail

Peel

Castle
Rushen
Douglas
Manx
Museum

Old Grammar
School
Castletown

Nautical Museum

Cregneash Village Folk Museum

Key to symbols

- ✠ Christian heritage
- Castle/Fort
- Historic house
- ♡ Romantic ruin
- ⛰ Humps & bumps
- Roman
- ✿ Garden/Park
- Industrial monument
- Pot luck
- ✕ Far from the crowd
- Great antiquity
- ▲ Cadw and Manx
  National Heritage sites

Scale

0 Miles 20

0 Kms 30

Created by Arka Cartographics Ltd. for English Heritage. © 1998.

Amlwch

Holyhead

Anglesey

Beaumaris Castle

Llandudno
Colwyn
Bay
Prestatyn

Holy
Island
Llangefni
Beaumaris

Rhyl

Menai
Bridge
Bangor

Conwy
Castle
Gonwy
Plas
Mahr
Abergele

Rhuddlan
Castle

Caernarfon
Castle
Caernarfon

Betws-y-
Coed
Denbi

Ruthin

Nefyn

Dolwyddelan Castle

Rug Chapel

Corwen

Porthmadog

Pwllheli

Criccieth
Castle
Harlech
Castle

Llangar Church

Cymer Abbey
Llanfyllin

Bardsey
Island
Barmouth
Dolgellau

KEY TO NUMBERED
UNITARY AUTHORITIES
2 SOUTH
GLOUCESTERSHIRE

Machynlleth

W A L E S

Newtown

Aberdovey

CARDIGAN
BAY

Aberystwyth
Llangurig

Strata Florida
Abbey
Llandrindod
Wells

Aberaeron

Tregaron

Builth Wells

Cardigan

Cilgerran
Castle
Lampeter
Llanwrtyd Wells

St. Davids
Bishop's
Palace
Fishguard

Talley
Abbey
Llandovery

Ramsey
Island
St. David's

Brecon

Carreg
Cennen
Castle

Carmarthen

Haverfordwest
St. Clears
Pen-y-Cae

Tretower
Castle &
Court

Skomer Island
Skokholm Island
Milford
Haven
Kilgetty

Laugharne
Castle
Kidwelly
Castle
Llanelli

Merthyr
Tydfil
Aberdare

Tenby

Pembroke

Caerphilly Cas

CARMARTHEN
BAY
Weobley
Castle
SWANSEA
Neath
Port Talbot
Pontypridd

Rhossili
The
Mumbles
Castell Coch

Oxwich
Castle
Bridgend

Porthcawl

216

B   C   D   E   F

212

A76   A74(M)   A7   A68   A696

E   F   G   H   J

▲220

Hadrian's Wall
See Map Pages 176-177

Brampton   ⚔ Lanercost Priory

Castle
Douglas

Kirkcudbright   Rockcliffe   SOLWAY
FIRTH

Prudhoe Castle

Derwentcote
Steel Furnace

⛪ Carlisle Castle   ✝ Wetheral
CARLISLE   Priory Gatehouse
Wetheral

Conse

16   Dundrennan
Abbey

Wigton   Alston

Maclellan's
Castle

Allonby   CUMBRIA   DURHAM

Maryport   A689   Auckland Ca
Deer House

Cockermouth

Penrith Castle   ▲ Mayburgh Earthwork   Barnard   Piercebri
Castle   Barnard Ro
Castle   Br

Workington   PENRITH
Clifton   ▲⛪ Brougham Castle
Hall   Countess Pillar

WHITEHAVEN   Keswick   Appleby-in-   Bowes
Castlerigg   Westmorland
Stone Circle   Arthur's
Round Table   Egglestone
Abbey

Egremont   Shap Abbey ✝   Brough   Bowes
Castle   Brough   Castle
Stanwick Iron Age Fortifications

15   Hardknott
Roman Fort   Ambleside   Tebay   Richmond
Richmond Castle

Ravenglass   Ambleside Roman Fort   Easby Abbe

Ravenglass Roman   Coniston   Windermere   Leyburn
Bath House   Kendal   Hawes   NORT

Bootle   Middleham Castle

Kirkby   YORKSHIR
Longsdale

Millom   Stott Park   Cowan Bridge
Bobbin Mill   Ingleton

14   Ulverston   Warton
Furness Abbey   ✝ Old Rectory   Settle
Carnforth

BARROW-IN-   Bow Bridge
FURNESS   Lancaster
Piel Castle   MORECAMBE
Morecambe   A59
Piel Island   BAY

Skipton

13   Fleetwood   LANCASHIRE
Salley Abbey ✝   Keighley
Garstang   Clitheroe   Pendle
Cleveleys   Whalley   Heritage Centre   BRADFO
Abbey Gatehouse   BURNLEY   W.
BLACKPOOL   PRESTON   YORKS
Lytham St. Anne's   BLACKBURN   Goodshaw   HALIFAX
Accrington   Chapel ✝   HUDDERSFIE

SOUTHPORT   Chorley   BURY   ROCHDALE
Ormskirk   BOLTON   OLDHAM   Holmfi

12   Formby   WIGAN   GREATER   MANCHESTER
LIVERPOOL   KIRKBY   SALFORD
BAY   BOOTLE   ST. HELENS   MANCHESTER
MERSEYSIDE   LIVERPOOL   WARRINGTON   STOCKPORT   Baguley Hall
BIRKENHEAD   WIDNES   Knutsford   Peveril Castle ♥
RUNCORN   Macclesfield   Buxton
Llandudno   Colwyn   Prestatyn   ELLESMERE   Nine Lad
Bay   PORT   Neston   CHESHIRE   Stone Cir
Conwy   Rhyl   Northwich   Winsford   Arbor Low
11   Castle   Abergele   Rhuddlan   Flint   Stone Circle &
Plas   Castle   CHESTER   Chester Castle   Sandbach   Congleton   Gib Hill Barrow
Mahr   Chester   Beeston   Crosses ✝   Leek
Denbigh   Roman   Castle   Sandbach
Mold   Amphitheatre   Crewe
Betws-y-Coed   Ruthin   Gresford   NEWCASTLE   STOKE-ON-
▼217   UNDER LYME   TRENT

218

E   F   G   H   J

A470   A494   A5   A41   A51

IRISH
SEA

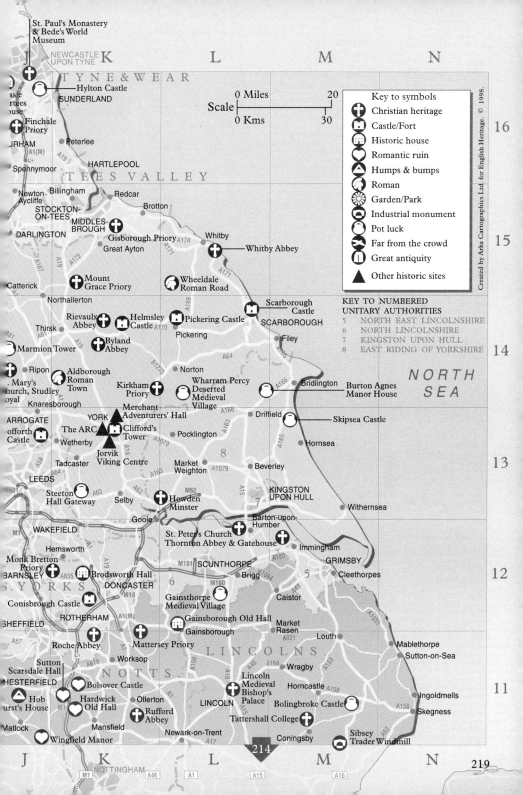

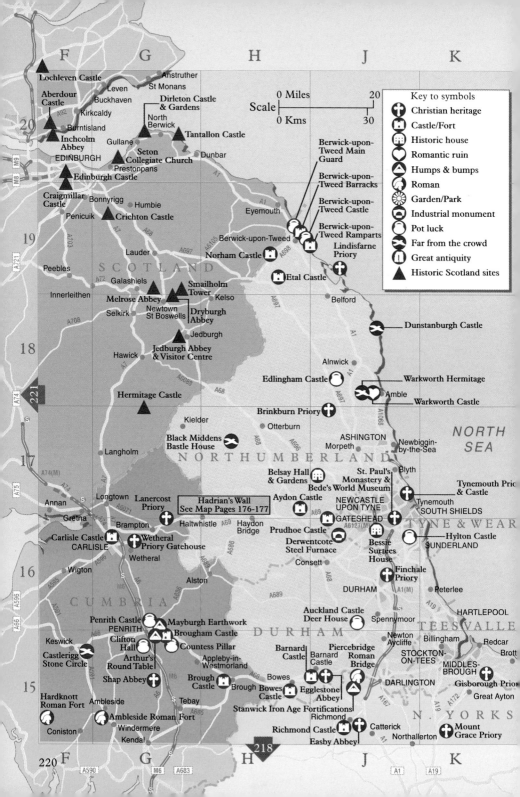

Key to symbols

- ✝ Christian heritage
- 🏰 Castle/Fort
- 🏠 Historic house
- ❤️ Romantic ruin
- ⛰️ Humps & bumps
- 🏛️ Roman
- 🌼 Garden/Park
- ⚙️ Industrial monument
- 😊 Pot luck
- 🦅 Far from the crowd
- 🎖️ Great antiquity
- ▲ Historic Scotland sites

Scale

0 Miles — 20
0 Kms — 30

F G H J K

20

Lochleven Castle
Anstruther
St Monans
Leven
Buckhaven
Aberdour Castle
Kirkcaldy
Dirleton Castle & Gardens
North Berwick
Burntisland
Inchcolm Abbey
Gullane
Tantallon Castle
EDINBURGH
Seton Collegiate Church
Dunbar
Prestonpans
Edinburgh Castle

19

Craigmillar Castle
Bonnyrigg
Humbie
Penicuik
Crichton Castle
Eyemouth
SCOTLAND
Peebles
Galashiels
A68
Lauder
Berwick-upon-Tweed
Norham Castle
Innerleithen
A708
Selkirk
Newtown St Boswells
Melrose Abbey
Smailholm Tower
Kelso
Dryburgh Abbey
Etal Castle
Berwick-upon-Tweed Main Guard
Berwick-upon-Tweed Barracks
Berwick-upon-Tweed Castle
Berwick-upon-Tweed Ramparts
Lindisfarne Priory
Belford

18

Hawick
Jedburgh
Jedburgh Abbey & Visitor Centre
Edlingham Castle
Alnwick
Dunstanburgh Castle
Warkworth Hermitage
Amble
Warkworth Castle
Hermitage Castle
Kielder
Otterburn
Brinkburn Priory

17

Langholm
Black Middens Bastle House
Morpeth
ASHINGTON
Newbiggin-by-the-Sea
NORTHUMBERLAND
Blyth
NORTH SEA

16

Annan
Longtown
Lanercost Priory
Hadrian's Wall See Map Pages 176–177
Haltwhistle
Haydon Bridge
Belsay Hall & Gardens
St Paul's Monastery & Bede's World Museum
Tynemouth Priory & Castle
Gretna
Brampton
Aydon Castle
NEWCASTLE UPON TYNE
Tynemouth
SOUTH SHIELDS
Carlisle Castle
CARLISLE
Wetheral Priory Gatehouse
Wetheral
Prudhoe Castle
Derwentcote Steel Furnace
GATESHEAD
TYNE & WEAR
Bessie Surtees House
Hylton Castle
SUNDERLAND
Wigton
Consett
Finchale Priory
Peterlee
Alston
CUMBRIA
DURHAM
A1(M)
HARTLEPOOL
Keswick
Penrith Castle
PENRITH
Mayburgh Earthwork
Brougham Castle
Auckland Castle Deer House
Spennymoor
TEES VALLE
Newton Aycliffe
Billingham
Redcar
Brott
Castlerigg Stone Circle
Clifton Hall
Countess Pillar
DURHAM
STOCKTON-ON-TEES
MIDDLESBROUGH
Arthur's Round Table
Appleby-in-Westmorland
Barnard Castle
Piercebridge Roman Bridge
DARLINGTON
Hardknott Roman Fort
Shap Abbey
Bowes
Barnard Castle
Gisborough Priory
Ambleside
Brough Castle
Brough Bowes Castle
Egglestone Abbey
Great Ayton
Ambleside Roman Fort
Stanwick Iron Age Fortifications
Richmond
N. YORKS
Windermere
Kendal
Richmond Castle
Easby Abbey
Catterick
Northallerton
Mount Grace Priory

A1068

A697

A1

15

Coniston

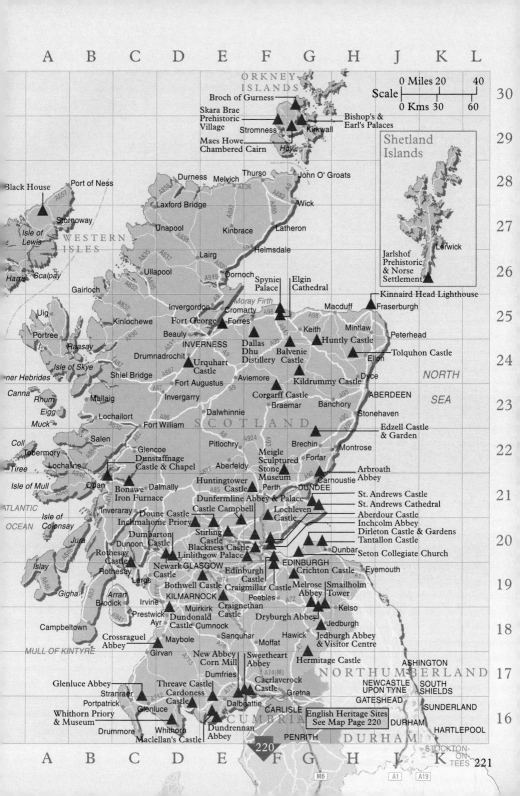

A B C D E F G H J K L

30

Scale

0 Miles 20 40

0 Kms 30 60

ORKNEY ISLANDS

Broch of Gurness

Skara Brae Prehistoric Village

Stromness

Kirkwall

Bishop's & Earl's Palaces

29

Maes Howe Chambered Cairn

Hoy

Shetland Islands

Durness   Melvich   Thurso   John O' Groats

28

Black House   Port of Ness

Laxford Bridge

Wick

Lerwick

Stornoway

Isle of Lewis

WESTERN ISLES

Unapool

Kinbrace

Latheron

27

Jarlshof Prehistoric & Norse Settlement

Harris   Scalpay

Gairloch

Lairg

Helmsdale

Uig

Ullapool

Dornoch

Spynie Palace

Elgin Cathedral

Kinnaird Head Lighthouse

26

Portree

Kinlochewe

Invergordon

Cromarty

Moray Firth

Macduff   Fraserburgh

25

Raasay

Beauly

Forres

Keith

Mintlaw

Peterhead

Isle of Skye

Fort George

INVERNESS

Dallas Dhu Distillery

Balvenie Castle

Huntly Castle

Tolquhon Castle

ner Hebrides

Drumnadrochit

Urquhart Castle

Ellon

Dyce

24

Canna

Shiel Bridge

Fort Augustus

Aviemore

Kildrummy Castle

ABERDEEN

NORTH

Rhum

Mallaig

Invergarry

Corgarff Castle

Braemar

Banchory

SEA

Eigg

Lochailort

Dalwhinnie

SCOTLAND

Stonehaven

23

Muck

Fort William

Pitlochry

Brechin

Montrose

Edzell Castle & Garden

Coll

Salen

Glencoe

Aberfeldy

Meigle Sculptured Stone Museum

Forfar

22

Tobermory

Lochaline

Dunstaffnage Castle & Chapel

Huntingtower Castle

Perth

DUNDEE

Carnoustie

Arbroath Abbey

Tiree

Isle of Mull

Oban

Bonawe Iron Furnace

Dalmally

St. Andrews Castle

21

ATLANTIC

Inveraray

Doune Castle

Castle Campbell

Dunfermline Abbey & Palace

Lochleven Castle

St. Andrews Cathedral

Aberdour Castle

Isle of Colonsay

Inchmahome Priory

Stirling Castle

Inchcolm Abbey

Dirleton Castle & Gardens

20

OCEAN

Dumbarton Castle

Blackness Castle

Tantallon Castle

Jura

Dunoon

Newark Castle

Linlithgow Palace

EDINBURGH

Seton Collegiate Church

Rothesay Castle

GLASGOW

Edinburgh Castle

Crichton Castle

Dunbar

Islay

Rothesay

Lergs

Bothwell Castle

Craigmillar Castle

Eyemouth

19

Gigha

Arran

Brodick

Irvine

KILMARNOCK

Craignethan Castle

Peebles

Melrose Abbey

Smailholm Tower

Muirkirk

Prestwick

Dundonald Castle

Ayr   Cumnock

Dryburgh Abbey

Kelso

18

Campbeltown

Crossraguel Abbey

Maybole

Sanquhar   Moffat

Hawick

Jedburgh

Jedburgh Abbey & Visitor Centre

MULL OF KINTYRE

Girvan

New Abbey Corn Mill

Sweetheart Abbey

Hermitage Castle

NORTHUMBERLAND

ASHINGTON

17

Glenluce Abbey

Stranraer

Threave Castle

Cardoness Castle

Dumfries

Caerlaverock Castle

Gretna

NEWCASTLE UPON TYNE

SOUTH SHIELDS

Portpatrick

Glenluce

Dalbeattie

CARLISLE

GATESHEAD

SUNDERLAND

Whithorn Priory & Museum

CUMBRIA

English Heritage Sites See Map Page 220

DURHAM

HARTLEPOOL

16

Drummore

Whithorn

Maclellan's Castle

Dundrennan Abbey

PENRITH

DURHAM

220

STOCKTON-ON-TEES

A B C D E F G H J K

M6   A1   A19

221

INDEX